WOMEN WORKERS IN THE SECOND WORLD WAR

WOMEN WORKERS IN THE SECOND WORLD WAR
PRODUCTION AND PATRIARCHY IN CONFLICT

Penny Summerfield

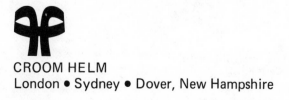

CROOM HELM
London • Sydney • Dover, New Hampshire

© 1984 Penny Summerfield
Croom Helm Ltd, Provident House, Burrell Row,
Beckenham, Kent BR3 1AT
Croom Helm Australia Pty Ltd, First Floor,
139 King Street, Sydney, NSW 2001, Australia
Croom Helm, 51 Washington Street, Dover,
New Hampshire 03820, USA

British Library Cataloguing in Publication Data

Summerfield, Penny
    Women workers in the Second World War.
    1. World War, 1939–1945 – Women
    2. Women – Employment – Government policy –
    Great Britain – History – 20th century
    I. Title
    331.4'0941   D810.W7

    ISBN 0-7099-2317-1

Typeset by Mayhew Typesetting, Bristol, UK
Printed and bound in Great Britain
by Billing & Sons Limited, Worcester.

CONTENTS

Figures

Acknowledgements

List of Abbreviations

1. Introduction   1

2. Pre-War   8

3. Mobilisation   29

4. Child Care   67

5. Shopping   99

6. Working Hours   123

7. Dilution   151

8. Conclusion   185

Appendix A: Extended Employment of Women Agreement   193

Appendix B: Women's Employment Statistics, Tables B1–B9   195

Bibliography   201

Index   211

FIGURES

3.1 Advertising for War Work Exhibition   39

3.2 Street interview during Ministry of Labour
    recruiting campaign   52

4.1 Outdoor activities at a wartime nursery in a north-
    western town, 1940   72

4.2 Wartime nursery in Sidcup, 1941   73

4.3 Demonstration for nurseries in Hampstead   78

4.4 Leaflet setting out nursery regulations   85

5.1 Inside an East End home   102

5.2 Mother working on household accounts   106

5.3 Meat queue   112

6.1 Outworker at work in her own home   144

7.1 Welder   164

7.2 Inspector   164

7.3 Capstan operator   165

7.4 Core makers   165

ACKNOWLEDGEMENTS

Many people have encouraged me to write this book, above all my D.Phil supervisor and friend Stephen Yeo, whose patient criticisms and suggestions have been invaluable. I am also indebted to Gail Braybon, whose work on women in the First World War has been a major stimulus, to Sylvia Walby, whose recently completed thesis on gender and unemployment has given me the courage of my convictions, and to Carol Dyhouse and Angus Calder for their careful and critical reading of the thesis on which this book is based. I am also most appreciative of the interest and support of members of the Women's Research Group at Lancaster University over the years. Numerous librarians and archivists have helped with the location of sources and I should like to give special thanks to Dorothy Sheridan of the Mass-Observation Archive. Janet Blacow, Chris Cowan and Maggie Lackey have contributed hours of typing.

One of the conclusions of this book is that even in the Second World War collective provisions for domestic work were limited and women had to depend upon their own families and friends for the support necessary for them to undertake work outside the home. This is no less true today and, while acknowledging with gratitude the collective child care facilities which have been available for my two children, particularly the University of Lancaster Pre-School Centre, I wish to thank especially warmly Joan Wood, my parents and parents-in-law and, above all, my husband Mark Easterby-Smith, for their part in creating the conditions in which this project could be brought to completion.

To Mrs Oliver and Mrs Shipley,
war workers of South Shields.

LIST OF ABBREVIATIONS

AEU	Amalgamated Engineering Union
ATS	Auxiliary Territorial Service
BEC	British Employers' Confederation
BOE	Board of Education
CCA	Churchill College Archive
Co-op	Co-operative Wholesale Society
DCIC	Deputy Chief Industrial Commissioner (MOL)
DC	Divisional Controller (MOL) (geographical divisions to which they belonged abbreviated in conventional way)
EWO	Essential Work Order
FBM	Federation of Boot Manufacturers
FWAB	Factory and Welfare Advisory Board (MOL)
LA	Local Authority
LEA	Local Education Authority
M-O	Mass-Observation
M-OA	Mass-Observation Archive
MOF	Ministry of Food
MOH	Ministry of Health
MOL	Ministry of Labour and National Service
MOS	Ministry of Supply
MRC	Modern Records Centre
NSDN	National Society of Day Nurseries
NUBSO	National Union of Boot and Shoe Operatives
NUGMW	National Union of General and Municipal Workers
NSAGB	Nursery School Association of Great Britain
PRO	Public Record Office
RC	Regional Controller (MOL) (geographical regions to which they belonged abbreviated in conventional way, e.g. NW North-west)
RWO	Regional Welfare Officer (MOL)
RCEP	Royal Commission on Equal Pay
ROF	Royal Ordnance Factory
TUC	Trades Union Congress
TGWU	Transport and General Workers' Union
WSS	Wartime Social Survey
WAAF	Women's Auxiliary Air Force

List of Abbreviations

WAC	Women's Advisory Committee (TUC)
WCC	Women's Consultative Committee (MOL)
WLA	Women's Land Army
WRNS	Women's Royal Navy Service
WVS	Women's Voluntary Service

1 INTRODUCTION

Women, war and social change have been subjects of interest and debate since the 1960s. Betty Friedan and, later, Juliet Mitchell argued that women's lives were profoundly changed for the better during the Second World War, because of the need for women's labour and the readiness of the state to intervene to release them from their homes for war work. After the war, they claimed, in both the United States and the United Kingdom, the reverse occurred. Women were not wanted in the labour force, state provisions were removed and a cultural offensive was launched to return women to domesticity.[1] Arthur Marwick argued against such views that some changes in women's experiences during the war have been exaggerated. He pointed for example to enduring ways in which femininity was represented and argued that conscription affected relatively few women. On the other hand, following the approach of Richard Titmuss in the 1950s, he argued that 'total' war inevitably altered some aspects of women's lives and that, contrary to the view that wartime changes were reversed after the war, women were rewarded for their participation with permanent changes, notably in terms of state provision for child care, access to men's jobs and equal pay. He argued that, above all, women gained in 'self confidence', a difficult proposition to verify historically.[2]

The interpretation developed here differs from those of both Friedan and Mitchell, and Marwick. In a nutshell, my argument is that, in spite of challenge and expectation of change during the war, continuity with pre-war attitudes and practices towards women was considerable in the areas of both domestic work and paid employment. In exploring these aspects of women's lives in wartime I have concentrated on state policy. This is both because the earlier debate was conducted in terms of its effects and because before investigating attitudes towards women during the war more widely I felt a need to clarify the meaning for women of the extension of the government's reach into social life demanded by the Second World War. It was, after all, a conflict not just between armies but, as the original expounders of the concept 'total war' put it, between the entire productive capacities and therefore civilian populations of the protagonists. It rapidly became apparent that there was not one but a set of policies towards women and that they could not be treated as 'background' separate from other attitudes, but were themselves a vital focus for ideas about women's place in social relations. The state was not, as I had assumed, a set of neutral structures. Wartime ministries were highly active brokers, mediating between entrenched views about women held in and out of government and the pressures of the war economy for ever-increasing numbers of women workers and maximum production. The deals achieved were enormously important in determining the extent to which these pressures were allowed to change gender divisions at home and at work during the war.

The focus of this book is, therefore, the making and implementation of official policy towards women during the Second World War. The Ministry of Labour and National Service is prominent, because of all government ministries it had the greatest responsibility for designing and implementing policies for the mobilisation of women. It is of course important to understand the context in which the MOL was working, so Chapter 2 outlines the history of women in the period before the war, concentrating on women's varied experiences in paid employment and in the home. The MOL met considerable problems in trying to move women from one type of job, whether in or out of the home, to another which counted as 'war work'. Chapter 3 looks at these difficulties and at the efforts of the MOL to reconcile mobilisation with conventional expectations about women's roles in the context of evidence about women's own attitudes to being mobilised.

Its experiences during the year 1940/41 forced upon the MOL the understanding that mobilisation could not be accomplished without taking account of the real work done by women in the home and it looked to other government ministries and outside interest groups to co-operate in the development of policies which would relieve women of all or some of this work. This process of negotiation, and the experiments which accompanied it, made public a conventionally private area. But the strength of the expectation that the domestic was a private zone was reflected in the great hesitation of government ministries and of groups like local authorities, retailers and industrial employers over assuming responsibility for any domestic activity. Thus the Ministry of Health and its local officers had very definite ideas about the limitations of their role in child care and about the correct place in it of the mother and the home and the Ministry of Food was more concerned to protect the interests of retailers than to promote the relief of the work of shopping. Industrial employers too were loath to involve themselves in domestic work of any sort and were wary even of changing the hours of work required of their workers to accommodate the time demanded by domestic work. Chapters 4, 5 and 6 examine the interplay between the assumptions of these groups about domestic work and the need to mobilise women and to sustain their productivity at work, in the three areas of child care, shopping and the hours of work.

In all three, principles were established which could have led to profound changes. Child care could have been transformed by the principle of collective responsibility embodied in wartime nurseries. Shopping and cooking could have been altered by new retailing practices in which the shop did the work for its 'members' and by the provision made by employers and local authorities for collective feeding. The gender identity of domestic work could have been changed by the recognition of the socially necessary labour demanded by the home, embodied in new ways of arranging working hours for men as well as women in industry. But although the logic of mobilisation of women for war pointed towards these goals, the steps actually taken contained no more than the seeds of change. The strength of conventional expectations within the government ministries concerned and among groups outside, including some women themselves, was such that change in every area of domestic responsibility was heavily constrained, in spite of interventions from those who saw change as desirable.

Finally, just as mobilisation put 'at risk' the gender division embodied in domestic work, so it created potential for change in the sexual division of labour within industrial work. Chapter 7 investigates the policy of 'dilution' of male by female labour, which was orchestrated by the MOL, though conducted by employers and trade unionists. The purpose of dilution was to promote the absorption of women into the industrial structure and the release of men into the armed forces. It could have broken down the division of 'men's' from 'women's' work, and the differentials in pay and status between them. In fact its implementation put into sharp focus the question of the desirable place of women in the workforce from the points of view of employers and male workers. The conflict arising from it demonstrates the tenacity with which industrial employers held on to the idea of the inferiority of women as a weapon which could be used against both men and women workers in order to cheapen labour. But this conflict had another outcome. By the end of the war some male trade unionist leaders spoke as though they had moved away from adherence to gender-based interests and understood men and women at work to have a common interest in job opportunities and equal pay. This would have been an important shift in trade union thinking but evidence about the practice of both the skilled and the general trade unions towards women throughout the war suggests that it was, like earlier demands from men for equal pay, a position adopted in order to protect the male rate and job, in fact underpinned by the conventional assumption that the two sexes had unequal rights of access to and remuneration for work.

This then is the shape of the book. Its theme is that the war economy placed the government in a position in which it had to make decisions about changing women's roles at work and at home. In doing so government ministries had to work with those groups whose own practices would be affected by changes in women's role. They included local authorities, retailers, industrial employers and trade unionists. The interests in and assumptions about women's place in social relations of each group were 'flushed out' by this process, in the sense that policy-making demanded that they be given overt expression. My conclusion is that these assumptions were remarkably resilient, to the extent that they profoundly constrained the provisions made for the changes demanded by the circumstances of war.

There is currently a debate among Marxists and feminists as to whether women's unequal position in society can be explained more adequately by reference to the structures of capitalism or patriarchy. Put simply, the analysis of women in capitalism depicts women as specially exploited workers. Capital requires them to be reproducers of both children and male labour power within the family and by virtue of this role they are available as a low paid and casual workforce should they be required in the labour market.[3] According to the analysis of patriarchy women work within the family not primarily for capital but for men. Under the marriage contract women work without remuneration, for their keep alone. Since the material basis of their existence in a patriarchal society is unpaid work within the family, marriage and family work (or the prospect of it) dominate women's lives, even when they perform paid work outside the home.[4]

The Second World War was clearly a time when women were needed in the labour market. The analysis of women's place in capitalism would lead one to expect that alternative arrangements would be made for domestic work so that women's entry into paid work could be facilitated, at least temporarily. The analysis of patriarchy, on the other hand, suggests that any arrangement which threatened the performance by women of unpaid work within the family and their dependence upon marriage, such as collective child care, or alternatives to shopping and cooking, or equality of hours, pay and opportunities at work, would be intolerable to men and would therefore be resisted. What follows is an interpretation of the history of women in the Second World War not just as the story of an interplay between the need to mobilise women and conventional expectations about their roles, but also as a moment of conflict between two modes of production, capitalist and patriarchal, which created considerable tension within the state since it represented not one side or the other, but both.

The research on which this book is based is of course limited in various ways. In particular, though concerned with the mobilisation of women for war, I do not deal with their recruitment for, and work in, voluntary organisations (e.g. the Women's Voluntary Service), nor the women's military services (the Auxiliary Territorial Service, the Women's Auxiliary Air Force and the Women's Royal Naval Service), nor the Women's Land Army, but I concentrate on women in industrial work. Research into all these areas is important for developing a complete picture of women in the Second World War and is, I hope, in progress.

A second limitation relates to sources of women's own reactions to and perceptions of war and the policies associated with it. Women's responses were vital to the development of policy and for this reason were investigated, interpreted and used by many of the different groups involved in, or trying to influence, policy-making. The evidence of women's own feelings which is used here belongs in the main 'within policy' since most of it comes from these official or semi-official observers of the wartime lives of women, who all had their own particular reasons for collecting and interpreting evidence in the way they did. This was particularly so of the various government ministries concerned, but also applies to bodies surveying public opinion and behaviour, such as the Wartime Social Survey[5] and Mass-Observation[6] and a motley of individual commentators. There is still great scope for constructing a history of women in the Second World War from women's own accounts of their wartime experiences, using both oral history and the wealth of wartime diaries and letters in the Mass-Observation Archive.[7] Such research would also provide insights into the mythologising of the war and women's part in it which has taken place since 1945.

Finally, official policy provides only one angle of vision on continuity and change in attitudes to women during the Second World War. Other possible sites of study include the labour movement, the feminist movement and the mass media. Some of these have been developed in other contexts, for instance by Gail Braybon in her important research into the attitudes to working women of members of the organised labour and feminist movements in the First World War,[8] and by Leila Rupp in her work on propaganda to women in the US and Germany in the Second World War.[9] Research in each of these areas in the British context in the Second World War needs to be undertaken. I hope that the concentration here on the government as a nerve centre in which the wartime pressure to maximise productivity and the restraining influence of patriarchal expectations about women's place met, clashed and had to be reconciled will form a useful context for such future research.

Notes

1. Betty Friedan, *The Feminine Mystique* (Penguin Books, Harmondsworth, 1965); Juliet Mitchell, *Psychoanalysis and Feminism* (Penguin Books, Harmondsworth, 1975), pp. 227–31.

2. Arthur Marwick, *Britain in the Century of Total War: War, Peace and Social Change, 1900–1967* (Macmillan, London, 1968), pp. 291–3; *War and Social Change in the Twentieth Century: A Comparative Study of Britain, France, Germany, Russia and the US* (Macmillan, London, 1974), pp. 159–61; 'Women's Fightback on the Home Front', *The Times Higher Education Supplement*, 10 September 1982.

3. *Inter alia*, Wally Secombe, 'The Housewife and Her Labour under Capitalism', *New Left Review*, 83, 1974; Jean Gardiner, 'Women's Domestic Labour', *New Left Review*, 89, 1975; M. Coulson, B. Magas and H. Wainwright, 'The Housewife and Her Labour under Capitalism: A Critique', *New Left Review*, 89, 1975; P. Smith, 'Domestic Labour and Marx's Theory of Value' in A. Kuhn and A.M. Wolpe, *Feminism and Materialism* (Routledge and Kegan Paul, London, 1978).

4. Christine Delphy, 'The Main Enemy: A Materialist Analysis of Women's Oppression', *Explorations in Feminism*, 3 (WRRC, 1977); for the debate on patriarchy see, *inter alia*, articles by Z.R. Eisenstein and H. Hartmann in Z.R. Eisenstein (ed.), *Capitalist Patriarchy and the Case for Socialist Feminism* (Monthly Review Press, New York, 1979); V. Beechey, 'On Patriarchy', *Feminist Review*, 3, 1979; S. Walby, 'Women's Unemployment, Patriarchy and Capitalism', *Socialist Economic Review*, 1983.

5. The Wartime Social Survey was part of the Central Office of Information, a government department. It responded to requests from different departments to report in depth, on the basis of population samples, on social matters vital to policy-making during the war. Three reports, duplicated for internal circulation but never published, were particularly concerned with women during the war: 'An Investigation of the Attitudes of Women, the General Public and ATS Personnel to the Auxiliary Territorial Service', New Series No. 5, October 1941; 'Women's Registration and Call Up', New Series No. 15, March–April 1942; G. Thomas, 'Women at Work: The Attitudes of Working Women Toward Postwar Employment and Some Related Problems. An Inquiry Made for the Office of the Minister of Reconstruction', New Series Regional 1.3, June 1944.

6. Mass-Observation was an organisation set up in 1936 by Tom Harrisson, an anthropologist, and Charles Madge, a sociologist. Its purpose was to observe

and investigate public behaviour and opinion. It is a major source in the following chapters, since it was extremely active during the war, both as an observer (in its own right as well as for individuals or organisations who commissioned it) and as a campaigner in 'the war to win the war', i.e. the struggle against suspected inefficiency (or at worst defeatism) in government or industry, in pursuit of full mobilisation and production for war. In this, a major concern was with the use of womanpower, hence the prominence given to women in M-O's publications such as *People in Production* (1942) and the abundance of material on women in the file reports, diaries, observations and replies to directives held in the archive.

7. M-O's diaries are beginning to be published. See, for example, R. Broad and S. Fleming (eds.), *Nella Last's War: A Mother's Diary 1939–45* (Falling Wall Press, Bristol, 1981). References in this book are to the originals in the M-O Archive.

8. G. Braybon, *Women Workers in the First World War: The British Experience* (Croom Helm, London, 1981).

9. L.J. Rupp, *Mobilizing Women for War, German and American Propaganda 1939–1945* (Princeton University Press, Princeton, 1978).

2 PRE-WAR

The pre-war history of women's paid employment and domestic work forms the setting in which the mobilisation of women for war took place and therefore has a vital place in this account of women in the Second World War. Some of the changes occurring in women's employment patterns between the wars, notably women's expanding proportions in industries like engineering and metals, presaged much more rapid developments on the same lines during the war, while other features, such as the dominance of textiles and domestic service, were reversed. Clarification of the interwar employment trends is important for discussion of the transfer of women to wartime jobs and their fortunes within them. Equally, the characteristics of domestic life and work for women, the ways it was touched by official policy before the war and the effects upon women of combining paid work with domestic labour constitute the background to the complex process of recruiting women from unpaid work in the home and official attempts to make provision for the domestic sphere during the war.

Employment Trends

The 1931 Census reported that a slightly higher proportion of women was in paid employment in 1931 than in 1921, 34.2 per cent compared with 33.7 per cent, representing a total of 6,265,000 women. Domestic service still dominated the picture, absorbing over one-third of women in paid work in 1931. Probably because of high levels of unemployment in some industries in the 1920s the number of domestic servants rose from 1.8 million in 1921 to 2.1 million in 1931,[1] in spite of middle-class complaints about the servant shortage and a strong current of dissatisfaction among working women.[2] The work was low paid, commanding only 5s to 10s a week for school leavers and 15s to £1 for women over 18, accommodation was often poor, hours were long and social life was severely restricted.[3] Most servants were single and two-thirds were under the age of 35. Wherever they could, women sought alternatives, though in doing so they often confronted prejudice. For example women made redundant by munitions firms at the end of the First World War who rejected offers of domestic placements because they wanted to stay in engineering were threatened with refusal of unemployment benefit and lambasted in the press.[4] Domestic service was seen as a 'natural' sphere of employment for women and it was repeatedly recommended, in and out of Parliament, as a solution to women's unemployment between the wars.[5]

In some areas domestic service was the only employment opportunity for women, but even in places where there was other work it remained important as a fall-back when preferred jobs failed, as the case of a young Londoner, Edith Hall, illustrates. Between the ages of 14 and 17 she worked in sequence as a production line worker in an electric lamp factory, maid of all work, daily maid, driller at His Master's Voice, shopgirl, maid of all work, maid in a large household, production line worker in a sweet factory and tea-trolley girl in another factory.[6] As this suggests, the industrial work available for young women often required no training and did not lead to permanent employment. This was less true of the minority of industries in which women were numerically dominant or formed a large proportion of the workforce, such as clothing, textiles, boots and shoes and pottery work. Here, training, acquired through the family, and relatively regular employment at least until marriage were the norm.[7]

However, textiles was a contracting industry in the 1920s and 1930s, and expansion was occurring in the so-called new industries such as commercial services, food, drink and tobacco, distribution, chemicals, vehicles, transport, engineering and metals. Not only did the numbers of women employed in these industries grow, but the proportion also rose, notably in those industries in which very small numbers of women had traditionally been employed, such as engineering, metals, gas, water and electricity and transport, implying that women were making greater gains than men from their expansion. For example, in engineering the proportion of women rose from 6.5 per cent to 10.3 per cent between 1923 and 1939. Analysing these trends the economist C.E.V. Leser wrote that they meant 'not so much that women took men's jobs as that women-employing sections of the industries concerned gained at the expense of men-employing sections'.[8]

Contemporary evidence supports this suggestion of the expansion of women's employment within a sex-segregated pattern. An official inquiry into the distribution of women in industry undertaken in 1929 gives details of the rising number of women in the light metal trades, pottery, bread and biscuits, tobacco, electrical fittings and scientific apparatus. The explanation offered, and frequently repeated elsewhere, was that women were inherently suited to the new, simplified processes introduced in such industries as a result of technical changes. The 1929 inquiry said of metals:

> The whole tendency in the light metal trades is towards a simplification of processes, and as the need for acquired skill or craftsmanship is eliminated and replaced by simple work of a routine character the work tends to be transferred from men to women or young persons.[9]

The report depicted as entirely natural the fact that women were always confined to semi- or unskilled work. It was seen as irrelevant for women to acquire skill, since marriage accompanied by withdrawal from paid work was assumed to be their universal destiny and women were believed to be intrinsically unsuited to heavy, dirty or wet work, regardless of the fact that traditional women's work, such as domestic service, work in laundries and textiles, and indeed much so-called light work in metals and engineering, was all these things. Women were also said to possess dexterity and tolerance of monotony, which ideally suited them to the new types of work.[10]

The 1929 inquiry did, however, acknowledge in passing other causes of the distribution of women in industry than the naturalistic ones which it emphasised, notably 'custom', i.e. trade union restriction, and the relatively low rates paid to women. The purpose of restriction was to protect male workers from the competition for jobs and the threat of undercutting perceived in the employment of women. The key determinant of the success of restriction was therefore the degree of control which male workers had over the labour process. This itself depended on the strength of trade union organisation, the level of unemployment and the degree of technical change.

For example, in branches of engineering where technical change made the least impact between the wars and the craft unions were strongest, such as locomotive construction, shipbuilding and marine engineering, the entry of women was almost entirely prevented. But in branches such as motor vehicles, where the specialised machine tool had become established for certain parts of the production process, women's entry varied according to regional union strength and the level of male unemployment. In Coventry the proportion of women metal machinists was 18 per cent, whereas in Manchester and the North-east, which suffered higher unemployment levels and were particularly well organised, the proportion was less than 4 per cent.[11] In electrical engineering and scientific instrument making, scattered through the

Midlands and the South, particularly London, women formed a much higher proportion of the workforce: over 40 per cent of those employed by firms making electrical apparatus and cables in 1939.[12] These branches of engineering were making fuller use than any other of the possibilities of break-down of production through the manufacture by repetition processes of separate components and flow-line assembly. The entry of women was not seen as dilution of the male labour force in the way that it was in other branches of engineering. Rather, the work upon which women were employed was labelled from the first 'women's work' and male union organisers accepted or even dismissed it as a separate category earning separate rates.[13] One of the cruel ironies in women's employment between the wars was that in spite of this union-sanctioned, sex-stereotyped sectionalisation, women in such branches of engineering were frequently accused of taking men's jobs.[14]

The strategy of the male-dominated unions in these trades towards female membership was either to deny it altogether, as in the case of the Amalgamated Engineering Union, the foundry workers' union, the metal working unions and the electrical trade union, or to try to recruit women, arguably in order to subsume their specific interests in those of men. This had historically been the case in many of the textile and clothing unions and Sheila Lewenhak suggests that it was the approach adopted by the Transport and General Workers' Union and the National Union of General Workers between the wars. The latter absorbed the National Federation of Women Workers in 1920, a move criticised by some feminists as flying in the face of women's interests. The same kind of drift occurred at the level of the TUC with the merging of the Women's Trade Union League into the Women's Group of the General Council, which was dominated by the male secretaries of unions in industries with a large proportion of women employees. The National Women's Advisory Committee which replaced it in 1931, and which reported annually to the TUC conference of unions catering for women workers, was in constant danger of being marginalised by the TUC General Council to which it was answerable.[15]

Sectionalisation also characterised women's employment in white-collar jobs, such as those falling into the categories 'clerical' and 'commercial'. Though employment opportunities for women expanded in these occupations, the jobs allocated to women such as stenography and work on typewriters and adding machines, were considered the least skilled and were stereotyped 'women's work', unsuitable for men,[16] who clung to the higher status, higher paid branches. All the same, as in manual, so in white-collar work, women were publicly criticised for taking it, as if they were undermining male employment chances. 'Better Pay and Smarter Clothes for Women: Unemployment and Patched Pants for Men', read a *News Chronicle* headline to an article on women secretaries in 1934.[17] Even highly educated women faced difficulties if they tried to move out of the sectors labelled 'women's work' into the higher reaches of the professions. In 1925 only three women were accepted into the administrative grades of the civil service and only nine more were deemed to have qualified between 1926 and 1935,[18] a fact worth remembering in the following chapters when looking at the part played by women civil servants in mobilising women workers. Even after the Sex Disqualification Removal Act of 1919, under which all professions except the top grades of the civil service had to admit women, the proportions were tiny.[19] Women were concentrated in the ranks of the professions with the lowest status and least remuneration, such as nursing and elementary school teaching.[20]

In some of these professional and white-collar occupations there was no tradition of trade unionism and much employer hostility to it. Women teachers, local government officers and civil servants were exceptional in the strength and vigour of their organisations, though divided from the support of the rest of the union movement by the 1927 Trades Disputes and Trade Union Act which made it illegal for public service unions to affiliate to the TUC. They were the only organised women workers to mount a consistent campaign for equal pay between the wars, though they made the claim on behalf of the single professional career woman, rather than women workers in general.

So the general picture is that, even though the number of women in employment was expanding between the wars, women workers were compressed in a few industries and occupations and, whether manual or non-manual, the trend was towards their containment in the narrow segments where the work was labelled 'women's work' and was regarded as non-skilled. Employers' demand for women's cheap labour pulled women in one direction and the resistance of male workers to competition and undercutting pushed them in the other, in the context of rapid technical change. Meanwhile it was widely claimed that women's distribution in employment was the natural result of their innate characteristics and inevitable destiny.

Paid Work and Family Life

So far the discussion has been of women in general, but in fact distinction has to be made between young single and older married women workers. Young women dominated the employment picture, especially in the newer areas of women's employment. In textiles 76 per cent of women workers in 1921 and 68 per cent in 1931 were under 35, whereas in the three industries metals, electrical apparatus and scientific instruments approximately 90 per cent of the women workers in both 1921 and 1931 were under 35. As well as being young, the majority of these women were single. The national figures for all occupied women in 1931 show that 77 per cent were single, 16 per cent married and 7 per cent widowed or divorced.[21]

The large number of young single women in employment struck some observers as more free-wheeling and independent than ever before.[22] But this was a superficial judgement based on factory girls' rejection of shawls and clogs and adoption of high heels, ready-made costumes and permanent waves. The findings of oral historians are that the family was still dominant in working women's lives. Often girls did not decide for themselves about their careers but relatives and family friends secured openings and provided training and a young woman's wage was not automatically her own. Customs varied, but the expectation that a girl would 'tip up' her entire weekly wage, often literally into the folds of her mother's apron, was still strong and in many cases the practice ceased only when the girl married.[23] A young woman worker's financial contribution was the direct equivalent of the labour contributed by the girl who stayed at home and devoted herself to domestic work.[24]

In spite of evidence of considerable family dependence upon the income of young single women, it was widely accepted that a young woman should not earn as much as a man, since she herself was viewed as dependent, initially upon her father and later upon her husband. Women in industrial work earned on average about half of the male wage and those in white-collar work about three-quarters between the wars.[25] However, the ideology of female dependence was contradictory. Almost a fifth of all adult women did not marry between 1921 and 1939, largely because of the demographic imbalance between the sexes arising from heavy emigration of men in the late nineteenth century and male war casualties during the First World War.[26] The expectations of the family were that an older unmarried woman would stay at home contributing her income and taking over household affairs when her mother died. In such cases the single woman frequently assumed responsibility for dependent relatives, such as an aged father and younger siblings.[27] The fact that many single woman workers, particularly women civil servants, were supporting others strengthened the resolve of those campaigning for equal pay when confronted with the tenaciously held belief that, as Vera Brittain put it, 'men have dependants to keep, while women work only for pin money'.[28] But it also caused some single women to argue against the removal of the marriage bar, of which more shortly, both because the dependent status of wives might weaken their case and because their competition for jobs might 'take the bread from the spinsters' mouths'.[29]

In spite of the relatively large proportion of women who did not marry, the spinster was still regarded as odd, though she might derive a tinge of glamour from her interwar claim to be an unmarried war widow.[30] Marriage and dependency within it were the norm. Vera Brittain quoted Charles Cheers Wakefield advising parents not to consider an 'alternative vocation' to marriage 'as a permanency' for their daughters, who required no more than 'a small wage, some leisure and more freedom'.[31] Young women's employment patterns were at least partly the result of the deep-rooted internalisation of such views by both girls and their families.[32] The Pilgrim Trust reported, 'The girl of 14 tends to drift into the most remunerative employment immediately available, keeping the alternative of marriage always in view and hoping that she will sooner or later be freed from the fulfil-ment of a function in industry.'[33] However, as Margery Spring Rice warned, this 'crown of a woman's life' turned out all too often 'to be one of thorns'.[34]

The practice of imposing a marriage bar in many occupations was one of the most concrete ways in which the ideology of the male breadwinner and female dependant was expressed. It was formally applied within the civil service, in banking, retailing and against women teachers by many local education authorities.[35] But 'white blouse' occupations were only those where it operated most rigidly. It was the unwritten practice to dismiss a woman on marriage in many industries[36] and reinforced the emphasis on youth in the age profile of women workers. Younger women, especially 14-18-year-olds, were cheaper to employ and, from male workers' point of view, did not stay long enough to compete for promotion. Prejudice against older women abounded among employers, although the women might be only as old as 35, and it became increasingly difficult for a woman to find a new job the older she became, whether single or married.

Unemployment hit women in their forties and fifties disproportionately hard in the 1920s and 1930s[37] and unemployment benefit was frequently denied them. A clause introduced to unemployment insurance legislation in 1921 required applicants to prove that they were 'genuinely seeking work' before they received benefit, but women running homes and families were easily construed as not doing so and women dismissed on marriage were trapped in the bind of being denied benefit until they had 're-established' themselves in industry.[38]

The realities of low male wages and high rates of unemployment meant that marriage did not mark the end of paid working life for many women. Marriage bars did not operate in work like charring and outwork which was done for a pittance in or near a woman's own home,[39] but the punitive rates of pay in this sector gave rise to many cases of women seeking to keep their original jobs by concealing their marriages.[40] There was in addition a small but growing proportion of married women with a 'legitimate' status in the occupied female population. The overall figures were 13 per cent in 1921 and 16 per cent in 1931, concealing higher proportions in a small number of industries, such as textiles, hosiery-making, boots and shoes and the pottery industry. Whereas 23 per cent of the women in textiles were married in 1921, the proportion was 36 per cent in 1931.[41] The explanation for such instances of tolerance in the context of generalised male prejudice against married women at work is twofold. Firstly these were 'women's' industries, divided from others such as mining or heavy engineering which had developed locally as exclusively male occupations. Secondly sexual division existed with these industries, as well as between them and others. The sex-typing of work, already discussed, was a continuous development, affecting industries which employed large proportions of women as well as those they were just beginning to enter. In some cases the differentiation of types of work and rates of pay received by men and women served to protect men from 'intrusion' by women, single and married. To give just one example, in hosiery women were being removed from the primary knitting process between the wars by the action of the hosiery unions forbidding them to work on certain knitting frames and were increasingly confined to making up the garments, a development justified on the grounds that these jobs, such as linking, cutting, mending and machining, required female dexterity.[42] Within 'female' industrial sectors employers frequently treated married women as particularly dispensable workers, who could be used to plug holes in the production process at certain times of the week or year but did not have to be continuously employed.[43] Such 'short-time' arrangements meshed with the counter-pull of housework and family demands upon married women which, in the absence of other provisions for domesticity, inevitably interrupted their availability for work.[44]

But even in areas where industrial work was the norm for single women, and a relatively large number of married women also worked in the mills or factories, there were pressures on married women not to work outside the home if their husbands' wages made private domesticity remotely possible. Such attitudes were not universal, as evidence of the egalitarian approach to marriage of Burnley weavers indicates, but they were widespread.[45] The complexities of the patriarchal expectation that women would renounce paid work on marriage are nicely illustrated by the case of a Nottingham woman whose mother refused to mind her child while she returned to hosiery work with the comment, 'You had the baby, you look after it; your husband married you, let him keep yer.' The mother explained that she did not want her daughter to be dragged into the double day of industrial and domestic work. However, she would take her grandchild while her daughter did her own housework. Ironically, on these occasions she occupied herself by making hairnets, outwork which earned her a pitiful sum, but which, like childminding and taking in laundry or lodgers, was not incompatible with the expectation that she would be home-centred.[46]

Domestic Work

We have seen that the proportion of married women in the female workforce was rising between the wars, particularly in the women-dominated industries, even though expectations that married women would not do paid work were strong. It is worth asking questions about the nature of the domestic labour which married women workers combined with paid work and about the official help, if any, which they could get with this family work. Answers are important in order to understand both the responses of married women to mobilisation during the war and the official approach towards collective provision for domestic work.

The work of washing perhaps best illustrates the arduousness of domestic work for working-class women between the wars. Reference is often made to an increase in 'labour-saving devices' in the home in this period as an explanation of the gradual expansion of women's employment, but few of those which saved the labour of washday had reached the majority of homes. The Women's Health Enquiry Committee found that even a self-contained water supply was a rarity possessed by less than 10 per cent of the working-class homes it visited.[47] If cold water had to be fetched, it went without saying that hot water had to be boiled up on a stove or in a copper. In such accommodation, commented the author of the committee's report, 'far from there being any labour-saving devices the bare necessities of a decent existence may be extremely difficult to obtain'.[48]

Verbatim descriptions of washing day collected by Mass-Observation in Bolton in 1939 indicate that the process usually took at least 24 hours, beginning with steeping clothes in washing powder and water on, for instance, Sunday night, going through the stages of wringing, mangling and scrubbing, boiling, rinsing, blueing and dollying, and ending, all being well, on Monday night with ironing and possibly mending. If the weather was bad the last stages of the chore were protracted. The clothes had to be dried indoors on a 'maiden' and it might be days before the family 'saw the fire'.[49] Cleaning the house involved some of the same problems as doing the family wash, such as the need to fetch and heat up water and the sheer graft of scrubbing and mopping, while cramped accommodation 'full of beds' added to the difficulties. Washing up also required heated water and usually had to be done after each meal because of the shortage of pots, crocks and cutlery.[50] For women going out to work there were three ways of coping with the family wash. The help of other members of the family, principally older daughters, could be enlisted in the evenings, or the wash could be sent to relatively expensive laundries, or it could be taken to the public wash-house provided by the local authority, but, though the facilities and space of the wash-house made the task easier and quicker, women interviewed by M-O were reluctant to use them because they were 'rough' and it was 'degrading' to carry dirty washing across the street, complaints suggestive of a shrinking against the public display of personal poverty common to potential users of many kinds of public assistance.[51]

Shopping, cooking and child care were other vital components of domestic labour. Shopping between the wars was characterised by a great variety of specialist shops, which added to the time it took to shop. Official wartime discussions referred to twelve types of shop in the area of food alone, even though 'multiples' selling different types of produce under one roof, such as Sainsbury, Woolworth and the Co-operative Societies, were on the increase.[52] The practice was highly socially stratified with services like deliveries and purchase on account for the wealthy, while the working-class wife had to buy small quantities daily while she had the cash, after which she had to appeal to buy 'on tick', not seen as equivalent to the credit extended to the rich. However the working woman was helped by touring barrow boys and also by the late opening hours of most shops. Under the Shops (Hours of Closing) Act of 1928, the legal closing times were 8 p.m. and 9 p.m. on late days, and many small general stores stayed open till midnight or simply opened in response to any request. Children were frequently engaged to help.[53]

As with washing, so with food storage and cooking facilities; labour-saving devices were not within reach of most working-class families. Refrigerators were luxuries and, though gas and electric cookers were on the increase, coal-fired ranges were still common. Even cooking utensils tended to be in short supply.[54] Public feeding of any sort was minimal and was provided as a safety net to prevent ill health and malnutrition, mainly among babies and children, and certainly not as a service to help working women.

Free or subsidised food was provided for cases considered deserving by groups like the Salvation Army in areas of high unemployment and it was possible to obtain free food and milk for sickly babies and for pregnant women at the local Maternity and Child Welfare Centres, whose uneven establishment by the different local authorities under enabling legislation of 1918 was accounted for like that of nurseries (see below) by the presence or absence of local initiative and enthusiasm.[55] After 1934 school children could obtain one-third of a pint of milk a day, either free or at a price subsidised by their LA and by 1939 half the elementary school population was receiving daily milk.[56] Under the 1906 Education (Provision of Meals) Act parents could obtain free school dinners for their children, which of all the measures mentioned so far would have been most helpful to working mothers. But application had to be approved by the LA and the meals were frequently provided by charitable organisations in their own premises. Such conditions constituted a disincentive to potential applicants and in 1938 only one child in 35 was receiving a regular free school dinner.[57] This meant that the mothers of over 4 million school children had full responsibility for their children's midday meal. They either had to provide a 'bait tin', send the children to a friend or relative, or be at home themselves at midday. Much the same was true of feeding husbands. Only the most progressive factories, numbering about 1,500 out of literally thousands of separate enterprises, contained canteens for their workers.[58] Some offered facilities for heating up food brought from home, others access to a tea trolley and others nothing at all. In some areas there were public bake-houses where a working woman could leave a meal cooking for members of the family to collect and in most towns there were fish-and-chip and hot-meat-pie shops, though (like getting clothes laundered) ready-cooked food was relatively expensive.[59] In all, shopping and cooking absorbed a major part of the working-class housewife's day and presented a significant logistical problem to the woman out at work.[60]

Child care is possibly the most difficult domestic responsibility to delegate, for all that the case for its delegation is clear as far as women doing paid work are concerned, since it was, and is, incompatible with most forms of paid work, apart from possibly charring and outwork. For this reason more consideration was given to child care than to any other aspect of domestic work in the development of wartime mobilisation policy, so it is important to clarify the pre-war provisions upon which wartime developments were based.

The day-time care of children under five took place in three different types of institution under two different authorities, the Ministry of Health and the Board of Education, between the wars. Only one type of institution, the MOH day nursery, was provided with the working woman's needs in mind and even in this case places were not available for the children of any woman in paid work, but only those whose mothers were considered to be working of necessity, i.e. because they were unmarried, deserted or widowed. Other day nursery children came from homes considered particularly poverty-striken, unhealthy or neglectful. Selection was conducted under Poor Law conditions and if actual disgrace was not attached to the use of a public nursery then the label of misfortune certainly was. Under pressure of public expenditure cuts the number of day nurseries declined from 174 in 1919 when the MOH took responsibility for them under the Maternity and Child Welfare Act, to 104 by 1938, taking 4,291 children.[61]

Nursery schools had even less to do with the needs of working mothers. Some were private, middle-class institutions which developed in the nineteenth century under the influence of the educational theorist, F.W.A. Froebel. Others were pioneered by socialists like Robert Owen, and later the McMillan sisters, to give children from poorer families 'a fair start' in educational terms. Largely as a result of the McMillans' pressure, coupled to a general concern about the physical and mental conditions of the population during the First World War, recognition was given to the nursery school in the 1918

Education Act. However, as with so much legislative provision for women and children, the clause relating to nursery schools was permissive. As LAs might, if they chose, provide them for two- to five-year-olds, with 50 per cent funding from the Board of Education.[62] In 1919 the Board had under its control, via the LAs, 19 nursery schools and by 1938 only 118 had been established or approved, catering for 9,504 children, in spite of unrelenting pressure from the Nursery School Association of Great Britain founded in 1923 and from Women's sections of the Labour Party.[63] Nursery schools, which worked school hours, from 9 a.m. to 3.30 or 4 p.m. and observed school holidays, were concerned both with children's mental development and also, as a prerequisite, with their physical well-being. But the needs of the mother were not of foremost concern, if considered at all, and the nature of provision was not well suited to the woman going out to work.

The other type of institution under the Board of Education, the nursery class, had originated by default rather than design, as a result of a tendency among late-nineteenth-century parents to send children from the age of two or three to the local elementary school. In 1900–1901, 616,000 under-fives were on elementary school registers, representing 43 per cent of the three–five-year-old age group.[64] The nursery class was, however, under attack. The 1902 Act established that grants would be paid only for those over three and in 1905 the women Inspectors of Schools urged exclusion of all children under five, on the grounds that they were neglected at school and should be home with their mothers. The proportion of under-fives at elementary schools subsequently fell, from 43 per cent in 1901 to 17 per cent in 1919, but the practice of sending under-fives to school died hard.[65] To mothers the arrangement had the advantage that elementary schools were local and that under-fives could go and return with older children, which lessened the difficulty of the incompatibility of the hours of schooling and working. From the point of view of head-teachers, under-fives filled desks in a period of falling birth rate and administration grudgingly accepted the classes since they kept young children off the streets. In 1938, 170,000 children out of 1,750,000 three- to five-year-olds were attending nursery classes, fewer by far than in 1901 but more than either of the other nursery institutions took. Total nursery provision covered barely 10 per cent of the under-five-year-old population.[66]

Working mothers inevitably had to fall back on minders. Thus in Preston, for example, women in full-time work paid relatives or neighbours as much as 10s a week for child minding.[67] Opinions were divided on the practice. The nannies of the wealthy were of course exempt from public criticism, but working-class minding was often deplored, for instance by the Pilgrim Trust, on the grounds that minding gave children an 'abnormal background' which led to all sorts of dire consequences including juvenile delinquency.[68] Health Visitors in Preston, on the other hand, believed that the minded children whom they visited were 'well cared for', in almost all cases by relatives.[69] For mothers, minding had the advantages of flexibility of hours and a personal, informal relationship between mother and minder. But there was no guarantee that these would always work to the advantage of mother and child and minding had the disadvantages of needing to be individually organised, of depending on the local availability of minders and of a tendency to be both temporary and expensive. Institutional forms of care also had disadvantages. Above all, there were not enough of them. But they were at least relatively permanent, cheap and reliable.

This brief review of some aspects of domestic work between the wars suggests that even though a growing proportion of married women was working, the material conditions of domestic life and the extent and nature of public provision for domestic work were not conducive to combining paid and unpaid work. In view of the weight of domestic work it is not surprising that women's health suffered[70] and, once it started to deteriorate, the breakwaters were flimsy. Only women in insured employment (just over half of those in paid work) were entitled to free or subsidised medical attention, apart from limited care relating to maternity[71] and even so there is little evidence to suggest that women in paid work were any more healthy than housewives. The high levels of sickness and disablement among working women took government officials administering the insurance scheme completely by surprise.[72] Poor nutrition among women, in part the result of feeding the man of the family first on the basis that a 'bread-winner' must be kept fit, and untreated problems, many of which arose from inadequate maternity care, such as dysmenorrhea, anaemia, headaches, haemorrhoids, rheumatism, varicosity and prolapse, may have been as characteristic of women in work as of those at home.[73]

The issue of women's health in relation to work, more than any other, split the women's movement between the wars. Legislation which was ostensibly intended to protect women's health was suspected by some feminists of being aimed in fact at protecting men from the competition of women workers, in the same tradition as trade union restriction. For example, Vera Brittain complained that the 1926

Lead Paint (Protection against Poisoning) Act 'virtually closed the paint industry to women', though she and others believed that lead had as harmful an effect on the male reproductive capacity as on the female.[74] The 1929 inquiry into the distribution of women in industry concluded that the rising numbers of women in industry showed that protective legislation did not have the effect of restricting women's employ-ment.[75] However feminists like Sylvia Anthony pointed out that it did have negative effects. Wages were depressed in the sections of industries where women were concentrated as a result of exclusion from others and legislation restricting, women's working hours had led to their removal from some industries. For example the 1920 Employment of Women, Young Persons and Children Act prohibited the employment of women on night work and the 1937 Factory Act reaffirmed this, laid down a maximum 48-hour week for women, limited their overtime hours and prohibited Sunday work. Feminists claimed that this legisla-tion had led to the removal of women from industries like flax, jute and tinplate which worked a shift system.[76]

In fact the legal restrictions on women's employment immediately before the Second World War amounted to no more than the exclusion of women from work with lead and from underground work in mines, plus the restrictions on their hours mentioned above. The legislation on working hours was, in addition, riddled with 'let-out' clauses permit-ting the employment of women at forbidden times when 'pressure of work' required it.[77] More important (though frequently overlooked) determinants of women's concentration in unskilled, low-paid occupa-tions were the numerous agreements on 'trade practices' between trade unions and employers which, as we have already seen, effectively closed whole sectors of industries to women. Observing this, Anthony and Brittain argued for the replacement of protective legislation by a law preventing discrimination between men and women which would effectively outlaw gender-based restrictive practices.[78] Inevitably this earned them the hostility of the male trade union movement and the Standing Joint Committee of Working Women's Organisations was also unsympathetic. Their strategy was to insist on the enforcement of protective legislation, which they supported on the grounds that it could eventually be extended for the benefit of men as well as women, but that women needed it immediately, both because of their natural constitutions and their maternal function, actual or potential. Their efforts were devoted to organising women and raising their wage rates, through the Trade Boards in cases of very low pay. Some women trade unionists supported the male demand for a 'family' wage, on the grounds that it would be better if married women did not have to go out to work.[79] When Anthony argued that women could be employed harmlessly on night work if they were 'certain of returning home to a cooked meal, a bed prepared for them, and complete lack of responsibility for domestic chores',[80] their reaction was that such things simply would not await working women in the immediate future. Many women trade unionists felt that therefore women should be legislated out of working arrangements such as night work or work during pregnancy, which combined with domestic conventions to the detriment of their health. Two conferences were held on the subject of protective legislation for women in 1926. Vera Brittain described the tension which arose as a 'class passion' roused by the gulf 'between middle-class theory and working-class anxiety'.[81]

What, in sum, was the position of women workers in and out of the home on the eve of the Second World War? It could be represented as an uneasy compromise between capitalism and patriarchy. There was a growing demand for women's labour, but women were concentrated in a few industries and occupations, frequently in sectors where the work was dubbed women's work, was considered unskilled and was paid at discriminatory rates. Even though, overall, women probably did not experience a higher rate of unemployment than men, their employment tended to be more episodic and irregular and their rights to benefits when out of work were more often denied than in the case of men, since they were expected to be dependants. Women workers in both industrial and white-collar occupations were overwhelmingly young and single, but such women experienced high expectations that they would not only earn their own keep until they married, but that their earnings would form an integral part of the family budget.

For the majority of married women, home life between the wars was, as a material reality, not conducive to combination with paid work. In addition many married women were denied the chance to try to combine the two, as a result of both the demands of husbands and families that they would work exclusively at home and the imposition of marriage bars particularly in better-paid industries and occupations. For all that women in and out of paid work were having smaller families, the weight of domestic work in unsatisfactory conditions, especially when combined with ill-paid work outside the home, had a corrosive effect on their health.

Women's collective struggles for change, though vigorous between the wars, were fragmented and polarised apparently along class lines, though the division was also between those who regarded domestic relations of production as fixed and wanted to change the way women were employed in paid work to accommodate them and those who wanted women to occupy a position of equality with men as workers within capitalist production and believed that, if necessary, domestic relations would have to change.

Government intervention into women's work and home life between the wars was minimal. With regard to work much of it, for instance protective legislation, constrained women's opportunities to do paid work. As far as it touched home life the aim of government policy was to help the very poor or 'disadvantaged' to survive, in other words to support those who could not subsist as a man's dependent, such as the widow or the unmarried mother. The official emphasis was less on mothers themselves than on their children. What is more, all policies affecting the home, be they the provision of welfare centres for pregnant mothers and young children, or nurseries with municipal wash-houses, were permissive, so that there was no guarantee that the thin safety net intended to preserve families from destitution existed in every area. No policy offered married women any encouragement to work, even though a rising proportion of women either wanted or were compelled to do so.

It was in this context that the labour market was transformed by the advent of the Second World War. Responses to the change were bound to be varied. But this sketch of women's pre-war position suggests that a number of general problems would confront a government trying to mobilise women for war. Firstly, there was the question of whether women would move spontaneously from industries where they were traditionally located to unfamiliar ones where war needs created a demand for their labour power. Secondly, the willingness of married women to add paid work to their existing work load was uncertain in view of both the real weight of domestic chores and the pressure of convention and in view of the sparse public provision for private house-work. Thirdly, the acceptability of women to both employers and male workers in many sectors of industry was in doubt. Underlying all three was the fundamental question of whether the demand of wartime production for women's labour power would transform the sexual division of labour in domestic and paid work, or whether such a profound change would be resisted.

Notes

1. *Census of England and Wales*, 1921, Occupation Tables (HMSO, 1924); *Census of England and Wales*, 1931, Occupation Tables (HMSO, 1934).

2. There is now a wealth of sources on domestic service, including accounts written by ex-domestic servants, e.g. M. Powell, *Below Stairs* (P. Davies, London, 1968) and W. Foley, *A Child in the Forest* (BBC, London, 1974) and many published by the Federation of Worker Writers and Community Publishers, e.g. Daisy Noakes, *The Town Beehive* (QueenSpark Books, Brighton, 1975) and Edith Hall, *Canary Girls and Stockpots* (WEA, Luton, 1977). Oral historians have also collected evidence e.g. Pam Taylor, 'Daughters and Mothers – Maids and Mistresses: Domestic Service Between the Wars' in Clarke, Critcher and Johnson (eds.), *Working-class Culture: Studies in History and Theory* (Hutchinson, London, 1979).

3. Information on pay and conditions comes from the above, e.g. Noakes (1975), p. 47, and Foley (1974), pp. 213 ff., as well as from feminists such as V. Brittain, *Women's Work in Modern England* (Noel Douglas, London, 1928), pp. 30–33 and Elaine Burton, *What of the Women?* (Frederick Muller, London, 1941), pp. 194–5.

4. G. Braybon, *Women Workers in the First World War* (Croom Helm, London, 1981), pp. 186–90.

5. *Parliamentary Papers*, 1919, xxix, Cmd. 67; Pilgrim Trust, *Men Without Work* (Cambridge University Press, Cambridge, 1938), p. 260; Sylvia Anthony, *Women's Place in Industry and Home* (G. Routledge and Sons, London, 1932), p. 232.

6. Hall (1977) pp. 28–33, 36–7 and 40.

7. *Census of England and Wales*, 1921, Occupation Tables (1924); Joanna Bornat, 'Home and Work: A New Context for Trade Union History', *Oral History*, V, No. 2, 1977.

8. C.E.V. Leser, 'Men and Women in Industry', *Economic Journal*, 1952, p. 330.

9. *Parliamentary Papers*, 'A Study of the Factors Which Have Operated in the Past and Those Which Are Operating Now to Determine the Distribution of Women in Industry', Cmd. 3508, December 1929 (HMSO, London, 1930), p. 13.

10. Supporting evidence can be found in J.B. Jefferys, *The Story of the Engineers, 1800–1945* (Lawrence and Wishart, London, 1945) and E. Ahrends, *Women and the Labour Force: The London Metal Industry 1914–1938* (Women's Research and Resources Centre, London, 1976).

11. R. Croucher, 'Communist Politics and Shop Stewards in Engineering 1935–46' (University of Warwick unpublished Ph.D. thesis, 1978), p. 31 and Tables 7 and 9.

12. P. Inman, *Labour in the Munitions Industries* (HMSO, London, 1957), p. 80.

13. Royal Commission on Equal Pay, *Minutes of Evidence* (HMSO, London, 1945), 3 August 1945, paras. 3366–7 and 3373–4.

14. See, for example, Hall (1977), p. 30.

15. Sheila Lewenhak, *Women in Trade Unions: An Outline History of Women in the British Trade Union Movement* (Benn, London, 1977), pp. 173–5, 186–92 and 205.

16. *Census of England and Wales*, 1921 and 1931; W. Holtby, *Women in a Changing Civilisation* (Lane, London, 1934), p. 112.

17. Holtby (1934), p. 100.

18. Neil A. Ferguson, 'Women's Work: Employment Opportunities and Economic Roles 1918–1939', *Albion*, 1963, pp. 61–5.

19. Anthony (1932), p. 16; Charlotte Haldane, *Motherhood and Its Enemies* (Doubleday, New York, 1928), p. 107.

20. Ferguson (1963), p. 60; Anthony (1932), pp. 16 ff.

21. *Census of England and Wales*, 1921, Occupation Tables (London, 1924), Table 2, and 1931, Occupation Tables (London, 1934), Table 3.

22. Cicely Hamilton, *The Englishwoman* (Longmans Green, London, 1940), p. 22; J.B. Priestley, *English Journey* (Heinemann with Gollancz, London, 1935), p. 196.

23. Bornat (1977), pp. 108–9; Elizabeth Roberts, 'Working Wives and Their Families' in Theo Barker and Michael Drake (eds.), *Population and Society in Britain 1850–1980* (Batsford, London, 1982), p. 146.

24. See, for example, Foley (1974), Hall (1977) and Pilgrim Trust (1938), p. 231.

25. Ferguson (1963), p. 66.

26. Royal Commission on Population, 'Report', Cmd. 7695 (HMSO, London, 1949), p. 23.

27. Bornatt (1977), p. 109.

28. Brittain (1928), pp. 192 ff.

29. Ibid., pp. 194–5.

30. Holtby (1934), pp. 128–31.

31. Brittain (1928), p. 196.

32. See, for example, E. Roberts, 'Working-class Women in the North-west', *Oral History*, V, Autumn 1977, pp. 9–10.

33. Pilgrim Trust (1938), p. 231. The Trust was a fund controlled by a group of religious, academic and political figures for use by voluntary organisations. *Men Without Work* was the report of its inquiry in the 1930s to discover the 'effect of long unemployment' and the 'work that voluntary societies could do for the unemployed'.

34. Margery Spring Rice, *Working-Class Wives: Their Health and Conditions* (first published by Penguin Books, London, 1939; this edition Virago, London, 1981), p. 95.

35. Hamilton (1940), pp. 24–5; Strachey, 'Married Women and Work', *Contemporary Review*, CXLV, 1934, p. 335; Burton (1941), pp. 119 ff. The London County Council withdrew its application to teachers and medical staff in 1935 after a referendum of the staff association had shown that three-fifths of women wanted it to go and in the light of shortages of these workers. See Lewenhak (1977), p. 226.

36. Hamilton (1940), p. 25; Sandra Taylor, 'The Effect of Marriage on Job Possibilities for Women and the Ideology of the Home: Nottingham 1890–1930', *Oral History*, V, Autumn 1977, p. 54.

37. Pilgrim Trust (1938), pp. 251, 244–6, 237.

38. B.B. Gilbert, *British Social Policy 1914–1939* (Batsford, London, 1970), p. 95. The Labour government of 1929–31 removed the 'genuinely seeking work' clause in 1930 but it was reintroduced under anomalies regulations of 1931. See Gilbert (1970), pp. 96 and 163. See also TUC Pamphlets and Leaflets, 1940/12.

39. Spring Rice (1981), p. 158.

40. See, for example, M-OA, 'Diary of an Inspector of Taxes', 1939–44; Hall (1977), pp. 45 and 48; Taylor (1977), p. 54.

41. *Census of England and Wales*, 1921, Occupation Tables (1924), Table 4 and 1931, Occupation Tables (1934), Table 1.

42. Lewenhak (1977), p. 213; Taylor (1977), p. 49.

43. RCEP, *Minutes of Evidence*, 27 July 1945, para. 2962.

44. Roberts (1982), p. 143.

45. Ibid., p. 147; D. Gittins, *Fair Sex, Family Size and Structure 1900–1939*

(Hutchinson, London, 1982).

46. Taylor (1977), p. 55.

47. Spring Rice (1981), pp. 135–40. (The incomes and average family sizes suggest that the sample came from the 'D' and 'E' sections of the manual working class.)

48. Ibid., p. 136.

49. M-OA, Topic Collection 4, Box 5, File G, 'Washing Habits, 1939'. M-O questioned a sample of 60 working-class housewives in Bolton. (There is a brief explanation of Mass-Observation in Chapter 1, note 6.)

50. Hall (1977), p. 8; Spring Rice (1981), pp. 97–8.

51. Spring Rice (1981), pp. 131 and 142; M-OA Topic Collection No. 4, Box 5, 'Washing Habits, 1939'.

52. The twelve were grocer, butcher, greengrocer, dairyman, fishmonger, fruiterer, baker, cake shop, confectioner, pork butcher, cooked-meat shop, egg retailer. See PRO Lab 26/61, memorandum on 'Shopping Difficulties', Ministry of Food, 27 August 1941 and minutes of a conference between Ministry of Labour, Ministry of Food, Retailers' Associations and Shop Assistants' Unions, 18 September 1941.

53. See Neil Griffiths, *Shops Book, Brighton 1900–1930* (QueenSpark Books, Brighton, 1978), pp. 14–15; Foley (1974), pp. 29–31; Hall (1977), p. 17; Albert Paul, *Poverty, Hardship But Happiness* (QueenSpark Books, Brighton, 1975), p. 11.

54. Spring Rice (1981), p. 98.

55. See S.M. Ferguson and H. Fitzgerald, *Studies in the Social Services* (HMSO, London, 1954), pp. 146 ff.

56. Ibid., p. 155.

57. R.M. Titmuss, *Problems of Social Policy* (HMSO, London, 1950), p. 149.

58. CCA, BEVN 2/3, Sir A.W. Garrett to Ernest Bevin, June 1942.

59. Roberts (1982), p. 161.

60. See G. Mitchell (ed.), *The Hard Way Up: The Autobiography of Hannah Mitchell, Suffragette and Rebel* (Virago, London, 1977), p. 112. ' "The tyranny of meals" is the worst snag in the housewife's lot. Her life is bounded on the north by breakfast, south by dinner, east by tea, and on the west by supper, and the most sympathetic man can never be made to understand that meals do not come up through the tablecloth, but have to be planned, bought and cooked.'

61. Ferguson and Fitzgerald (1954), pp. 177–8.

62. Board of Education Consultative Committee, *Infant and Nursery Schools* (HMSO, London, 1933), Chapter 1.

63. Ferguson and Fitzgerald (1954), p. 178; T. Blackstone, *A Fair Start: The Provision of Pre-School Education* (Allen Lane, London, 1971), pp. 42–50.

64. Blackstone (1971), p. 28.

65. Ibid., pp. 28–33 and 57.

66. Ferguson and Fitzgerald (1954), p. 178.

67. Roberts (1982), pp. 158–9, note 92.

68. Pilgrim Trust (1938), pp. 239–41. The Trust's patriarchalism is summed up in the following statement. 'The existence of a group of women in Blackburn who, despite the tradition of continuous work in the mills and despite the low standard of wages earned by their husbands, yet feel the claim of the family to their whole attention, is, we believe, an indication of social progress.'

69. Roberts (1982), p. 157.

70. Spring Rice (1981), pp. 28–9 and p. 26. Evidence of husbands helping working wives with domestic work exists, but for every one who helped there appears to be another who did not. See, for instance, C. Hall, 'Married Women at Home in Birmingham in the 1920s and 1930s', *Oral History*, V, 1977, p. 75;

D. Gittins, 'Women's Work and Family Size Between the Wars', *Oral History*, V, 1977, pp. 95-6; Roberts (1982), pp. 151-2; Spring Rice (1981), p. 94 and 103-6.

71. Spring Rice (1981), Chapter 1. See also Ferguson and Fitzgerald (1954), p. 30 and p. 28, note 4.

72. J. Lewis, 'In Search of a Real Equality: Women Between the Wars' in F. Gloversmith (ed.), *Class Culture and Social Change* (Harvester, Brighton, 1980), p. 222.

73. Spring Rice (1981), pp. 49 and 37.

74. Brittain (1928), p. 26.

75. *Parliamentary Papers* (1930), p. 28.

76. Anthony (1932), p. 134.

77. RCEP, *Report* (1946), pp. 109, 102; Lewenhak (1977), pp. 211-12, 234. Seventeen out of 31 sections of the 1937 Act dealt with permissable exceptions and the Act was believed not to have led to the reduction of hours before the war. See also TUC Pamphlets and Leaflets, 1940/12.

78. Anthony (1932), pp. 125-6; Brittain (1928), pp. 186-7.

79. Lewenhak (1977), Chapters 13 and 14.

80. Anthony (1932), p. 137.

81. Brittain (1928), p. 25.

3 MOBILISATION

The war effort reached its height in terms of the size of the workforce in 1943. The number of men and women in Great Britain in paid employment was 22,285,000 compared with 19,750,000 in 1939.[1] As far as women were concerned there was a rise from 6,265,000 recorded as 'occupied' in 1931 to an estimated 7,500,000 in 1943.[2] A major shift in the distribution of women in the employment structure, and in their age profile and marital status, accompanied this expansion. These changes need to be described and discussed briefly but the focus of attention here is on how they were accomplished. At the beginning of the war the government's approach to women's employment was laissez-faire, as it was in the First World War and in the interwar years, and only gradually did the Ministry of Labour undertake the deliberate mobilisation of women. In doing so, policy-makers experienced a major dilemma. In essence the problem was whether the demands of wartime production for an increased supply of female labour should be allowed to take precedence over the demand for women's labour in the home, or whether intrusion upon women's conventional domestic roles, particularly those of married women, should be avoided. In trying to resolve the dilemma, policy-makers searched for a compromise between the two spheres of activity, domestic and industrial, such that neither would be profoundly changed.

By 1943 the picture of women's employment described in Chapter 2 had been transformed. Between 1939 and 1943 1.5 million women joined the 'essential' industries, a change reflected in the fact that the number of women in insured employment increased by nearly one-third in four years.[3] It was the industries in which the proportion of women was relatively small before the war which increased their numbers and enlarged their proportions of women most dramatically. For instance, the number of women in engineering rose from 97,000 to 602,000 between 1939 and 1943 and the proportion of women workers in the total rose from 10 per cent to 34 per cent. Large increases also occurred in the metal and the chemical industries, vehicle building, transport, gas, water and electricity, and shipbuilding, though here the starting point was so low that any increase would have looked great. By 1943 women represented 33 per cent of the total number of employees in these industries, compared with 14 per cent in 1939. The number of women in some white-collar occupations also expanded, for instance by 50,000 in commerce and by 540,000 in national and local government, from 17 per cent to 46 per cent of the workforce.[4] (See Table B7.)

On the other hand, numbers dropped in occupations which had employed mainly women before the war. For example, in textiles the number of insured women fell from 656,000 in 1939 to 456,000 in 1943 and in clothing the numbers fell from 462,000 to 317,000 in 1943. In these cases pre-war contraction advanced rapidly in wartime, but the pattern was the same in all industries in which there were high proportions of women before the war, including some in which the numbers of women had been expanding, such as pottery and leather goods, food, drink and tobacco, distribution and consumer services. In addition to all these changes there were, by September 1943, 470,000 women in the armed forces.[5]

Even though the proportional increases of women in the 1920s and 1930s in industries like metals and engineering were as nothing compared with those which occurred during the war, it did mean that at the start of the war there was a core of women already working in these industries and others outside who had been employed in them earlier in their lives. One survey of women aged 18–59 employed in industry in 1943 found that 71 per cent were in paid work at the time that war broke out. Of the 45 per cent of this group working as 'machine and tool operatives' and 'assembly and repetition workers' in 1943, nearly half (47 per cent) had been 'machine and assembly workers' before the war, though of course not necessarily in the same firm or even industry. The rest had come from a range of other occupations: 28 per cent had been 'distributive workers, waitresses etc.', 19 per cent had been 'labourers and domestics' and 6 per cent had been in the 'professional administrative and clerical' category.[6] (See Tables B5 and B6.) Women who were not in paid employment immediately before the war formed 22 per cent of the total sample and 6 per cent had come straight from school but, apart from the school leavers, the majority had done paid work at some time before the war, usually prior to marriage. The last paid occupation of a minority was on munitions in the First World War.[7] All this suggests that the extent to which the women employed in 'war work' were entirely new either to this type of work, or to paid work generally, has often been over-stated by both contemporaries, for instance in the pages of the *Engineer*, and by historians such as Henry Pelling and Alan S. Milward; for all that the amount of movement within the employment structure was enormous.[8]

Other major changes in the female labour force during the war were in the marital status, age structure and regional distribution of the women employed. In 1931 only 16 per cent of all women over 14 in paid employment were married. This had risen to 43 per cent in 1943. The age profile was turned upside down. In 1931 the largest proportion of women workers, 41 per cent were aged 18 to 24, but this had shrunk to only 27 per cent in 1943, and whereas a mere 16 per cent were aged 35 to 44 in 1931, 26 per cent were in this age group in 1943.[9] (See Tables B3 and B4.) Finally the increase in the numbers of women in insured employment was unevenly spread over the country. Its impact was greatest in those regions where there had been few such opportunities for women before the war, such as Wales where the number more than doubled and the northern, south-western and eastern regions where the number rose by 50–70 per cent between 1939 and 1945. In contrast the increase in the number of women in insured employment in London and the South-east and in the North-west (principally Lancashire) and North-east (Yorkshire) was small, because of both evacuation (from the South) and the high proportion of insured women in these areas before the war.[10]

From Contraction to Compulsion

How were these profound changes in the employment structure achieved during the war? In the first eight months, September 1939 to May 1940, no steps were taken by government to redistribute women in the workforce. They were expected to move in response to the changing demand (or the lack of it) for their labour, without government intervention, as they had in the First World War. Men, on the other hand, were liable for direction by government under the force of law from the outset. Male conscription was a step taken in 1916 and there was no hesitation about repeating it in 1939. Under the National Service (Armed Forces) Act, passed on 3 September 1939, all men aged 18 to 41 could be called up for service in the armed forces. In December 1941 the upper age for men's call up was raised to 51.[11] Statutory exemptions were embodied in the Schedule of Reserved Occupations first drawn up in January 1939 and designed to ensure that firms would, in the event of war, be able to keep all but the youngest of their skilled workers, by listing trades from which workers could not be called up above a certain age, which included most of the skilled trades in the munitions industries.[12] The Restriction of Engagement Order, introduced under Defence Regulation 58A in June 1940, stated that male workers in key industries (engineering, building, civil engineering and later mining and agriculture) could only be engaged through the Employment Exchanges or an approved trade union.[13]

In this period, women with special educational qualifications who expected the war to provide opportunities denied them in the 1920s and 1930s were disappointed when they rushed forward to volunteer. This is graphically illustrated by the experience of the Women's Employment Federation, which happened to be moving its offices on 4 September 1939. The rush of applicants was so great that 'even while the move was in progress interviews continued on the stairs, in the street and even inside the removal van, and the difficulty of keeping track of records and cards was severe. At that period over 200 interviews were given each day.'[14] But the Federation had trouble finding jobs for these volunteers. In November 1939 and February 1940 protests were made to MPs by the Federation of Business and Professional Women, which stated that more than half of the 6,872 women who had registered with the WEF were unemployed.[15] These qualified women were not alone in their disappointment. Women who applied for jobs with London Transport in November 1939 were also turned down. The employers preferred the promotion of men and reduction in the service to the employment of women. Discouragement must have been even greater to several thousand women already in industry who were thrown out of work. A total of 175,000 more women were unemployed in September 1939 than in August, whereas 75,750 fewer men were unemployed in September than in August[16] and, though total unemployment dropped below the August 1939 figure by March 1940, women's unemployment did not fall below that of August 1939 until February 1941. The problem was that many of the consumer industries in which women worked (such as tailoring, hosiery, boots and shoes) reduced their production on the outbreak of war and the women displaced were not rapidly absorbed into war industries.

After the change of government in May 1940, contraction was hastened by the official policy of concentration of industry. The purpose of the policy was to economise on raw materials, to make industrial plant available and to release labour. The definition of 'inessential' industries in which firms were closed changed during the course of the war, but during 1940 they included many of those in which there was a large proportion of women, for example, textiles, clothing, boots and shoes, paper, pottery, glass, hosiery, lace, gloves, perfumery. Production was 'concentrated' in 'nucleus' firms, which had to be outside munitions areas so as not to exert a drain on the local labour supply. It was hoped that the 'transfer of operatives to munitions and other war industries on a voluntary basis' would take place.[17]

However, the policy was bound to take effect slowly because negotiations between the Board of Trade and individual enterprises to be closed had first to be completed successfully. And the Ministry of Labour found that it could never assume that all the women made redundant would in fact find their way into munitions work, since the policy was concerned only with redundancy and not with re-employment.[18] Janet Hooks, observing the process for the US Department of Labor, wrote,

> In actual practice the schemes supplied less new labor than was anticipated since considerable loss occurred in making transfers. The release of a specified number of women did not add the same number to munitions manufacture. Some workers thrown out of employment were lost sight of altogether, some remained jobless or drifted into occupations other than munitions, and many eventually filtered back to their original employment.[19]

By the middle of May 1941, women trade union leaders had become aware of the severe problems that were emerging from the point of view of women workers. Miss Elliott, National Woman Officer of the General and Municipal Workers' Union, spoke of 'considerable alarm among the textile, hosiery and clothing workers as to the way in which those who were displaced as a result of concentration would be reabsorbed'.[20] Nevertheless the MOL was determined to maintain a laissez-faire approach. It refused to apply the registration scheme (of which more shortly) to women in industries to be concentrated[21] and rejected the idea of the planned withdrawal of women on the grounds that it 'would only invite criticism'.[22] It was clearly employers' criticism which worried the Ministry and not that of women whose first experience of mobilisation for war was redundancy, with neither an alternative job nor an invitation to seek one.

By the autumn of 1941, however, the shortcomings of the policy were becoming evident to civil servants and in Cabinet it was attracting fierce criticism. Beaverbrook, Minister of Supply (responsible for equipping the armed forces), complained that only about half the women released by concentration were working in munitions and he demanded official measures 'to recall these women for work in the war factories and to prevent a similar leakage to other concentrated industries'.[23]

One might ask why the Minister of Labour, Ernest Bevin, trade unionist and socialist, went along with laissez-faire principles which were in practice neither efficient nor humane. Bevin's views, informed by experience of the unpopularity of labour controls in the First World War, were in fact based on the 'voluntary principle'. He believed that women would respond better to recruitment, and work harder in their war jobs, if they undertook them of their own free will. Indeed, on taking office in May 1940, he had the power under Regulation 58A to direct anyone, man or women, to any task, but as far as women were concerned he preferred to persuade first and to compel only as a last resort.[24]

During 1941 he was in fact moving towards the compulsion of women, though he tried to maintain the spirit of voluntarism at every stage. The first step was the introduction of registration in March 1941. Under this scheme all women, whether in paid or unpaid employment, received an official invitation to register their occupation with the local Employment Exchange and on the basis of certain criteria (discussed below) women selected from this register were allocated jobs to which, if they demurred, they could be 'directed' under the force of law.[25] However, instructions to interviewers embodied Bevin's ideas about the benefits of voluntarism:

> The attitude to each particular person interviewed should be that she is the last person in the world likely to require compulsion and that she is only too ready to do voluntarily what is in the national interest . . . Willing workers are wanted and no trouble is too great to achieve this end.[26]

The group called upon to register was at first limited to those aged 19–40 and excluded women in concentrated industries on the grounds that they would be transferred more rapidly if they did not have to go through registration.[27] But, as it became evident that this was the opposite of what was happening, they were included[28] and, after 40-year-olds had been reached in the autumn of 1942, the upper age limit was raised first to 45 and then in 1943 to 50 amid cries of 'the conscription of grandmothers'.[29]

However, though registration may have helped to reduce the feeling of not being wanted in women who experienced concentration, initially it did little to increase the overall numbers of women recruited for war work. In August 1941 when a review was made of the first few months of registration, it was found that of 2 million women registered, 500,000 had been interviewed, but only 87,000 had been put to work in the Women's Auxiliary Services or on munitions.[30] Beaverbrook painted a picture of women deliberately evading essential work:

> There should be more expedition and ruthlessness in combing out women from non-essential occupations. Too many are still allowed to stay in kiosks and in the distributive trades generally which still absorb over one million women.[31]

The image was of a stubborn woman idly painting her nails in a station kiosk on a deserted platform, behind shelves sparsely filled with bars of chocolate and packets of cigarettes in short supply. This woman became a kind of bogy to the registration scheme. She was often cited by Ministry of Labour officials. For instance, in discussion of proposals to apply the Restriction of Engagement Order to women, two MOL officials referred to 'the worst offender' under registration, who 'takes work temporarily to satisfy the Department and then reverts to a life outside the field of work of national importance, and passes beyond the Department's ken in consequence'.[32]

MOL officials hoped that increased use of compulsion would catch her and this came in two forms. Firstly, concern about recruitment for the Auxiliary Territorial Service persuaded the government to introduce the National Service Number 2 Act which became law in December 1941. Its objective was to expand the supply of women to the women's services, but Bevin insisted that women should be given a choice between the services, civil defence and the munitions industries. His justification in Cabinet was, 'There was great advantage in people having a say in deciding the jobs for which they were best suited.'[33] However, Cabinet discussions focused not on the feelings of women towards conscription but on the reaction of men, particularly service-men, among whom Churchill and the service chiefs claimed there was 'strong feeling against *any* compulsion of women'. Nevertheless the majority of Cabinet members believed that soldiers would tolerate the call-up of single women and the Cabinet eventually agreed upon the compromise of exempting married women, 'although they should be allowed to volunteer'.[34] Call-up of all single women in the age group 20–21 began in January 1942.

The second way in which compulsion was extended was through the Employment of Women (Control of Engagement) Order, which came into force on 16 February 1942. Henceforth all women between the ages of 20 and 30 (with certain exemptions) could be employed only through Employment Exchanges which, it was hoped, would prevent employers in less essential industries privately taking on women whom the MOL might have wanted to send to more essential work.[35] In January 1943 the Order was extended to women up to the age of 40 and simultaneously it was announced that women could be directed not only into full-time but also into part-time work.[36]

All this meant that by 1943 the government was using considerable powers of compulsion over women and it is misleading to state, as the historian Arthur Marwick does, that 'conscription played a relatively minor role in the changes in women's employment during the war',[37] even though there were many problems in its implementation. Despite all the powers that members of the MOL had at their disposal by 1943, they remained concerned that women were 'misallocating' their labour power. The problem was now the opposite of the concentration dilemma, when women would not move into munitions. The withdrawal of women from industries categorised as less essential under the National Service Number 2 Act, was said to create 'an atmosphere of unrest among the remaining employees' who, fearful that their 'inessential' work offered no security, volunteered for the armed forces if they were young, or for 'some type of war work which will save them from further interference by the Local Office' if they were older. This voluntary movement was exactly what the devisers of concentration had wanted but had failed to achieve in 1941, but in 1943 it was seriously depleting the labour force in the concentrated industries which, as one official put it, were in fact 'hardly less essential whether to the war effort or to the life of the civil population' than munitions work.[38] Ministry officials now complained that women who removed themselves from industries like clothing and distribution were 'irrational' but in view of the way that concentration had made women redundant with no promise of a job, they seem anything but irrational. Finally late in 1943, an order was issued to compel employers to inform the Employment Exchange when a worker was due to be released so that she could be transferred without delay.[39]

In spite of the apparent humanity of Bevin's preference for voluntarism to direction, there are grounds for seeing it as quite mistaken. In terms of both efficiency and women's own experiences, the policy looks more like a continuation of the tradition of treating women as a marginal workforce than a real attempt to maximise women's co-operation with the war effort.[40] There were some who pressed Bevin to introduce the conscription of women earlier (William Beveridge for instance) and female critics abounded. For example, Ann Temple argued in the *Daily Mail* in March 1941, 'You've got it wrong, Mr Bevin', women would have 'responded magnificently' to appeals to volunteer if they had been organised properly, but 'in this war the voluntary system was doomed to failure from the very start by a stupidity, tactlessness and incompetence that made women draw back in dismay'.[41]

Personal Reactions to Mobilisation

Politicians and civil servants were certainly tactless in their tendency to blame women for the shortcomings of concentration (which had released a quarter of a million workers by April 1942 but had supplied less than half that number to war industry[42]), and for the weaknesses of registration. They did not look far into women's circumstances to understand the reasons for their lack of response. There is no doubt that some women, both single and married, considered it impossible to enter war work. In October 1941 32 per cent of a sample of 1,000 women between the ages of 17½ and 43 'apparently free to go into work or the Services' were unwilling to do war work of any sort. Nearly two-thirds of this group gave domestic responsibilities and that they would not like leaving home as their 'objection to war work or joining a service'. Women in different age groups stressed different aspects of these two objections. Older women emphasised their responsibility for dependants, especially young children, and younger women said 'that they did not want to leave home' and 'that their family would object'. Their attachment needs to be seen in the light of the relationship of single women to their families described in the last chapter. It was reflected in comments collected by both WSS and M-O, such as 'I'm rather used to home; I don't like the idea of going away very much,' which the WSS understood 'as the expression of a definite economic relationship'. 'Most working girls . . . give money and services to the home, and in return are enabled to live better than on their own.'[43] In addition many young single women had considerable domestic responsibilities. For example a working-class woman in her early twenties said, 'It's different for me, I've got no mother and I'm keeping house for my father.'[44]

The claims of domesticity upon women's time and energy are visible in their reactions to War Work Week exhibitions and parades. These recruitment drives were held around the country in 1941–2, to make women aware of the need to register and encourage them to

volunteer for war work. At the War Work Week held in Coventry in
November 1941, the parade and exhibition were spectacular. Women
from the various munitions factories of the town, GEC, Morris Motors,
Singer Motors, Standard Motors, Rootes, Wickman's, Daimler aero-
engines,

> led a procession through the main streets of the town dressed in
> overalls and gowns with 'V' signs embroidered on them, they rode
> on tanks and armoured military vehicles they had helped to make,
> and they sat at their machines mounted on lorries, filing, riveting
> and drilling aeroplane parts as they went along.[45]

There were in addition more women demonstrating war work in Central
Hall and there were recruiting speeches and talks.

However, one Coventry woman, aged 40 and middle class, was incensed by the suggestions that women who were not in paid work were
'shirking'. This woman had worked in munitions in the First World
War and was prepared to work part-time, but was told at the Employment Exchange that only full-time work was available. Her comment
was, 'We would get war in our homes if we took it.' She was particularly annoyed by a recruiting speech made by a Commander Thomp-
son in which he said, 'If you know anyone who is not working, make
them feel darn' uncomfortable by giving them the lash of your tongue.'
To this she said, 'I can tell you from my own experience that no
Coventry woman slacks. If we don't work it is because we have definite
reasons for not doing so.'[46] One poster carried by parading girl factory
workers said, 'Don't queue with the shirkers, join the women workers',
but many women felt that queuing for food in short supply and preparing it in such a way as to both feed and please a family was a major
task. For instance two working-class women said to each other, 'I
wouldn't mind doing half-time but you can't do full-time, can you?
Not with the shopping and the getting of meals,' and 'It'd be all right
if you could eat out in a café or a restaurant. But you can't in Coventry, can you?' Sometimes women gave up war work because of the
problem of shopping and cooking:

> My husband's on night shifts and I used to get home about six – it
> wasn't time to cook him his dinner and he was losing sleep doing it
> himself. Then they wanted us to stay and do overtime till 6.30 or
> more – I couldn't do that.[47]

Figure 3.1: Advertising leaflet for the War Work Exhibition held in Coventry in November 1941.

WAR WORK EXHIBITION
Central Hall, Coventry

Come and see Munitions being made!

ADMISSION FREE. Open Daily (except Sunday)
10 a.m. to 5 p.m.

WATCH OUT FOR THE MOBILE EXHIBITION
OF LATEST WAR PHOTOGRAPHS
A new display every week. Admission Free

Courtesy of the Coventry City Record Office and the Mass-Observation Archive.

Many women said they would work if it could be fitted in with home life, especially child care, and comments like the following were common: 'I often think I'd like to go to work if it wasn't for the child . . . if there was a nursery or something,' and from the mother of a seven-year-old: 'I feel I should be doing something, it's getting on my nerves [but] he's too little to leave for all the time between when school ends and when I or his father would get in . . . It's only him, it doesn't matter about my husband, I'd have put my foot down.'[48] However some were convinced that factory work and running a home were incompatible. A woman who had decided not to take up war work explained her decision with considerable anguish, based on her understanding of the place that home ought to occupy in wartime:

> I feel very guilty sometimes, but there's my husband to think of. I know our homes are not supposed to count any more now, and it's only my husband and myself, but you have to do *something* in a house, or you'd get overrun by rats and mice. I'd like to go to the exhibition — I was meaning to this afternoon, but then I thought, no, the work is from 8 in the morning till 7 at night, I couldn't do that.[49]

Many women's reaction to the appeal in November 1941 was simply 'I've got enough to do at home'.

One might question whether the views collected by M-O in one or two locations were held by women nationally. At first sight it appears they were not. In March–April 1942, 97 per cent of a large Wartime Social Survey sample of women stated that they believed that women should go into war work and nearly half said that they should be directed. Only a minority (14 per cent) actually opposed direction, on grounds such as 'women's place is in the home'. However, against this must be set the detailed information collected. Firstly, the support for direction of 27 per cent was conditional upon adequate attention being paid to the individual circumstances of women, particularly their home commitments. Secondly, the survey revealed that the most common question asked by these women at registration was whether local, part-time work would be available and the five most frequently mentioned problems were child care, the care of husbands, housework, shopping and health. Moreover, thirdly, fully three-quarters of women in the sample expected that they themselves would be exempt from registration and direction, meaning that the same women who advocated compulsion for women in general did not see it as applying to themselves, mostly either because they thought they were already doing essential work or because of unavoidable family ties.[50] A Mass-Observer commented with some justice in May 1942, 'Women already feel that the jobs they do whether it is being a housewife or typist or munition worker are important.'[51]

Men had a part to play in this, too. M-O collected some quite panic-stricken statements from men who did not believe that women should be required to do war work. For instance, in a debate at an air-raid warden's post in December 1942, Mr T, a working-class man in his thirties, said,

> If married women are called up home life will vanish, and it will be very hard to revive it after the war. Men coming home on leave will find that they can only see their wives for an hour or two a day. Men in reserved occupations will come back to cold, untidy houses with no meal ready. Friction in the home will be greatly increased, and with children evacuated there will be nothing to hold it together.

He was supported by most of the men at the post, though the women who spoke said these views were nonsense and all but one of the women voted against the motion that 'There should be no conscription of married women', which was, nevertheless, carried.[52] Many women contemplating war work referred, and deferred, to their husbands' opposition. For instance a working-class woman in her twenties said, 'I have thought and thought, but my husband doesn't want me to; that's the only reason why I don't because I know perfectly well I should have a much better time [but] he feels he's doing his bit and I ought to do what I can for him,' a statement which makes the patriarchal relations within this family very clear. It was rumoured that women were evading compulsion 'by having children and rushing to get married', but the only verbatim comment I have found suggesting this way out was made by a man to his wife:

> What's going to happen? Look at all the homes that are going to be broken up. It'll be a muck up. What would I do, now, if you were called up, E? It's no good kid, we'll have to get a little lad to keep you at home.[53]

Women's comments, if not men's, suggest a readiness to consider wartime employment if it could be fitted in with domestic work. Many women needed the money, especially in view of rising prices.[54] But the official campaigns did little to create confidence that the government would effectively arrange to alleviate the domestic burden. In March 1941, under the apocryphal headline 'Bevin Wants a Hundred Thousand Women, the State to Keep the Children',[55] the government launched a kind of national war work week to pave the way for registration, but the only mention of child care was a reference to 'recommendations' that local authorities set up day nurseries, and on hours of work all that was said publicly was 'Hours will vary at different factories'. A similar statement was made about wages and there was no mention of arrangements for shopping or part-time work. Further all that was said about leaving home was, 'It is essential workers should be mobile minded,'[56] a requirement expressed in the official language of labour supply, in which the most desirable women recruits were known as 'surplus, unskilled, mobile woman labour'.[57] But who were these women? Did they include women who were prepared to do some war work but considered their first duty to be to their homes and did not wish to be sent away, or only young, unoccupied women? In view of all the omissions in recruitment propaganda, an observer wrote that, 'There was much opinion, especially from middle-aged women that only the 20s and 21s were wanted even for volunteering,' and 'There is some feeling that only unemployed people who are doing *nothing* are wanted.'[58] Women working in the home did not regard themselves as doing nothing. Feelings of frustration among women mounted during 1941-2: 'I nearly threw a brick through the Ministry of Information van when it came our way,' said one Coventry woman with regard to her struggle to get suitable work.[59]

Not surprisingly, the numbers recruited at 'War Work Weeks' fell far short of the targets set. For instance in August 1941 Worcester aimed at 2,000 volunteer war workers and succeeded in producing 100, Finchley aimed at 1,000 and got less than 400 and a similar level of response was reported in Bradford in December 1941, where a diarist wrote:

> The number of Bradford girls who have volunteered for work is 498 – and that is higher than in any other West Riding town. So much for the 11,000 that are needed! It looks as though Bevin and Co. will have to use compulsion after all.

And in Littlehampton, Worthing, Chichester and Bognor in January 1942, at a time of military crisis in Malaya and Libya, only 211 war workers and 48 ATS were forthcoming.[60]

We shall see in later chapters that the assumption of many women, that their first responsibility was for shopping and cooking, caring for children, cleaning, washing and mending, in other words for expending the socially necessary labour time embodied in running a home and a family, was in fact shared in some government ministries. In 1940–41, however, the attention of those dominant in the MOL was focused on the wartime needs of the production machinery, ever hungry for workers, and policies addressed to striking a compromise between women's domestic role and the need for their labour power in industry followed rather than preceded the calls for recruitment. Thus the first official circular on child care was not issued to local MOL offices where registration started in April 1941 until June 1941, the first conference on shopping problems was not held until April 1941 and the first investigation into the organisation of women's hours did not begin until September 1942. The government never took an initiative on women's wages but left them to collective bargaining under dilution agreements which it encouraged but did not compel unions and employers' associations to make. The vagueness about mobility in the statement of March 1941 was inevitable in view of the fact that the MOL possessed no definitions of which women were 'mobile' or could be 'directed' under force of law. However, it was, as we shall see shortly, in the process of looking for them.

The Women's Consultative Committee and 'Household R'

A group of women was ready and willing to give the MOL advice on the question of how to mobilise women. MPs from across party lines, including Lady Astor, Irene Ward and Edith Summerskill, formed a parliamentary caucus called the Woman Power Committee in May 1940, which strongly criticised the government for its failures in the recruitment field throughout 1940–41. Linked to organisations like the Federation of Business and Professional Women, they belonged to the interwar feminist tradition, demanding, for instance, no conscription of women without equal pay. However their pressure 'for the appointment of a committee of women to act as an Advisory Committee on all questions of women's employment in wartime' was resisted by the MOL for eight months.[61]

This resistance was partly caused by the group members' place in the political spectrum. As a deputy secretary at the MOL put it, in the veiled language of the civil service, 'Miss Ward has been identified rather too closely with the movement and we have had to beware of political reactions.'[62] There was also resistance in the MOL to seeing gender as a relevant issue in policy-making, but the Deputy Secretary, F.N. Tribe, eventually recognised that, since MOL policies differentiated profoundly between men and women and since policy towards women so far had not been very successful, the MOL had necessarily to consider these matters 'on a sex basis'. Thus in January 1941 Tribe wrote:

> We do not find it necessary to have a man's committee to advise us on men's problems but I think we must recognise that the absorption of 2 million women into industry is going to be an enormous problem.

By now he was also aware of the danger of women's reactions to being ignored, writing, 'We do not want to court the antagonism of women's interests, either political or industrial', so the MOL would 'have to show that we are paying full regard to what may be termed the women's point of view' on the issue of recruitment. For these reasons he suggested the appointment of a committee constituted not just of members of the Woman Power Committee, but of a range of representatives. He decided that they should not discuss matters relating to either welfare or training, since women sat on the MOL bodies which dealt with these issues and he confined the brief of the new committee to advice on the recruitment and assimilation of women to industry.[63]

Tribe's recommendation reached Bevin in the context of pressure from women MPs for a debate on woman power, and it was accompanied by a note from Assheton, Bevin's Parliamentary Secretary, stating 'it will be impossible to avoid a women's committee of some sort', but offering assistance. 'Perhaps I could help by presiding over the ladies on your behalf. I think I could resist their charms.' The WCC was called into being, with Assheton in the chair, in March 1941.[64] Its members included two women trade unionists (Dorothy Elliott and Florence Hancock), the chief woman officer of the Labour Party (Mary Sutherland), two woman MPs (Edith Summerskill, Labour and Irene Ward, Conservative), the Chairman of the National Council of Girls' Clubs (Mrs W. Eliot), and two others, the Countess of Limerick and Miss M. Maxse, CBE. Caroline Haslett, President of the Women's Engineering Association and adviser on training to the MOL, also sat on the committee as a representative of the MOL.[65]

The main task of the WCC was to advise the Ministry on how to apply compulsion to women in its first phase, registration. Its members thus become the architects of compromise between the pressure of war for women's labour, conventional expectations about women's work at home and the voluntary principle, in the context of recruitment. F.N. Tribe specified the questions which the committee was to answer:

> I have in mind such questions as the ages at which women should first be registered under our new Registration Order. Should we begin at the age of 25 and work upwards to 30 and then downwards or should we begin at 20 and work upwards? Should we pay any special regard to the marital state of women? Should a young married woman without any family responsibilities be treated differently from a single woman?[66]

When it met, the WCC endeavoured to oblige, first deciding the order in which various categories of women should be registered and then turning its attention to the vexed question of exemptions on the grounds of the unpaid occupation of so many women — their household work.

It was decided that single women aged 20-21, not engaged in a full-time paid occupation, without responsibility for a household or for young children and not engaged in full-time study, were top priority for registration and could be regarded as 'mobile'. They were the type of labour most coveted by the Ministry of Labour which could apply to them its traffic-light map of the UK, on which they were moved from the green or amber to the scarlet areas, designated to have the most acute labour needs.[67]

The search for 'mobile' women became increasingly desperate during 1941. Women on the Unemployed Register were regularly interviewed and even tramps were closed scrutinised.[68] In September 1941 the WCC recommended a special Women's Panel to review resistant cases, because of the large number of women officially deemed mobile who were not prepared to move. Compulsion could ultimately be used, but the panel was to uphold the voluntary principle by reassuring women about the difficulties they had raised and persuading them of the necessity for transfer.[69] The clear case of a mobile woman was defined for the benefit of the Ministry of Labour Panel as:

> Single women and widows without domestic responsibilities . . . unless there are special circumstances involved, such as the case of an invalid relative. The fact that a woman is living alone with a mother or other woman relative is not regarded as an adequate

reason for not taking work at a distance unless the relative is aged or infirm.[70]

Obviously the kind of woman described by the journalist Elaine Burton,[71] living alone or with one other in a flat or house which she was loath to leave or for which she would have to maintain payment even if she was, in addition, paying for a billet elsewhere, would not be treated sympathetically by the panel. 'Domestic responsibilities' it seemed, were not considered to exist where a woman lived outside a conventional caring role in a family. This was put emphatically in the WCC's discussion of which married women should be regarded as available for work and which, if any, were mobile. The ruling was: 'In general married women living at home would not be expected to take employment at a distance (although of course they may do so if they wish'.) However, 'A woman (married or single) who is living alone and doing her own housework cannot be regarded as responsible for a household,' so she was certainly available for work locally and if single she was mobile. If she was married the question of mobility depended on 'whether she is looking after her house in her husband's absence either in the Army or working in another district'. If she was not, the instruction was unqualified. 'A married woman living alone away from her own home and without domestic responsibilities of the kind dealt with above should be regarded as fully available for work anywhere.'[72] But what was 'her own home'? If she had moved and resettled, one would imagine that the new residence was her home. The meaning of 'home' became explicit in discussion of the mobility of servicemen's wives.

The WCC discussed this at several meetings. It was thought that many servicemen's wives would not be responsible for a household if, for instance, they had moved in with their parents or parents-in-law. But while this suggested that they were mobile 'the fact that a woman might not be free when her husband came home on leave was a very real difficulty'. The appearance of mobility was even stronger where a wife had followed her husband to the area where he was stationed. Yet the advice it was decided to issue to interviewers was:

so long as the woman's husband is stationed in the district, she should not be required to leave her new home . . . because she has migrated with the deliberate intention of living near him and giving him as much of a home as, in the circumstances, is possible.

This thinking was influenced by the suggestion of the service chiefs and Churchill that the call-up of women would cause dissatisfaction among servicemen.[73] The WCC's discussion led to the conclusion that the supportive role of a serviceman's wife, to be free when he was on leave and in a position to give him 'as much of a home as possible' while he was stationed away, was sufficiently vital to the war effort to justify exemption from being moved to a 'scarlet' area to do war work. Clearly many servicemen's wives thought so too, even though their low allowance might compel them to take local work.

The MOL Umpire, however, took a different line. In adjudicating in disputes over unemployment benefit, he used the refusal of benefit to put pressure on insured women to enter war work, even when they considered it unsuitable or too far from their homes. Thus in February 1941 the following case was reported in the MOL *Gazette*. A woman button-hole machinist left her employment in London to join her husband, a soldier in training near Morpeth, and applied for unemployment benefit. She was offered employment at a munitions factory 200 miles away and refused to go. The insurance officer disqualified her from benefit, the majority of a Court of Referees to which she appealed reversed his decision on the grounds that munitions work was 'unsuitable' for a button-hole machinist, but the Chairman of the Court of Referees dissented and the Ministry of Labour Umpire upheld his judgement because the new job was 'work of national importance' and because her husband's army training in Morpeth was bound to be temporary. The Umpire's general ruling represents a clear statement of the view that the demands of production should predominate in wartime:

> Circumstances which in the days of peace may justify the refusal to apply for employment, may not justify such a refusal in the times of war, when citiziens are expected to subordinate, and with very few exceptions are ready and willing to subordinate, their personal convenience to the needs of the national emergency. One of the common experiences of the times is the separation of husbands and wives or members of families in the discharge of their moral obligation to render effective assistance in industry towards the support of the national effort to secure the defence of the country.[74]

The ruling could be seen as a wartime reinterpretation of the pre-war 'genuinely seeking work' clause. In contrast the WCC which had no authority over unemployment benefit implanted the patriarchal interest at the centre of recruitment policy, ensuring that wives would be exempt from direction far afield. 'Home' and the wifely role within it should not, in the committee's view, be subordinated to war industry, especially where servicemen were concerned: 'It was undesirable that the wives of men serving in the Armed Forces should be required to move to war work.'[75]

The Ministry of Labour and its Women's Consultative Committee had discovered that in order to mobilise women they had to get down to consideration of exactly what a 'home' was. The advice issued to Employment Exchange interviewers was that usually 'responsibility for a household' meant 'wives who were keeping their husband's homes', but that in the case of servicemen's wives 'it is however possible to place a wider interpretation on the meaning of the word "home" ', it could include places other than just the serviceman's own home over which the wife was presiding. But even this wider definition did not embrace *anywhere* that the wife happened to be. There were only two types of MOL approved alternative locations for 'home' – the parents' home, or lodgings near where the husband was stationed. Home, then, was not defined in relation to the wife herself but only to the husband.[76]

This definition of 'home' was considered adequate for interviewers to decide whether or not a woman was mobile. But it was a different matter deciding whether she was available for work locally. In the case of the serviceman's wife the WCC decided that there was no reason why she should not 'undertake local employment if available'. But the precise nature of the domestic responsibilities which would justify complete exemption from war work, distant or local, provoked lengthy discussion, leading to definition of what was known as the 'Household R' category.

The WCC approved the Ministry of Labour's emphasis in its advice to interviewers that any woman who at registration said she was looking after a household required an interview and careful scrutiny. 'It is only by going carefully into the circumstances of each case that a fair decision can be reached and it is not possible to do this at the time of first registration.' The WCC decided that a woman should be exempt from direction if she was running either a large household, containing two persons other than herself, or a small household, of one other person such as her 'father, husband or brother', and that the exemption should apply if she was 'helping her mother' or had help herself, either paid or unpaid. Thus not only a woman running a large or a small household as defined above, but also a woman who had 'reasonable domestic help' in running such a household was exempt, though the definition of 'reasonable domestic help' was left to the discretion of interviewing officers. They were told simply 'the size of the house needs to be taken into consideration' of what was reasonable.[77]

The exemptions of women with servants seemed generous to some women. For example the WSS collected comments such as 'people with money can do their bit towards the war by doing their own work and so releasing maids'.[78] The WCC's respect for domestic help presumably arose from the social backgrounds of many of the women on the committee, such as Lady Limerick, with whom the suggestion that some domestic servants were 'essential' had originated, though there were no objections from the trade union and labour women.[79] The exemptions could be seen simply as recognition of the work involved in running a household, defined principally, as we have seen, in relation to a man. But the permissiveness with regard to servants was felt by some women to represent an uneven distribution of the war effort among women: 'don't see why women should go about with nothing to do, having a cook and a nannie. If a working man's wife can do work, they can!'[80]

This aspect of MOL policy does not suggest the 'levelling effect' or 'equality of sacrifice' which many historians have perceived in the Second World War.[81] However, it would be mistaken to imagine that in practice all or most households automatically retained all their domestic servants, who were themselves not exempt from registration and interview. The Lord President in October 1941 made a point of emphasising that 'special means of withdrawing young women from domestic service' would have to be found in order to increase the numbers of mobile women. The introduction of conscription in December 1941 withdrew those aged 20 to 21 and by 1943 it had withdrawn those aged 19 to 24. But in March 1942, 57 per cent of domestic servants in the WSS's sample believed that they would be exempt and the employment of older people as servants continued. In spite of the growing labour shortage the most inveterate of the servant-employing class saw no reason to stop the practice and even believed that the Employment Exchanges should help them find servants, though they met mounting disapproval.

Women with children of school age or younger (i.e. up to the age of 14) were from the start regarded by the Ministry of Labour and WCC as clear cases for exemption. As far as 'a woman with young children of her own living with her' was concerned, 'a pledge has been given under the Registration for Employment Order that these women will not be called for selection interview'.[82] But the exemption was not quite so clear where the child or children were not the woman's own, 'whether relations or evacuees', though it was decided that 'even though it might be possible for her to make arrangements for the care of the child by someone else' it was not appropriate to expect such a woman to be available for work. Yet possibilities of exerting pressure in such cases were recognised: 'Where there is more than one woman in the household who is not at work, it should in general be assumed that the elder is in charge of the children.'[83] The younger would then presumably be available for work, except where circumstances justified 'additional help', as in the case of three or more young children. This help was cited as being 'paid or unpaid', thus as with housework so with child care, the woman who could afford to pay for help was afforded an easier war than the one who could not.

Nevertheless the guidance to MOL recruiting officers on exemptions under the Household R classification was welcomed in many quarters. Florence Hancock told the 1941 TUC women's conference (partly in self-congratulation since she was on the WCC), that it was 'the most human document which had issued from the Civil Service',[84] and the experience of many women during 1941 was that exemption was easy to obtain. Indeed some women alleged that interviewers put excuses into women's mouths, for instance:

> A friend in her 20s went to Labour Exchange on Friday for interview after registration months ago. 'I see you are married. Does your husband come home to his midday meal?' 'Yes'. 'Very well, I expect you have enough to do so we won't keep you.' The larger lunacy again.[85]

To some women such lenience was discouraging. Even if they expected to be exempt from direction, many hoped to be offered a choice of work from which they could select a suitable job given their circumstances.

But the determination of the WCC that the MOL should respect women's household responsibilities encouraged reluctance to interfere at all with women's unpaid labour in the home. In July 1941 a senior member of the MOL even suggested that Employment Exchanges should cease to bother to interview any woman who said at registration that she was 'engaged on household duties', so large was the proportion of interviewees placed in the Household R category in the first few months of registration. To the WCC, however, this went too far. Not every woman's domestic work was, they believed, a full-time occupation and to classify all such women as exempt would 'open the door to

evasion'.[86] It would also remove the stimulus to women in the Household R group to volunteer, a principle which had been firmly embedded
in the guidance to interviewers:

> It should be clearly understood that although no pressure should be
> put on women whose domestic circumstances fall within the classes
> referred to below, they can, and should be encouraged to take
> employment if they wish to do so, and can make the necessary
> arrangements.[87]

In fact the exemption of married women living in a conventional
home from compulsory mobility under registration and their complete
exemption from conscription were repeatedly questioned during 1942,
as the labour shortage in both the women's services and industry
became more acute. In particular it was argued by some members of
the WCC that childless married women should be regarded as mobile:
the importance of giving a husband 'as much of a home as, in the
circumstances, is possible' diminished in their eyes over the years.[88]
However the regulations were not changed, though pressure on married
women to volunteer mounted. For example, following the pattern of
other exemptions, women with young children were excluded from the
Control of Engagement Order, but the MOL made explicit its expectation that they would work. Since they were outside controls 'employers
will probably make very great efforts to induce such women to enter
their employment' and this was 'much to be desired'.[89]

However, it was evident to some members of the WCC that most
women faced genuine difficulties in trying to make arrangements for
their domestic work such that they could volunteer for war work.
Several of them believed that the successful voluntary recruitment of
married women required a huge increase in government intervention
to adjust the relationship between home and work. In September 1941,
Mary Sutherland made an emphatic statement to this effect:

> I am convinced that if the married women are to be mobilised effec-
> tively for the war effort, the question of organising work to meet the
> circumstances of the married woman needs to be considered much
> more thoroughly than has hitherto been the case. Married women
> who are considered available just cannot be fitted into an industrial
> organisation which is planned primarily to receive workers who have
> no other occupation.[90]

Figure 3.2: The pressure on married women to volunteer mounted. This picture shows a street interview during a Ministry of Labour recruitment campaign in the spring of 1942.

She and the other trade union and Labour members of the WCC had been intervening whenever the opportunity arose to achieve the re-organisation of work. For instance, in discussion of the controls over labour under the Essential Work Order (EWO), it was agreed that the hours of work which could be expected from a married woman were different from those of a man, thus 'married women with household responsibilities had special grounds for refusing to work overtime'. It was also agreed that domestic commitments constituted a valid reason for a woman to leave, though not for a man.[91]

The three areas identified by the WCC as presenting the main difficulties for women with domestic responsibilities, were feeding, child care and the hours of work which, as we have seen, were also thought by M-O and the WSS to be major impediments to recruitment. But although the WCC asked questions about them repeatedly, it was not allowed to discuss them because they were issues of 'welfare' and factory organisation and belonged in the province of the Factory and Welfare Department which had its own advisory board on which women sat.[92] We shall examine in the following three chapters the official steps taken to meet these problems and in particular the dilemma in which the government was placed by the tension between conventional expectations concerning each area and the wartime need for labour supply and stability.

Women's Perceptions of War Work

Even though domestic work was undoubtedly the greatest impediment to the mobilisation of women in 1940–41, it was not the only thing which discouraged recruitment. Some women were inhibited from volunteering by their perceptions of industrial work and workers and, in addition, some employers were reluctant to take on women.

As we have seen, the introduction of new types of machinery and the development of mass production methods between the wars expanded the sector of employment in which women were permitted to work in many industries and the war speeded this up, particularly in engineering. But the simplicity and repetitiveness of many of the jobs offered led some women to reject such work as a new opportunity not worth having. The largest proportion of replies to the WSS question 'If you have any objection to War Work what is it?' was that is was 'too monotonous and uncongenial'.[93]

Women watching 'War Work Week' demonstrations made many

comments to this effect. For example in Worcester in August 1941 a Mass-Observer overheard the following conversation:

> 'It looks so easy, but I don't think I'd like it – monotonous, doing the same thing all the time.' (F30C)
> 'I couldn't do that – I'd go crazy, just putting those things in all day.' (F20B)
> 'My, you wonder they don't go all crackers. Quite crackers.' (F20C)
> 'Some people go balmy after a time, my mother said, in the last war. They can only stand it for a few weeks, some of them, then they go balmy.' (F20C)[94]

Similar comments were overheard at the war work demonstration in Coventry in November 1941. A 25-year-old working-class woman was demonstrating testing mica by inserting a steel blade into wads of several thicknesses. She claimed 'there is some skill in this' but on seeing her at work a woman of the same age and class remarked to her friend, a WAAF, 'Oh I do think this work looks monotonous. Fancy sitting down doing that all day. What do you think about?' The WAAF replied, 'You can day-dream I suppose. But most jobs mean doing the same thing every day – housework for instance.' The first woman rejected the comparison. 'Oh no, that's not really the same – of course we've all got to do something, but really all this is monotonous.' Another woman agreed, but thought there might be some saving graces: 'You do see things forming under your hands though, and that must make you feel you are really helping the war effort. But I should think the work is horribly monotonous.'[95] But an upper working-class woman of 35 expressed disappointment about the type of work on offer, specifically related to the fact that in her opinion you did *not* see things forming under your hands. She had worked in a wireless factory before the war:

> I want a job like my old one, but I can't find anything like it. That was interesting. We used to make about seven wirelesses a week, so we were doing different things following on all the time. Not like this, going on the same. It's monotonous. I wonder how many she has to turn out a day? And standing all the while too – of course you sit down at that job (pointing to a girl checking sizes of holes in capstans) and there's no noise, but wouldn't it be awful. I'd go potty doing that all day. And you haven't done anything when you've

finished. You haven't made anything. These jobs are only fit for young girls — 14-year-olds could do that.[96]

There was frequently a further dimension to women's rejection of the factory, which also applied to the ATS. Both were perceived to be recruiting women from the bottom of the social hierarchy. For example, a Mass-Observer recorded an upper-working-class woman of 25 at the Coventry war work exhibition in November 1941, saying:

They've got a very low class of girls in the factories now and I think the exhibition is to encourage a better class. I've heard from several sources that they're a a low type at present and they're dirty. Not dirty from the factory I mean, the oil and grease is different. But dirty heads and that sort of thing. They've got a lot of imported labour from slums and Irish girls. They want to get girls from offices but I've heard lots of girls say they wouldn't work in a factory for anything. And that's the reason — that the girls are such a rough lot.[97]

Such comments could be multiplied. Conscription, starting at the beginning of 1942, crystallised the negative feelings that many women had towards work in munitions factories and there were reports that women working in jobs which might not now be regarded as essential, especially clerks, typists and shop assistants, were doing their best to avoid conscription into lower-status munitions factories. M-O, in *People in Production*, summed up the attitude: 'Typists and shop-assistants tend to feel that it would be falling to a lower level to take a dirty manual job. Men also dissuade their womenfolk . . . for the same reason.'[98]

The 'low class' of factory girls, as perceived by women outside work, was associated in many instances with immorality. For instance one Bedford housewife keeping a wartime diary wrote in December 1941:

My husband had a spot of bother at work today. Since women have come into the factories the moral tone leaves much to be desired. Wives of serving soldiers, women with little self-control and fewer scruples, acts as magnets to silly young men, and to silly older ones too. Disgusting evidence of impropriety was found on my husband's tool box and he at once saw red. At the same time a flagrant case came under his direct notice and he caused quite a stir by insisting

on action being taken . . . Can it be wondered at that nice girls
hesitate to enter factories?[99]

Such allegations, also made about women factory workers in the
First World War, were generated to no small extent by men hostile to
women's presence in the factories.[100] The suggestion was almost always
of enticement by women rather than harassment by men. In the Second
World War the image of immorality stuck in particular to the Auxiliary
Territorial Service and, as in the case of the factories, was associated
with, or perhaps another way of expressing, the feeling that the women
serving there were of a low social class. Whether ill-founded or not, the
image undoubtedly made recruitment more difficult.[101]

Partly to counter this, the idea that the munitions factories and
women's services were social melting pots was vigorously propagated
for the purpose of recruitment, meshing with wartime propaganda
about 'national unity' and 'equality of sacrifice'. A typical image was of
the factory 'levelling' women from different parts of the social
hierarchy through the overalls which made them look alike and the
noise of the machinery which blurred the differences in their speech,
and a common belief was that 'the wives and daughters of dukes
enjoyed the novel experience of working in factories along with everyone else'.[102] However, contrary to these images, documentary and
statistical evidence suggests considerable continuity of class segregation.
For instance Inez Holden's novel about the night shift at a factory
making photographic equipment in 1940–41 emphasised that the
appearance of non-working-class women, let alone 'the wives and
daughters of dukes', in the factory, was exceptional. A girl nicknamed
Feather worked at Braille's:

> I did not know why this girl was in the factory . . . She was not of
> the working class and I thought she was the sort of girl who would
> have been 'ladying it' at a First Aid Post attached to some auxiliary
> service. Perhaps something had happened to shake up her journey
> in the slow coach of security.[103]

In some factories personnel managers tended to allocate the women
supplied so as to perpetuate the social composition they had been used
to before the war. For instance one manager felt so sorry for the
'striking blonde from a beauty parlour and a brunette from a gown-
shop' whom he described as a 'better type' than the usual factory girls
that he arranged staff jobs for them.[104]

These suggestions of far less social mixing in the war factories than either wartime propaganda or post-war images convey are confirmed in statistical terms by the WSS. The economic classification of women by the income of the 'chief wage earner' in the woman's household (be this a man or the woman herself) revealed that a higher proportion of women war workers were in households in which the chief wage earner got up to £5 per week than the proportion of such households in the population as a whole (87 per cent as opposed to 75 per cent). The conclusion was that

> women in the higher income groups have gone into other forms of National Service and that the group from which the greatest proportion of working women has been drawn is that of the semi-skilled and skilled workers with wage rates of £3 12s 0d to £5 0s 0d.

Educational attainment was another useful guide to class composition since secondary education was fee paying with a small proportion of local authority scholarships until 1944. In engineering and metals 86 per cent of the women had received elementary education only and in terms of occupation 94 per cent of women on assembly and unskilled repetitive work and 96 per cent of machinists and hand-tool operators came into this category.[105] Undoubtedly the incidence of 'wives and daughters of dukes' in factories was greatly exaggerated and even ex-clerks were relatively rare.

The evidence of social homogeneity in the factories is important not only as an indicator of the continuity of class in the so-called 'people's war', but also for the fact that the social policies eventually developed to cope with the domestic work of war workers were, necessarily, aimed at a predominantly working-class rather than a socially undifferentiated clientele. However, women's perceptions of factory work and factory workers did not engage the attention of government as a recruitment problem. Members of the WCC pressed for improvements in women's pay and opportunities for promotion, but the possibility that women were discouraged from entering war work because they regarded the work itself as boring or 'low class' was not considered.[106]

The same could not be said of industralists' reluctance to employ women. Both the WCC and the professional journal, the *Engineer*, made numerous accusations that employers were 'supine' about the use of women dilutees, that they were not employing them as freely as they had in the First World War and were exaggerating the 'need for

special training' and that they were simply 'resistant' and 'unenter-
prising' especially in the machine-tool industry and the shipyards.[107]
The reasons appear to have been twofold. On the one hand, there was
prejudice against using women as such as employees, especially certain
categories of women, such as older and Irish women, and, on the other,
there were fears of the industrial unrest their employment might
produce.

It was alleged that some employers, including government departments, simply preferred men. Elaine Burton wrote, 'Most firms seem to
be taking on in every case men of over forty before giving women a
chance. It is only when it is impossible to find a man suitable that a
woman is called in.' In such cases a younger rather than an older
woman was inevitably employed, contrary to the concentration agreements which stated that a condition of becoming a 'nucleus' firm was
that the firm should release young workers and take on older ones.[108]
As the WCC discovered, the age group denoted by the term 'older
woman' was remarkably large. Numerous letters from women indicated
'that there was still a marked disinclination to take on women over 40',
and some said that even younger women were considered too old.[109]
For 'older' women the experience of rejection at Employment Exchanges was embittering. For example a London woman told an observer:

> They say they want women, but they don't want women in this war.
> I've tried and tried to get work and I can't . . . I go along and they
> won't take me. Say I'm too old. I'm 41 — in Russia women of 60
> and 70 do things.[110]

Between the wars, as we saw, the great majority of women in both
industrial and clerical work in the 1920s and 1930s was under 35.
The evident reluctance of employers to take on women over this
age in 1940–41 suggests that the pre-war pattern was by no means
solely a product of women's choice, but also one of employers' preference.

The WCC, angered by the evidence of discrimination, pressed the
MOL to mount a campaign during 1941 to force employers to use
older women but, though some Regional Controllers who dealt directly
with problems of labour supply favoured tighter regulations on the
employment of older women, the official position remained that it
was simply 'a question of educating and influencing employers'.[111]
The views of some employers were, however, hard to change; for

example, a welfare manager, nicknamed 'Illfare', was quoted as saying in 1943:

> 'If you ask my candid opinion girls and women are a very expensive form of labour, and a darned nuisance! . . . The women are poor stuff and the girls are worse! They don't want to work at all . . . It's the older women — over 31 — that I hate . . . Look at those!' (They were two small blue-covered books which he flung on his desk with passionate loathing) 'Those belong to two women who signed on only last week and haven't even turned up to work, Wasting my time!'[112]

As this manager's comment suggests, the reasons for the particular misogyny towards 'older' women were that they were thought to be prone to irregular attendance and to be less adaptable than younger women. But these 'reasons' seem to have been embedded in a deep-rooted assumption that women just did not do paid work after their twenties or at the latest their early thirties. It was only gradually, through the registration scheme, that the age profile of women in paid work shifted from a very heavy concentration of women under 25, tailing off thereafter, to almost equal percentages in each age group, 18–24, 25–34 and 35–44. The fact that the same proportion was over 45 in 1943 as in 1931 (16 per cent), suggests that employers would in fact take on older women only under pressure of official direction, which did not begin for those aged 46–50 until the autumn of 1943.

Prejudice against Irish women was also strong. The views of a Birmingham labour manager, who wanted to replace two male welders, are probably typical:

> At Labour Exchange I see Female Vacancies Supervisor, ask for women for the job. She says the sort they get now are either afraid of the blow pipe and the sparks or don't like the dirt and heat . . . I see a girl there who looks intelligent enough to be trained. Supervisor goes over to her. Comes back and says, 'She's an Irish girl — domestic servant.' I say hastily, 'No thank you!'

On another occasion, he reluctantly accepted an Irish woman. 'She's Irish (I groan) . . . However I daren't refuse her.' Welfare managers expressed surprise when the negative stereotypes of Irish women ('dirt and drunkenness') were not confirmed.[113] As with older women special steps were taken to try to persuade employers to drop prejudices based on the untenable idea that all Irish women, like all older women, were unreliable and even, in the case of the Irish, immoral, but the official historian described the MOS's task of inducing its contractors to employ Irish workers as 'by no means always easy'.[114]

Concerning women in general, employers' prejudices were that they could not (under the 1937 Factory Act), or would not, work the hours required, e.g. on Sundays, or a day and a night shift alternately, that employing women required 'considerable expenditure on lavatory, canteen and other accommodation', that women had high rates of absenteeism and that women conscripts supplied under the National Service Number 2 Act were unwilling and therefore indisciplined. Women who had had no industrial experience and who had been excluded from the 'craftsman's tradition' were considered to be a special problem since they had no sense of factory discipline.[115] All these things had roots in reality, but as reasons for not employing women they were inadequate, as a government committee hastened to point out, because they were all remediable. It was not necessarily desirable to require long hours and night and Sunday work from any worker on a long-term basis. Lavatories and canteens benefited all workers. Changes in management styles (from 'Illfare' to welfare) and training would help reduce absenteeism, indiscipline and bad time-keeping.[116]

In spite of the guarantee about job protection offered to working men in the relaxation agreements governing dilution of male by female labour (see Chapter 7), hostility towards the entry of women into male-dominated trades sometimes fed the prejudices of employers reviewed above, particularly where employers feared that industrial unrest might be a consequence of dilution. The most notorious cases were those of shipbuilding, metal manufacture and the airframe industry, where employers faced the opposition of the strong craft unions such as the boilermakers and sheet-metal workers and, because they feared trouble, met the efforts of MOL inspectors to persuade them to employ women with constant opposition. The MOL restrained the essentially middle-class feminist Woman Power Committee from launching a recruiting drive in the shipyards for fear of worsening the situation. Variations in the strength of union opposition meant that, overall, there were wide differences in the degree of dilution between regions and factories on identical work.[117]

How far working men were right to fear the mobilisation of women and how far the policy of dilution was conducted so as to offer them protection will be discussed later. The important point here is that it was not only women's attitudes to home and to industry but also employers' and male workers' desire to keep gender relations as they were which impeded the process of mobilisation.

Conclusion

Some of the reasons for the slow pace of recruitment in 1940–41 have been discussed in this chapter: the misplaced expectation in government that the concentration of industry would transfer women automatically to 'essential' industries, the priority-ordering as between home and work which many women made and many men insisted upon, and its sanctioning by the 'Household R' exemption in the context of the absence of facilities for alleviating domestic work, women's perceptions of factory work and workers and the attitudes of employers to potential women workers, which were often ageist as well as sexist.

However, by the middle of 1943 an increase of 1.5 million women in the 'essential' industries had been achieved and the regional, marital and age distribution of women workers had changed profoundly. By now the employment of women was constrained within a legal framework which was entirely new since 1940. Registration covered all women aged 19–50, those aged 19–30 were liable for conscription, 20–40-year-olds could be engaged only through a MOL Employment Exchange, any woman could be discharged from an undertaking scheduled under the Essential Work Order only with the permission of the MOL national service officer and if a woman did leave a job the MOL had to be notified with a view to transferring her. Finally, those aged 18–40 deemed to have household responsibilities preventing full-time work could be directed into part-time work. There were, as we have seen, grounds on which women could be exempt from these regulations, most notably simply being married was enough to secure exemption from conscription and having a child under 14 living at home automatically exempted women from both direction under the Registration Order and engagement only through an Employment Exchange under the Control of Engagement Order. Exemptions could be secured by other women on the grounds of 'domestic responsibilities' which placed them in the 'Household R' category and the deference to women's expected role at home was so great that a married woman running a home with only one man in it, and with domestic help, might legally escape direction into full-time work.

It is striking that in their deliberations about mobilisation the WCC
and the MOL did not see themselves as having to defend the family
against a threat from women stimulated by wartime opportunities.
There was an almost complete absence of fear that women would desert
matrimony or the family for war work. Thus the worry when married
women were declared exempt from conscription in December 1941 was
not that women would get divorced so that they would be sent into the
women's services, but that the ruling would encourage women to rush
into marriage, and the Cabinet decided that a single woman conscript
who then married would not be released: 'Any other course would put
a premium on reckless marriages.'[118] Discussions were not based on
fears of the family disintegrating, but on fears of women disappearing
into their families and thus depriving the state of their labour power.
The approach of the WCC was one of respect for the attachment of
women, and men, to the conventional role of women in the home,
while simultaneously seeking ways of loosening these ties for the
benefit of the labour supply. Thus those women who were exempt,
including women with young children, were under pressure to volunteer for work and many eventually did so: by 1943 an estimated 43
per cent of women in paid employment were married and about one-
third of them had children under 14.[119] However, in 1941 when this
pressure was initiated, many members of the WCC believed that married
women running homes would not be able to volunteer without profound changes in the organisation of both home and factory and they
pressed for government intervention in the domestic sphere. Such
reorganisation potentially disturbed the conventional gender divisions
at home, between home and work, and at work. The question to take
with us into the following chapters is this. Would a government, whose
recruitment policy was so closely informed by the assumption that
the 'proper' nature of marriage and home was a location for a woman
defined not in relation to herself but to the man or child whom it was
her duty to nurture, permit profound change in order to secure the
voluntary mobilisation of housewives and mothers? We shall look first
at two areas of domestic work, child care and shopping, and then at
two aspects of industrial work, hours and job allocation, in pursuit
of some answers.

Notes

1. H.M.D. Parker, *Manpower: A Study of Wartime Policy and Administration* (HMSO, London, 1957), Table II, p. 483.
2. Wartime Social Survey (WSS), 'Women at Work' by Geoffrey Thomas, June 1944, Appendix II, p. 30. Since there was no census in 1941, one has to rely for all wartime population data on surveys and estimates.
3. G.M. Beck, *Survey of British Employment and Unemployment 1927-1945* (Oxford University Institute of Statistics, Oxford, 1951), Table 40.
4. Ibid., Table 41.
5. Central Statistical Digest, *Statistical Digest of the War* (HMSO, London, 1951), p. 9.
6. WSS (1944), p. 9.
7. Ibid., Table 12, pp. 7 and 10.
8. See, for example, *Engineer*, 19 December 1941; H. Pelling, *Britain and the Second World War* (Collins, London, 1970), pp. 187-8; A.S. Milward, *War, Economy and Society 1939-1946* (Allen Lane, London, 1977), p. 219.
9. WSS (1944), Table 1, p. 1.
10. Beck (1951), p. 78.
11. Parker (1957), pp. 150 and 163.
12. Inman (1957), pp. 34-5.
13. Parker (1957), p. 122.
14. V. Douie, *The Lesser Half: A Survey of the Laws, Regulations and Practices Introduced During the Present War Which Embody Discrimination Against Women* (Women's Publicity Planning Association, London, 1943), pp. 30 ff.
15. *Evening Standard*, 22 November 1939; V. Douie, *Daughters of Britain: An Account of the Work of British Women During the Second World War* (Women's Service Library, London, 1949), p. 9.
16. Beck (1951), Table 45.
17. J.M. Hooks, *British Policies and Methods of Employing Women in Wartime* (United States Government, Washington, 1944), pp. 16-17. The full list was: pottery, blown glass, hosiery, lace, gloves, perfumery, carpets, toys, cutlery, jewellery, silver and electroplate, light leather goods, corsets, suspenders, sports goods, fancy plastic goods, photographic goods, mechanical lighters, combs, linoleum, lighting fittings, musical instruments, pens, pencils, cotton, woollen and worsted, paper, boots and shoes, linen and silk.
18. PRO Lab 26/130, Minutes of third meeting of the Women's Consultative Committee, 26 March 1941.
19. Hooks (1944), p. 17.
20. PRO Lab 26/130, seventh meeting WCC, 13 May 1941.
21. Ibid., fifth meeting WCC, 16 April 1941, memo WCC 8.
22. PRO Lab 8/470 'Transfer of Women from Retail Distributive Trades', G.H. Ince to Mr Wiles, 10 July 1941.
23. PRO Cab 67/9, 'MOS Labour Needs', memo by Minister of Supply, 20 October 1941.
24. Allen Bullock, *The Life and Times of Ernest Bevin, Vol. II, Minister of Labour 1940-1945* (Heinemann, London, 1967), pp. 29, 44-6, 126; PRO Lab 26/130, seventh meeting WCC, 13 May 1941, memo WCC 13.
25. SR and O 1941, No. 368, 15 March 1941, Registration for Employment Order.
26. PRO Lab 26/130, fourth meeting WCC, 4 April 1941, memo WCC 5, though see WCC 14 for the limits to free choice.
27. Ibid., fifth meeting WCC, 16 April 1941, memo WCC 8 and seventh

meeting WCC, 13 May 1941.

28. Ibid., eighth meeting WCC, 28 May 1941, memo WCC 17. Ninth meeting WCC, 18 June 1941, memos WCC 19 and 20.

29. Parker (1957), p. 292.

30. PRO Cab 67/9, WP (G)(41)115 'MOS Labour Needs', memo by Minister of Supply, 20 October 1941. See also H.M.D. Parker (1957), p. 284.

31. PRO Cab 67/9, WP(G)(41)115.

32. PRO Lab 8/479, Kingham to Gould, 23 August 1941; Tribe to Parker 31 July 1941.

33. PRO Cab 65/20, 121st Cabinet conclusions, 28 November 1941.

34. Ibid., 110th Cabinet conclusions, 10 November 1941 and 121st Cabinet conclusions, 28 November 1941. See also W. Churchill, *The Second World War, Vol. III, The Grand Alliance* (Cassell, London, 1950), p. 455.

35. SR and O 1942, No. 100, 22 January 1942, Employment of Women (Control of Engagement) Order.

36. TUC Pamphlets and Letters, 1943/16, report of thirteenth annual conference of unions catering for women workers, 17 April 1943.

37. A. Marwick, *War and Social Change in the Twentieth Century* (Macmillan, London, 1974), p. 159.

38. PRO Lab 8/492, 'Withdrawal of Women from Less Essential Industries', correspondence with Board of Trade, 21 April 1942.

39. Douie (1949), pp. 12 ff.

40. Bevin, however, professed himself well satisfied, telling 8,000 women at the Albert Hall in September 1943: 'It is true there are sanctions in the background but in the main you have responded because you felt the nation's need and have looked upon directions as determining where you should go ... Behind it is the voluntary submission to discipline of a whole people' Bullock (1967), p. 255.

41. M-OA, File Report 615, quoting *Daily Mail*, March 1941.

42. Hooks (1944), p. 17.

43. Wartime Social Survey, 'An Investigation of the Attitudes of Women, the General Public and ATS Personnel to the Auxiliary Territorial Service', New Series No. 5, October 1941, Question 5, pp. 6 and 46.

44. M-OA, Topic Collection, 'Women in Wartime', Box 1, File A, 21 October 1941.

45. *Coventry Evening Telegraph*, 24 November 1941.

46. M-OA, Town Box, Coventry, File 3708, 'War Work, Coventry, 1941', 18 November 1941.

47. Ibid., 22 November 1941.

48. M-OA, Topic Collection, 'Women in Wartime', Box 1, File A, 20-21 October 1941.

49. M-OA, *People in Production: An Inquiry into British War Production. A Report Prepared by Mass-Observation for the Advertising Service Guild* (John Murray, London, 1942), p. 176. Emphasis in original.

50. Wartime Social Survey, 'Women's Registration and Call Up', New Series No. 15, March-April 1942.

51. M-OA, File Report 1238, 'Appeals to Women', May 1942.

52. M-OA, Topic Collection, 'Women in Wartime', Box 1, File A, debate at warden's post 31, 16 December 1941.

53. Ibid., 21 October 1941 and 25 November 1941.

54. Ibid., and interviews with the author: I.W., July 1977; Mrs S., November 1977.

55. Bullock (1967), p. 76.

56. M-OA, File Report 615, 'An Appeal to Women', 20 March 1941.

57. Parker (1957), p. 150.

58. M-OA, File Report 625, 'A Note on Woman Power', 1 April 1941. Emphasis in original.

59. M-OA, Topic Collection, 'Women in Wartime', Box 1, File A, 20 November 1941.

60. M-O (1942), p. 150.

61. PRO Lab 26/59, 5 June 1940. On the origins of WPC and pressure for equal pay, see Harold Smith, 'The Problem of "Equal Pay for Equal Work" in Great Britain During World War II', *Journal of Modern History*, 53, 4, 1981, pp. 656 and 659.

62. PRO Lab 26/59, 6 January 1941.

63. Ibid., 18 January 1941 and 18 February 1941.

64. Ibid., 26 February 1941.

65. PRO Lab 26/130, Women's Consultative Committee, minutes of meetings, 1941.

66. PRO Lab 26/59, F.N. Tribe to Secretary, 18 February 1941.

67. PRO Lab 26/130, second meeting WCC, 9 March 1941; Parker (1957), p. 284.

68. PRO Lab 8/414, 'Investigation Carried Out at Casual Wards on 3 and 4 June 1941 to Encourage Regular Employment'.

69. PRO Lab 26/130, memo WCC 29, 12 September 1941.

70. Ibid.

71. Burton (1941), p. 16.

72. PRO Lab 26/130, fourth meeting WCC, 4 April 1941, memo WCC 24.

73. Ibid., eleventh meeting WCC, 16 July 1941, memo WCC 24.

74. *MOL Gazette*, February 1941.

75. PRO Lab 26/130, eleventh meeting WCC, 16 July 1941.

76. Ibid.

77. PRO Lab 26/130, second and fourth meetings WCC, 9 March and 4 April 1941, memo WCC 6.

78. WSS (1942), p. 20.

79. PRO Lab 26/130, second meeting WCC, 9 March 1941.

80. WSS (1942), p. 20.

81. For example, Arthur Marwick (1974), p. 151 ff; Gordon Wright, *The Ordeal of Total War 1939–45* (New York, Harper, 1968), p. 246 ff.

82. PRO Lab 8/479, correspondence with regional offices, 1 October 1941 and Gould's notes on draft Restriction of Engagement Order, 17 November 1941.

83. PRO Lab 26/130, fourth meeting WCC, 4 April 1941, memo WCC 6.

84. TUC Pamphlets and Leaflets, 1941/6, 19 April 1941.

85. M-OA, Topic Collection, 'Women in Wartime', 'Diary of a Sheffield Housewife and Clerk', 21 December 1941.

86. PRO Lab 26/130, twelfth meeting WCC, 30 July 1941.

87. Ibid., fourth meeting WCC, 4 April 1941, memo WCC 6.

88. PRO Lab 71/5, memo 177, 'Manpower', 22 October 1941 (the 'special privileges' of servicemen's wives were questioned); PRO Lab 26/63, WS 16, Women's Services (Welfare and Amenities) Committee, 29 May 1942 (Edith Summerskill of the WCC sat on this committee and suggested the conscription of childless married women); M-O (1942), pp. 170–1; M-OA, Box 276, 'Children, Day Nurseries, 1941–2'; *News Chronicle*, 3 September 1943, for the views of some women outside policy-making.

89. PRO Lab 8/479, 17 November 1941.

90. PRO Lab 26/130, correspondence from Miss Sutherland to WCC, 9 September 1941.

91. PRO Lab 26/130, second and third meetings WCC, 9 and 26 March 1941, JCC 42, NSO memo 1.

92. Bevin created the Factory and Welfare Department of the MOL and its advisory board in June 1940 when he took over the administration of the Factory Acts from the Home Secretary. The Department appointed Local Welfare Officers and the Advisory Board (FWAB) was particularly concerned with the 'welfare of the worker outside the factory'. It was composed of representatives of employers, voluntary bodies and trade unions and there was a small overlap in membership between it and the WCC. See Ferguson and Fitzgerald (1954), p. 183, and Parker (1957), pp. 121, 394.

93. WSS (1941), p. 9.

94. M-O (1942), pp. 151–2. M-O's coding indicates sex (F female), age and social class (A upper, B middle, C artisan, D unskilled).

95. M-OA, Town Box, Coventry, File 3708, 'War Work, Coventry, 1941', 18 November 1941.

96. Ibid., 21 November 1941.

97. Ibid.

98. M-O (1942), p. 152.

99. M-OA, 'Diary of a Housewife, Bedford', December 1941.

100. See Braybon (1981), especially Chapter 5.

101. See WSS (1941); Edith Summerskill, 'Conscription and Women', *The Fortnightly*, CLI, March 1942; PRO Lab 26/63, Women's Services (Welfare and Amenities) Committee, 29 May 1942.

102. Margaret Goldsmith, *Women at War* (Lindsay Drummond, London, 1943), p. 193; Douie (1949), p. 12.

103. I. Holden, *Night Shift* (Bodley Head, London, 1941), p. 13.

104. M-O (1942), pp. 164–5.

105. WSS (1944), p. 6.

106. See PRO 26/130, third meeting WCC, 26 March 1941.

107. *Engineer*, 29 November 1940, 3 January 1941, 4 April 1941, 11 July 1941, 11 September 1942.

108. Burton (1941), p. 104.

109. PRO Lab 26/130, seventh meeting WCC, 13 May 1941.

110. M-O (1942), p. 145.

111. PRO Lab 26/130, seventh, tenth and twelfth meeting WCC, 13 May 1941, 2 July 1941 and 30 July 1941.

112. A. Williams Ellis, *Women in War Factories* (Gollancz, London, 1943), p. 34.

113. M-O (1942) pp. 94–5, 87 and 165, M-OA, Topic Collection, 'Industry', 1941–7, Box 140, Report on Tube Investment Ltd, 1942, p. 94.

114. Inman (1957), p. 168.

115. *Engineer*, 25 July 1941; PRO Lab 26/133 memo on wartime nurseries (concerning under-use at Hungerford because of hours required by Vickers-Armstrong), 9 April 1941; *Engineer*, 28 March 1941, 1 August 1941; M-O (1942), p. 163; M-O, *War Factory* (Gollancz, London, 1943), p. 17.

116. Select Committee on National Expenditure, 'Seventeenth Report, 1940–41, Labour in Filling Factories', (102) iii 291.

117. Select Committee on National Expenditure, 'Seventh Report, 1941–2, Supply of Labour', (75) iii 123; PRO Lab 26/59, 6 January 1941 (MOL rebuttal of Irene Ward's offer to visit the shipyards).

118. PRO Lab 65/20, 121st conclusions, 28 November 1941.

119. WSS (1944), pp. 1 and 4.

4 CHILD CARE

Before the war official provision for child care was seen essentially as compensation for 'inadequate' maternal care and was offered on a selective and discriminatory basis. As we saw in Chapter 2, responsibility was divided between the Ministry of Health which was responsible for day nurseries and the Board of Education under whose authority came nursery schools and classes. Neither government department exercised an energetic policy towards the under-fives and in addition many local authorities, upon whom implementation largely depended, were uninterested. Since the orientation of policy was towards the welfare of the child rather than the freedom of the mother, the issue of child care was seen as totally separate from that of labour supply and there was no tradition of MOL participation in child care policy.

The war of course changed this, though the MOL was initially reluctant to get involved. Before May 1940 its position was reactive rather than proactive. Only if employers complained of a shortage of married women's labour 'owing to the absence of day nursery facilities' would the MOL look to their provision.[1] It is unlikely that it would have been much troubled had this remained the policy, in view of the degree of interest of most employers in their women workers' domestic circumstances. However on taking office in May 1940, Bevin informed the MOH that nurseries would have to be supplied in advance of the recruitment of married women, who would be needed in large numbers in war industry. He repeated this message emphatically both within his own ministry and in public. For example in the context of conscription of single women to the armed forces in the autumn of 1941 he wrote:

I have to look to married women not previously employed to supply much of the necessary additional power for industry. From that point of view the provision for the care of the children is now a matter of the first importance to the war effort.[2]

But even though Bevin changed the MOL approach and tried to push child care policy towards plentiful provision of collective facilities, others vitally involved in policy-making resisted this change. Surprisingly, they included some officers within Bevin's own ministry, notably

67

a Miss Mary Smieton who occupied the relatively senior position of Assistant Secretary in the Factory and Welfare Department. She was insistent throughout 1940-41 that MOL policy was not, as Bevin implied, vigorous expansion but that as before the MOL

> is only concerned to suggest the provision of nursery care where the employment of married women with young children is necessary to satisfy the demands of industry in wartime, bearing in mind that it is not the Ministry's policy to encourage such employment except where it is the only means of filling labour demands.[3]

Miss Smieton's response to external pressure for wider provision from, for example, the National Society of Day Nurseries indicates that she doubted whether mothers with young children should work except as a last resort, even in wartime. By implication she opposed the idea that nurseries were a good thing in themselves for children as well as mothers and that they should be provided everywhere on a permanent basis.[4] In contrast Bevin was quite encouraging to voices from the Labour Party urging him to use the wartime opportunity to make the provision of nurseries universal, 'thus bringing about a great piece of Socialist policy'. He saw this long-standing Labour Party objective as quite compatible with the MOL's need for nurseries to expand the supply and promote the stability of women workers.[5] Views like those of Miss Smieton were, however, held strongly in the other government department on which nursery policy depended, the MOH. In fact Miss Smieton had a counterpart there, with whom she liaised closely, a Miss Zoë Puxley, Assistant Secretary in charge of Maternity and Child Welfare.

The MOH had considerable power within policy-making since the pre-war day nurseries, rather than the nursery schools, were seen as appropriate models for wartime nurseries and the MOH was responsible for this type of nursery under the 1918 Act. As we saw in Chapter 2 it had presided over a reduction in the numbers of day nurseries in the interwar years and there is evidence that Miss Puxley was personally involved in making closures.[6] During the war the MOH retained overall control. The MOL merely recommended the provision of a nursery in any area where it decided that the labour supply situation demanded one. The MOH, which provided capital costs and contributed to maintenance, reserved the right to check whether a nursery was really necessary, as well as to decide upon standards of premises and staffing. The nursery was actually set up by the Local Authority concerned (which also contributed to running costs) through their Maternity and Child Welfare Committee headed by the Medical Officer of Health.[7]

The making of nursery policy in the context of these complex administrative and political relationships was fraught with tension between, broadly, the desire to make any arrangement necessary to recruit women and preference for continuity with pre-war child care practices, even if this prevented the mobilisation of some women. As we have seen the division did not coincide neatly with the boundaries between the two ministries concerned and in addition it spilled over into the localities where ultimately policy had to be implemented. Underpinning the tension was the fundamental question of the acceptability of change in the relationship between mothers, children and home and a redefinition of the scope of collective child care. Out of this tension there arose considerable pressure to adopt a policy which would reconcile conventional expectations about child care with the need for an increased supply of women workers and this was highly significant in determining the extent of change which actually took place.

This chapter therefore concentrates on the struggle between a 'work' and a 'welfare' perspective in wartime child care policy and on the constraints imposed by this policy on the 'potential' within collective provision. It is thus distinct in its approach from other recent research in this area, notably that of Denise Riley.[8] The focus of her useful article 'War in the Nursery' is a critical assessment of the idea that post-war psychiatric theories of the threat to social stability posed by the maternally deprived child informed the closure of wartime nurseries and 'travelled' into popular thinking to pave the route back home for the woman war worker. Although she traces policy-making briefly, from the Ministry of Health perspective, she does so as a setting for conflicting ideas about the socio-psychological impact of wartime collective care. She does not discuss in detail what she characterises as the 'administrative, ideological dilemma of how the nurseries should be understood, as a "Welfare service", as an index of future socio-educational policy, or as a limited reaction to the immediate necessities of war and the labour process'.[9] It is with the ideological practices of the two ministries, which developed in conflict as a result of their different reactions to the demands of production for the mobilisation of women from 1940–43, that this chapter is concerned.

The four crucial issues in the development of nursery policy were the regulation of nursery premises and staffing, assessment of the demand for nurseries, interpretation of the use made of them and determination of the relationship between the nursery and the minder. In what follows each issue is pursued separately though of course in practice there was considerable convergence.

Premises and Staffing

The MOH's efforts to apply pre-war standards of premises and staffing to wartime nurseries demonstrates how reluctant it was both to question its own earlier policy decisions, and to allow mobilisation to take precedence over them. On assuming responsibility in July 1940, Miss Puxley warned the MOL to respect MOH authority in the area of child welfare:

> No doubt you will have your hands full with the welfare of the workers. The care of the babies of women munitions workers is rather remote from industrial welfare and I am anxious to keep it in the hands of the Maternity and Child Welfare Specialists.[10]

However the MOH's specialists appeared to be largely concerned with setting high standards but refusing the funds which would make them attainable. Not surprisingly their professional expertise was repeatedly challenged.

For example the 'specialists' decreed that 25 square feet per child in a day nursery and 40 in a residential nursery and facilities to play and sleep were necessary. But the MOH refused to sanction building or the purchase of suitable property 'save in extreme cases'.[11] Under these arrangements premises for nurseries could not be found in several towns supporting ordnance factories, including Chorley, Hereford and Redditch, in August 1940 and the MOH insisted that the stringent space requirement be reduced to 20 square feet per child.[12] In spite of the change many local officials remained convinced that the MOH was loath either to pass any premises as fit or to provide funds for adequate conversion. For example a health visitor involved in a project to convert a police station in Tooting into a nursery complained to a Mass-Observer in January 1942 that the MOH was blocking all progress: 'They say that they've never spent more than £800 on any nursery yet.'[13]

Under pressure from the MOL to enlarge the supply of nurseries the MOH agreed to alter its practice to the extent of offering pre-fabricated huts. It nevertheless announced that only 'a limited number of these huts are available' in May 1941 and by October there were abundant complaints from local MOL officials that supplies were so limited that there were simply no huts to be had.[14] Ironically, although the huts met the ministry's cubic footage requirements, authoritative outsiders pointed out that they were really quite unsuitable for nursery use. Lady Allen of Hurtwood, an architect and one of the leaders of the Nursery Schools Assocation of Great Britain, wrote that the windows were too high for children to see out of, the internal fixtures were at adult and not child height, poky passages robbed the huts of 'freedom and space', yet the play room was undivided, a real problem for a nursery taking children of all ages up to five. This picture was confirmed by some of those working in 'hutment nurseries'. Anxious to criticise constructively, Lady Allen supplied a better design for a prefabricated nursery, which was eventually accepted by the MOH.[15] Thus did that ministry 'lower' its standards.

However it was still quite capable of turning down nursery plans, frequently justifying its rejection on health grounds. For example, when confronted with a plan to put MOH huts in the garden of a 'smaller type of house' in Birmingham, the ministry objected, claiming to have learnt never to repeat such experiments from 'the disastrous experience of epidemics, involving deaths, in schools which evacuated themselves in a hurry as nursery parties at the beginning of the war, without due regard to the space rules of the Ministry of Health'.[16] The MOL replied that the lower space standard had in fact stood the test of experience, but did not ask the really pertinent question, which was why the Ministry offered huts to solve the accommodation problem, only to turn down arrangements using them on the grounds that they did not provide enough space.

The MOH also claimed that infectious disease would roar through the nurseries if its pre-war staffing standards were relaxed. Each nursery of 40 children was to be in the charge of a matron and her helper, who had to be State Registered Nurses with children's hospital or nursery training. In addition there had to be probationers and assistants in the ratio of one to five children. A nursery or infant school teacher was 'desirable'. This array of staff meant an overall ratio of one to between three and four children.[17]

MOL officials, however, questioned whether such a ratio was strictly necessary and found evidence of well-run nurseries which did not keep to it rigidly. The head of Tottenham nursery with a ratio of one to seven explained that she preferred this relatively low proportion of staff because 'the personal relations of the staff to each other are easier when

Figure 4.1 and 4.2: The Ministry of Health insistence on nursing qualifications for nursery workers was questioned during 1941. In these photographs nurses are supervising outdoor activities at wartime nurseries in 'a north-western town' in September 1940 (4.1) and in Sidcup in the autumn of 1941, where a working mother is shown looking on (4.2).

Figure 4.1

Figure 4.2

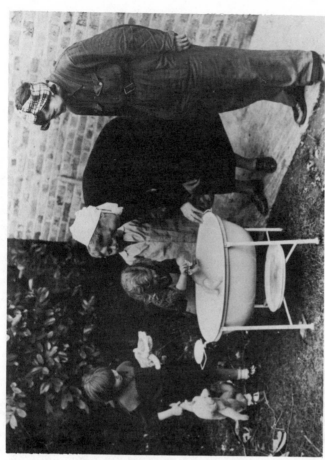

the numbers are small', and she attributed outbreaks of illness not to staffing ratios but to the absence of any 'spare rooms that could be used for isolation'. This matron was a State Registered Nurse but she and others questioned whether SRNs were the most appropriate people to supervise the under-fives.[18] The matron of a Coventry nursery admitted anxiously 'that she had plenty of experience with sick children but none with healthy children' and there were suspicions that nurses tended to leave children in high chairs or play pens 'with nothing interesting to do', an image supported by a newspaper photograph of Moynihan House Nursery in Leeds, which shows children in cots and at tables on a railed-in balcony being attended to by nurses wearing enormous white head-dresses.[19]

During 1941 questions were repeatedly asked inside and outside the MOL about the appropriate qualifications of the staff of wartime nurseries (who were, of course, assumed to be women). Both nurses and teachers were in short supply and the recruitment of women to war industry was becoming more pressing. Bevin urged 'dilution' in a memorandum of October 1941 and eventually the MOH was persuaded to turn from nursing qualifications to reliance on women's 'inborn love of little children'. A two-week course and a local authority interview now qualified women for 'war emergency work' as members of the 'Child Care Reserve', and ex-nannies and volunteers young and old were welcomed.[20]

Ironically the MOH's original high staffing ratios were used to support the claim that nurseries contributed little to the wartime supply of labour. Miss Smieton, from within the MOL, argued in January 1941 that 'almost as many staff may be taken up in looking after the children as may be released for the factory' and her view was repeated by deprecators of the nurseries both during and after the war. In fact official assessments made in 1943 suggested that they caused a considerable net gain to the labour supply (possibly as much as 90 'releases' for every 100 children cared for) and that this was magnified further by the fact that the age and qualifications of many nursery staff meant that they would not themselves have undertaken industrial work.[21]

With the relaxation of MOH regulations on both premises and staffing came an increase in the supply of nurseries from only 14 in October 1940 to 165 a year later and 1,345 in the summer of 1943. Hutted nurseries contributed about half of this expansion.[22] Wartime pressure on the labour supply had forced the MOH to become involved for the first time in the provision of nurseries on a large scale to free mothers from child care and in so doing had exposed many of its rules as un-necessary or even inappropriate. At the end of the war the insistence of wartime critics that the health of children would not suffer from the relaxation of MOH standards received corroboration from the MOH's Chief Medical Officer himself. In his report for the war years, published in 1946, he said that 'When day nurseries were first contemplated . . . grave danger from infection was anticipated,' but that, in fact, 'the great majority of the children who attended war-time nurseries bene-fited from nursery life under war-time conditions' especially the 'fresh air, good feeding and regular rest periods'. This positive assessment was, however, unusual and was rapidly submerged in a welter of evidence, both medical and psychological, purporting to show that institu-tionalised care was not good for children.[23]

The Demand for Nurseries

The issue of whether or not mothers really wanted wartime nurseries was even more crucial to their provision than that of the standards of premises and staffing appropriate for them. The administrative pro-cedure was that when a MOL Divisional Controller (renamed Regional Controller during 1941) claimed there was a need for a nursery, the local Medical Officer of Health made his or her own inquiry into the likely demand for one and reported the verdict to the MOH. Only if the ministry supported the claim did the Medical Officer set about convincing the local council that they should make provision. Given the different dispositions of the two ministries towards the relationship between collective care and mobilisation, this aspect of the history of the wartime nurseries bristles with claims and counter-claims and, since local officers tended to express themselves in less guarded terms than their superiors in London, the reasons, or suspected reasons, for reluct-ance to provide nurseries were made more explicit.

The first MOL survey of demand for nurseries was undertaken by the Divisional Controller in the North-west in April–May 1940. He decided not to ask employers whether nurseries were necessary to increase their supply of women workers, nor did he ask women outside paid employment whether they would take work if there was a nursery, but instead tried to find out how women already working coped with child care. Using a large sample from Chorley ROF he found that the children of over 17 per cent of the mothers working there were cared for in 'unsatisfactory' ways. This was not a moral judgement but

referred to the permanence and stability of the arrangement. He therefore urged that nurseries should be set up in and around Chorley,
especially in view of the fact that in the future many thousands more
women would be working there.[24]

Bevin himself saw the results of the survey and was impressed and
other DCs were told to make inquiries in their own areas between May
and August 1940. Most however did not ask women workers directly,
but consulted employers, who frequently said there would be no need
for nurseries because they did not want to employ married women. As
a result replies from half the divisions were negative, but an 'urgent
need' for nurseries was identified in four areas, the Midlands, North
Midlands, Scotland and of course the North-west.[25] This information
was referred to the MOH, which asked its senior Regional Officers to
evaluate it. Drawing on evidence from Medical Officers of Health, who
sometimes consulted employers and sometimes Health Visitors, these
MOH officials replied that the need was in fact even less than the MOL
claimed. For instance the MOL said there was an urgent need in
Nottingham, at the heart of the North Midlands, but the MOH reply
was as follows: 'The Medical Officer of Health made a complete
enquiry from all factories in the County Borough and in almost every
case was told there was no demand and that the number of young
married women was small.' Similar comments were made about other
key industrial towns in the North Midlands, the Midlands and the
north-western divisions and there was later said to be no need in Scotland or Wales. In view of this denial of need during 1940, it is not
surprising that only 14 nurseries were open by October 1940.[26]

When MOL DCs were asked to assess the demand for nurseries
again early in 1941 several were highly critical of the methods previously used. Employers were largely indifferent, Employment Exchanges did not keep records of the number and ages of women's
children at registration and even lists of women who said they would
use a nursery if they had a job were often fallacious guides to the need
for a nursery, since the question they were asked was so hypothetical
and actual use so dependent on the specific circumstances of the job
and the nursery. Further, as two DCs pointed out, the women were
uncertain about how to answer because they did not know what was
behind the question. 'The same women questioned by different people
give entirely contradictory answers according to what they assume to
be the desire of the questioner,' wrote one official and another added,
that when women were asked at Exchanges 'whether they can make
proper provision for their children . . . many women argue to themselves

that if they say they cannot provide for their children they will be considered as not available for work and consequently reply that they can make satisfactory provision whatever the difficulties may be'.[27]

The point made by several DCs was that it was impossible to express demand in the precise numerical terms required by the MOH and the local authorities, which frequently wanted a daunting list of data including proof of employers' difficulties in recruiting women, lists of names of potential women workers with young children and details of whether or not they would use a nursery. MOL officials claimed that there were plenty of other reliable indicators, for example the frequency of inquiries to the Employment Exchanges about day nurseries and other types of child care, such as school meals and after-school play centres, and the opinion of a wide range of different groups, including local voluntary bodies such as Citizens' Advice Bureaux, Co-operative Women's Guilds, Women's Voluntary Service branches, Trade Union branches, etc. In addition they had evidence of voluntary nurseries struggling to meet the need for places, many of which, such as those at Leeds and Dewsbury, were said to be 'overcrowded' and to have 'long waiting lists'.[28]

However when confronted with evidence from voluntary bodies, medical officers suddenly became aware of the problem of bias. They 'may not be always entirely disinterested' they complained and on the same grounds the MOH preferred to disregard the widespread pressure for nurseries which mounted after May 1941.[29] The TUC's women's conferences passed motions urging wider provision in 1941 and 1942, Labour Party women pressed for action, a Birmingham Day Nursery Campaign Committee came into being in June 1941 and *ad hoc* groups of women were formed in many parts of the country, including Tolworth, Greenford, Eastbourne and Worthing. *Picture Post* ran an article by Anne Scott James, 'We Want More Nursery Schools', in October 1941 and reported in June 1942, 'Hampstead Mothers Stage Baby Riot to Demand More Day Nurseries'. A Women's Parliament held at Conway Hall, London, in January 1942, and widely reported in the press demanded, 'More Nurseries Soon for War Babies', as did one held in Glasgow on 25 January 1942 and at a meeting called by the MOL in February 1942 for women to 'voice their grievances' one of three demands was 'provide more nurseries for children of working married women'.[30] However, the chairmen of local authority committees were said to 'place more reliance' on Health Visitors' evidence than on any other. As a result a situation could arise like that in Ealing, where the Medical Officer claimed 'lack of evidence of need' whereas the DC

Figure 4.3: Mothers pressed for nurseries increasingly energetically during 1941/2. This demonstration took place in Hampstead, north London, during an MOL recruiting drive in the spring of 1942.

Courtesy of BBC Hulton Picture Library.

insisted, 'In this instance as it happened there was more real evidence that a Day Nursery was urgently required than in any other part of the Division.'[31]

It did not take long for MOL officials to become convinced that Medical Officers were thoroughly biased against nurseries. A MOL memorandum of February 1941 summed it up:

Although in some areas, where the Medical Officer of Health approves of day nurseries, the proposal has been made willingly, in the majority of areas the Medical Officer of Health greatly prefers that women with young children should remain at home and does not feel inclined to make much effort to persuade his Council to incur their share of the cost.[32]

The allegation that many Medical Officers dressed up their prejudice that 'a mother's place is in the home' as evidence of lack of demand for nurseries, was repeated increasingly angrily during 1941-2, not only by MOL officials but also by some of those pressing for increased provision.[33] Several DCs questioned whether *any* evidence of demand was necessary in advance of nursery provision, arguing that if nursery places were made available they would be filled, whatever was said beforehand.[34]

MOL exasperation with claims that nurseries were not wanted, in the face of its conviction that they were vital for mobilisation, led to efforts to circumvent the Medical Officers by addressing strongly worded circulars to the mayors of towns where the MOL considered provision to be inadequate, which at the end of 1941 including Birmingham, Coventry, Gloucester, Liverpool, Crewe and Leeds. At the end of 1941 Bevin asked for their 'personal interest and help in a matter of real and vital importance to the allied cause', to which the mayors replied instantly, mostly professing their full support and earnest endeavours.[35] As we have seen, after the end of 1941 the numbers of day nurseries did rise, though the figures were often inflated by the inclusion of nurseries planned and in preparation with those actually open.[36] However, even while they were on the increase, MOL officials found that they had to be constantly on their guard against MOH attempts to close nurseries on the grounds of under-use.

The Use Made of Nurseries

The biggest onslaught came in April 1943 when the MOH claimed that it had evidence that average attendance at many nurseries opened before 1 July 1942 was less than 50 per cent. The MOL view was that the MOH survey failed to relate nursery opening hours to crucial factors such as employment practice and family habits and thus, by overestimating the maximum hours of use, underestimated average attendances. The figures were based on a six-day week, whereas in fact small numbers of children attended on Saturdays for several reasons, for instance that some employers used only half the workforce at weekends, some women took Saturdays off with or without permission and others left their children at home with other members of the family at these times, thereby saving themselves the standard 1s per day nursery fee. RCs insisted that more realistic attendance averages should be calculated and many asserted that even if they were not filled to capacity the nurseries in their areas should not be closed.[37] The upshot was that only 43 nurseries out of a total of 1,345 in July 1943 were closed and even after the end of the war MOL officials managed in the name of labour supply to save some from instant closure, even though the withdrawal of MOH funding in 1945 and the reluctance of local authorities to foot the whole bill sounded the death knell of many nurseries.[38]

In general evaluation of the use made of nurseries was, like assessment of the demand for them, a matter of interpreting ambiguous evidence. When the MOH suggested that nurseries were under-used (and that by implication demand had been over-estimated) MOL officials responded that use depended largely on the terms on which nurseries were offered. Cost, accessibility and publicity were important to take-up, but the questions which stood out as vital were the hours for which nurseries were open and the group of women to whom places were available.

The long hours for which a munition worker was away from home each day were a major characteristic of such work. Although there was a movement to reduce women's hours during the war, which we shall examine in a later chapter, in the summer of 1942 two-thirds of Royal Ordnance Factories still employed women for 55 or more per week, which meant a ten-hour day plus travelling time which could be lengthy.[39] For instance, women spent up to four hours getting to and from Chorley ROF in Lancashire, as well as walking large distances between the factory gates and the workshops which were scattered over a large area for safety. The nurseries in the Chorley area were said by the MOH to be under-used and local MOL officials believed that this was accounted for by the long hours coupled with a 'general dislike of that particular factory'. The local Medical Officer of Health, on the other hand, interpreted it as a sign of profound 'opposition to the idea of a nursery' in the area.[40]

Miss Smieton from within the MOL, argued at one point that the long hours required of factory workers meant that they would not be able to use the nurseries at all, without harming their children. She described graphically how mothers would have to get the children up early in the morning and collect them in the dark of the evening, concluding, 'This is bad for the child.'[41] Despite her responsibility for factory welfare Miss Smieton did not think in terms of the effect of this on the woman worker nor of solutions which would have made her life easier, but argued from a perspective on child welfare which itself was not necessarily valid, especially if nurseries had, as they were supposed to, somewhere for children to sleep. Many other observers both within and outside the MOL disagreed with her, advocating much longer hours for nurseries than the typical seven to twelve, especially after the relaxation of the provisions of the 1937 Factory Act under Emergency Orders, which permitted women to work on shifts around the clock. A factory welfare officer in Cardiff said:

> The nurseries could not fill the needs of shift workers unless they were run on a 24-hour 7 day a week basis. At present they are open from 9.0 a.m. until 5.0 p.m. on 5 days a week. This seems to be the reason why the war nurseries are half empty.[42]

However the MOH opposed residential child care for women war workers. Miss Puxley explained to the MOL that 'such Homes are carried on largely under the Poor Law for neglected and deserted children'. This was not in itself an argument against providing them for the children of war workers, but Miss Puxley deftly switched cause and effect, making the institution appear to create the condition which had in fact been the reason for its establishment:

> once a child is taken from its parents for the night as well as the day, the family tie is apt to be completely loosened, and before long a neglectful parent would probably cease to take responsibility for her child altogether.[43]

Her prejudices were played upon by Miss Smieton who claimed to know that 'Many mothers are unwilling to have their children away from home at night,' a point which Miss Puxley rapidly added to her own armoury of objections, stating a week after she had received Miss Smieton's memo, 'Experience still seems to show that only a very few women want their children cared for by night as well as by day.'[44]

But on what 'experience' did Miss Smieton and Miss Puxley, assistant secretaries in Ministries housed in London offices, draw when they made such judgements? They relied, presumably, on information from their local officers. As far as the surviving files are concerned, the last information they had received on the subject of night nurseries was in the summer of 1940, when the MOL Controllers of four divisions (the North-west, the North-east, Midlands and the North Midlands) had indicated that there was a need for them. Miss Puxley's claim that the force of 'experience' was behind her arguments against residential nurseries was in fact a way of dressing up her view (and that of the

MOH) that the family was preferable to the institution in all but extreme cases of family failure. 'Generally,' she wrote, 'there is a father or an older schoolchild who can look after the smaller child during night shifts.'[45] The reference to the idea that a man might take responsibility is rare in discussions of child care but the context is important. The father and the schoolchild (meaning in 1941 a child under 14) were suggested because they were alternatives to maternal care which avoided collective provision. They were not recommended in their own right.

However, in spite of the opposition, the demands of war production for women to work round the clock slowly pushed the MOH into allowing the lengthening of nursery hours. During 1942 some residential nurseries were permitted in industrial areas and some day nurseries were allowed to take children overnight, thus becoming '24-hour' nurseries, to cater for shift workers. Leeds, for example, eventually had both varieties and Birmingham boasted 'Children's Hotels', open day and night, but different from conventional residential provision in that mothers took home their children at week-ends or when they were free.[46] The MOH retained some control by ruling that only one-third of the number of day places might be occupied at night. Protest against this rule from MOL officials, and comments made by women in Leeds who regretted having to impose child care on their mothers when they were 'on nights' and would have preferred 24-hour nurseries, suggest that in some cases at least mothers felt that it was better for their children to be cared for in a nursery than at home, at night, in the special circumstances of doing war work. Women at the TUC's women's conference in 1941 supported such views, arguing forcefully that in view of the shift system 'the best way to provide for the young children is by the provision of resident nursery schools or residential nurseries, well away from factories or military objectives, and as near the mother as is convenient with safety and giving her a chance to visit them'. They argued that experience of such arrangements rapidly removed any doubts that women might have about them.[47] So much for Smieton and Puxley's denials on the grounds of 'experience' at the beginning of 1941 that mothers would not be prepared to use residential nurseries.

The case of residential child care emphasises the resistance of those concerned with 'welfare' to changes in order to accommodate the needs of production. They had to concede some ground, but nevertheless effectively upheld conventional social values against the encroachment of the pressures of wartime mobilisation. Children should be looked after by their mothers, privately, at home, preferably all the time, but definitely at night if not by day. However, it is worth pointing out here that it is by no means clear that women's own advantage lay entirely with the MOL in this struggle between 'welfare' and 'production'. As far as the issue of residential nursery accommodation was concerned, they were losers in respect to policies built exclusively on either. Why should production rob women, or men, of home life? Why, on the other hand, should the welfare of their children mean that they must be confined to caring for them privately at home?

Where residential nurseries were set up, women applying for places in them found strong overtones of the pre-war practices of provision only for those in poverty or distress. One woman concluded that they were 'really only for waifs and strays, or at any rate not for the children of women who earn a fair wage by working eleven hours a day in the factory'.[48] In most day nurseries the process of selection was far less overt. But it nevertheless occurred, officially sanctioned at least at first by the philosophies of the Ministries involved. Thus the MOH definition of the day nursery was that it was 'a cloak-room for the children of women workers' and was 'for the benefit of the mother' as opposed to arrangements 'for the education of the child' based on the part-time nursery school. The MOH implied that use of such 'cloak-rooms' should be limited to those mothers who 'had' to work, which at first was felt to exclude any who could be said to be working to 'supplement' their husbands' incomes, even if they had been called up. The low level of servicemen's wives' allowances meant, however, that they were rapidly absorbed into the 'deserving' category.[49]

Initially the MOL also favoured a selective admissions policy for nurseries though on labour supply rather than 'welfare' grounds. In the interests of the recruitment of women for munitions it was declared in June 1940 that 'The Day Nurseries are intended to provide for the children of women recruited for work in Government factories or factories having Government contracts.'[50] But this principle came under fire repeatedly during 1940–41, as distinctions between what was 'war work' and what not became more obviously invidious. They ignored the interrelatedness of the labour supply, as the concentration policy had done, and in practice the working arrangements of non-essential workers like bus conductresses and shop assistants often meant that use of a nursery was more convenient for them than for munitions workers. The implications for nursery admission were gradually appreciated in the MOL and were given emphatic statement in January 1941:

it does not matter whether it is the child of a munition worker who is cared for or the child of any other mother . . . provided she is employed on work of national importance which in these days covers almost every form of employment.[51]

In spite of the changes in the MOL's approach, there is evidence to suggest that women in many areas believed that admission was only for certain categories of person. An article in the *South Wales Echo* stated:

Many working mothers seem to take it for granted that some condition, rule or proviso will make *their* babies ineligible . . . 'but I won't work in a war factory − I'm on the trams' . . . 'But my husband isn't in the Army; he works on the dock.'[52]

Moreover, the simple fact that there was an absolute shortage of nursery places made it inevitable that many nurseries operated their own selection procedures. By one estimate places were available for at the most 25 per cent of the under-five-year-old children of women war workers in 1944[53] and evidence from London and Leeds suggest that those in charge (mostly of course State Registered Nurses) tended to use the pre-war MOH criteria giving priority to hardship cases, in spite of the wartime MOL policy that places should be available for the children of any woman who would work. Thus at a St Pancras nursery places were given first to those considered 'needy' such as an Englishwoman married to an Austrian who had been interned, a mother whose ex-convict husband had left her with two children and expecting a third and an unmarried mother who would have to lose her job if she could not find somewhere for her child. At Moynihan House nursery in Leeds, 9 of the 35 children were 'illegitimate', and the rest were mostly the children of servicemen. These groups were widely understood by women themselves to be those for whom nurseries were provided. At some nurseries the long established poor law tradition of regarding only the clean poor as deserving was upheld. The Chief Health Visitor supervising Wandsworth nursery explained to a Mass-Observer, 'We've instructed Matron not to take them in if they're dirty.'[54]

In spite of their wartime role and the vast expansion in their numbers, a 'waifs and strays' image clung to the nurseries in official literature and media coverage. For instance in the leaflet appealing for women to do 'war work in War Time Nurseries' the nursery was presented as a kind of wartime charity, in such a way as to tug at the heart strings of kind women who might help: 'The nation has a duty to

Figure 4.4: This leaflet, setting out nursery regulations, was picked up in Coventry in November 1941 by a Mass-Observer.

CITY OF COVENTRY
PUBLIC HEALTH DEPARTMENT

DAY NURSERIES

These Nurseries are intended for children aged six months to five years. Infants under six months can also be admitted at the discretion of the Medical Officer. Only children of women recruited for work in munitions and other factories essential to the war effort will be accepted. Mothers must not bring to the nursery children who may be suffering from any infectious disease or who have been in contact with another child suffering from such a disease. Should any child develop an infectious disease during the day, mothers are asked to give their consent to the child's removal to the City Isolation Hospital, Whitley, Coventry.

DAY NURSERY ⎰ 1/6d. a day for first child.
FEES ⎱ 1/- a day for any other child of the same family.
Meals will be provided.

HOURS OF OPENING.
7-30 a.m.—8 p.m. (Saturday included, but Sunday excluded).

Mothers should provide the following:—

FOR CHILDREN UP TO 1 YEAR—Hair Brush. Change of napkin and knickers to be brought daily in which the child may return home. Articles should be marked with name

CHILDREN AGED 1—5 YEARS—Brush, comb, tooth brush change of shoes. A change of knickers will be required and a clean handkerchief. Articles should be marked with the name.

85239/9/48. 500. (12).

Courtesy of Coventry City Record Office and the Mass-Observation Archive.

safeguard the health and well-being of its children. Above all there are the bombed-out babies, the evacuated children, and the children of war workers, to be cared for.'[55] Coupled to the idea that nurseries were places where middle-class women might offer service was the notion that they could offer much needed 'training and guidance' to the children left in them, implying that the sort of women who went into war work left something to be desired as mothers.[56] In some accounts the mothers themselves were supposed to learn from their contact with the nursery, for example in a book celebrating women's war work Peggy Scott wrote:

> The mothers appreciate the interest in their children which makes the nurse come to see them, and they learn from her how to use dried egg and other wartime foods. They are quick to notice also that the Nursery School teachers manage their children better than they do themselves and they are glad to try the plans the teacher suggests.

In this account a doctor was quoted to give authoritative emphasis to the idea that the nursery was a temporary stopgap for needy women in the war emergency: 'In normal times children were better with their mother and father: it was the whole foundation of British life.'[57]

It is perhaps not surprising that some nurseries were 'under-used' in view of the way that they were publicly presented and perceived. Yet patterns of use varied enormously, even within single towns. For example in Cardiff there was excess capacity in under-advertised huts and a waiting list of over 100 at a large centrally positioned and well-established nursery, a pattern repeated elsewhere.[58] Confusion among women about eligibility must have been further heightened by the variety in provision. Nursery schools and nursery classes in elementary schools co-existed with various types of day nursery and not every nursery was open all day (let alone all night). In particular those which originated with the evacuation scheme, as nursery centres, were open for even shorter hours than nursery schools. They evolved out of a work-welfare dilemma arising from evacuation but came to occupy a special place in wartime child care policy.

It was initially assumed that nurseries could not be provided in areas from which parents were advised to evacuate their children (evacuation areas), on the grounds that they would constitute targets. (For the same reason factory crèches were frowned upon by both the MOH and the MOL for all that a few progressive employers provided them.[59])

However, members of the MOL complained that the non-provision of nurseries in evacuation areas, which were by definition centres of war production, would have a disastrous effect on the recruitment of women there and in 1941 it authorised its local officers to urge mothers to evacuate their young children.[60] However, it proved difficult to find billets for under-five-year-old evacuees, because, unlike school-age children, 'the householder normally has them on her hands all day long'. As a solution nursery centres were set up in reception areas by voluntary groups. They were cheap because voluntary, they took only two- to five-year-olds, they could be seen as a charity for the deserving and as part-time institutions they meshed into conventional patterns of home life.[61] They were well liked by both Miss Puxley of the MOH and Miss Smieton of the MOL. In fact Miss Smieton advanced the claim that, quite apart from their role in solving evacuation problems, they could contribute to labour supply, on the grounds that they were a suitable form of provision for areas where there was thought to be insufficient demand for a full-time nursery, even though the recruitment of women was necessary. But how could the hours of a nursery centre (9 to 11.30 a.m. and 1.30 to 4 p.m.) be reconciled with the hours of work expected from most women workers? Such nurseries were at the opposite extreme from the 24-hour service that many other MOL officials demanded. Miss Smieton proposed that the shortfall should be covered by the use of paid minders, who would collect children, take them to their own homes, give them meals and look after them till their mothers picked them up on their return from work. This suggestion was embodied in the June 1941 circular on wartime child care arrangements as one variant in a 'flexible' system.[62]

Even though they formed a small proportion of wartime nurseries, the future lay with the part-time nursery. Part-time provision for two- to five-year-olds, rather than full-time for all ages, was the form of nursery which LEAs were advised to provide to meet their responsibilities towards the under-fives laid down in the 1944 Education Act.[63] As far as wartime child care was concerned, the meshing of part-time nurseries and minders in Miss Smieton's thinking in 1941 presaged the development of a policy advocating the use of child minders as complete alternatives to wartime nurseries, which gathered momentum as a result of the MOH–MOL alliance forged between the Misses Puxley and Smieton.

Childminding and the Wartime Nurseries

When members of the MOL and MOH 'discovered' child minding in the war, the practice was at first said to indicate that nurseries were unnecessary. For example, the Divisional Controller for the North-east wrote in June 1940:

> It is customary for women in the textile and clothing industries to continue in employment after marriage and to arrange for their young children to be left in the care of relatives or neighbours. Already an increasing proportion of married women in the West Riding are returning to industry, and as no difficulties in regard to arranging for the care of the children have been brought to our notice, it is assumed that the practice of leaving their babies in the care of grandparents or the woman next door is being resumed. It is not therefore anticipated that the need for the provision of Day Nurseries will be widespread.[64]

However this conclusion was rapidly contradicted by the logic of the mounting demand for labour which caused minders themselves to be called up or urged to volunteer. Exemption was only available under the registration and conscription schemes if the children for whom a woman was caring were her own and reports soon mounted of a growing shortage of minders.[65] This did not stop Medical Officers of Health from using evidence of the practice of minding as one among their battery of arguments against the need for nurseries in such areas of intensive employment as Manchester, Wigan, Coventry and even Birmingham during 1940–41,[66] but nevertheless the MOL view that the minder system had no long-term viability in wartime dominated in this period, informing the presentation of the first official minding scheme as no more than a stopgap in places where nurseries were slow to materialise.

This first minding scheme, known as the Registered Daily Guardian scheme, was introduced in February 1941. Its key features were that it was seen as temporary and that it was subject to a relatively high degree of local authority intervention. Thus in June 1941 the MOL stated, 'It is the policy of the Ministry to encourage the provision of nurseries where this will meet the need,' and only in special cases where 'quick or extensive provision' for child care was necessary was the Registered Daily Guardian scheme to be implemented. Minders were to be selected and inspected by the local authority through its

Maternity and Child Welfare Committee, who would also pay part of their fee of 1s a day per child and check that they did not take more than three children. The other part of the fee came from the mother and some minders were authorised to take children for 24 hours. Only a few towns used the scheme, notably Birmingham and Leeds, and in total there were 2,000 registered minders caring for 5,000 children in 1942, a relatively small proportion of the probable eligible population.[67]

However, minding as an alternative to collective child care was favoured not just by many Medical Officers but also by Miss Puxley in the MOH and Miss Smieton in the MOL and in November 1941 the Registered Daily Guardian scheme was superceded by a second minder policy, that of the 'volunteer housewife' which differed from the first in several key respects. Where minders had previously been advocated to fill the gaps in nursery provision, nurseries were now presented as the last resort when all possible minding arrangements had failed. Responsibility for making arrangements now rested with women workers themselves and only where they failed to find a minder was the local authority to step in, by compiling lists of women who wanted to work but did not know a minder and of potential minders who did 'not know a friend or neighbour whom they can help', and by making an 'initial introduction' of members of one group to the other.[68]

Apart from this, local authority responsibility was minimal. No government subsidy was now offered, a change justified on the grounds that women did not really want one: 'Experience so far has suggested that both parties prefer in this matter to make their own financial arrangements,' but in fact underpinned by the local authorities' dislike of being put in the position of debt collectors and the MOH's eye for economy. Only in cases where the mother and the minder could not agree terms was the government 'ready to afford financial assistance' which would be made through the old Registered Daily Guardian scheme. There was a strong suggestion that this option should not be used, however: 'It is not suggested that the Maternity and Child Welfare Authority should take any initiative in regard to the introduction of such a scheme.' In contrast to the preoccupation with regulations where nurseries were concerned, there was no general supervision or set of standards. Only in those cases where the local authority made the 'introduction' did they need to 'satisfy themselves in advance that the conditions for the care of the child are satisfactory'. Otherwise it was expected that in the majority of privately made arrangements standards would be upheld simply by Health Visitors who 'in pursuance of their usual duties' would 'be in contact with young children'. There was no indication of how information about private arrangements would reach them and the guidance on standards was limited to the recommendation that three children per minder should be the limit. And there was no mention of cubic footage, facilities indoors and outdoors for play and sleep, medical inspection, 'occuptional training' or special qualifications, as there was in the case of nurseries.[69]

A government circular announced the new policy in December 1941. It opened with a dramatic statement of the urgent need for women workers:

> To meet the needs of our own Forces and to provide the aid which has been promised to Russia, a rapid increase in production and consequently in the numbers of women employed in the key factories is essential.

It then went on to present private minding as the normal method of catering for the vast majority of their children. It stated that child care required the 'co-operation of the responsible local authorities, of voluntary organisations and of all people of good will in the district', but above all the 'women of the district themselves' had to make 'the greatest single contribution'. They

> must between them carry out the two tasks of looking after the children and working in the factories . . . the housewives in one street who cannot go out to work themselves might well undertake the care of the children of those mothers in that street who are at work or who are ready to undertake war work. In this way there will be real partnership in the war effort.

Only when minders were impossible to find would the LA have to provide other facilities. These 'may take the form of the provision of wartime nurseries', which was still important, 'a duty to the nation . . . which needs no emphasis', but effort to set them up was now to be concentrated just on 'key areas'.[70] In reality the new policy meant there would be no state help in arranging, nor any financial contribution from the state towards the child care which women needed in order to participate in wartime production.

The out-manoeuvring of the nursery did not pass unnoticed, however. There was considerable opposition within the MOL to the precedence given to the minder over the nursery in the draft of the circular. For instance, Bevin's Parliamentary Secretary wrote:

> The TUC and our Factory and Welfare Board . . . put these arrangements well ahead of any others in their programme, and are extremely reluctant to give any blessing to anything in the nature of 'childminding'. We had a good deal of criticism for instance at the last meeting of the Board about semi-official minding.

He advised that alternatives to nurseries should be expressed as 'in the meantime' ones. Bevin himself tried to redress the balance between nurseries and minders, at least in the covering letter to recalcitrant local authorities, which was recast to read 'minding arrangements . . . will not be sufficient, and it is imperative that more War-Time Nurseries should be established'.[71] Nevertheless in the final version of the circular, ML Circular 128/74 covering MH 2535, there was no change in respect of the priority ordering of minders and nurseries, even though several other changes had been made. These included dropping the term 'volunteer foster parent', which was used for 'minder' in the draft, 'because of the possible association with foster mothers who look after illegitimate children'. They became 'volunteer housewives' in the circular – a curious term in view of the fact that minders were presumably already housewives by virtue of their exemption from war work and were actually volunteering for child care not housework. However, it was a contortion necessary if the stigma attached to both 'foster parent' and 'child minder' was to be avoided.[72]

In addition to opposition to the new policy within the MOL there was disquiet, even outrage, outside. Newspapers carried rather hysterical statements deploring the revival of the Victorian practice of 'baby farming' and neither of the voluntary organisations involved in nursery work was happy about private minding arrangements. The Secretary of the Nursery Schools Association was furious about the shift in policy: 'the minding system is a scandalous one, as the Government sponsors it, but takes no responsibility for any harm to the children while in the charge of the foster mothers.'[73] In February 1942 an angry resolution was passed at a conference of working women's organisations (which included trade unions, Women's Co-operative Guilds, and Labour Party women's sections) declaring their protest

> against the circular (Ministry of Health 2535) sent on December 5 to local authorities, which suggested that most of the young children of

married women at work outside their homes must be cared for by means of private arrangements made by the mothers.

The view of the Standing Joint Committee of the organisations, which was endorsed by the conference, was that the elevation of private minding was an evasion of the government's promises that the children of women war workers would be properly looked after. Further, 'such private arrangements as are suggested cannot safeguard the welfare of the children, and, because of their uncertainty, must lead to absenteeism and loss of production'.[74] Miss Sutherland, National Woman Organiser of the Labour Party and a member of Bevin's Factory and Welfare Advisory Board, spelt out the objections of organised working women to minders in *News Review*. She said that they accepted the 'carefully planned' Registered Guardian Scheme was a stopgap but were publicly opposed to giving the 'volunteer housewife' precedence over the nursery. This would lead not only to inadequate care of children and instability among women workers, but also to inactivity on the part of local authorities who would think 'that they would only have to cope with a paltry residue of children whose mothers had failed to park them on friends or relatives'. The *News Review* report concluded, 'A sneaking feeling, had Mary Sutherland, that somebody, somewhere in the MOH, was against nurseries all along.'[75]

Women workers might have been expected to prefer informal minding arrangements because of their freedom from the disadvantageous aspects of nurseries, such as the dominant role of 'specialists', the stigma attached to the use of nurseries and the rigid and limited hours of many of them. However, in as far as there is evidence, the attitude of women to minders other than close blood relatives was remarkably negative. At the 1941 TUC women's conference, a man representing the hosiery unions suggested in debate that minders were more popular with mothers than nurseries, but none of the women spoke in agreement and one asserted, 'The minder system was not good enough.'[76] Mass-Observers inquired about the minding scheme in several different towns during 1940–41 and reported many negative reactions. For example in Leeds an investigator 'canvassed the Hyde Park Ward on the subject and could not find anyone to support the scheme' in June 1942. 'Typical comments' were that it was 'baby farming', that their children were likely to 'get the wrong end of the stick' and that you could not trust a stranger with your child. Eighty per cent of the women asked in five London boroughs in March 1942 were against having their children looked after by 'neighbours'. As in Leeds, women felt that minders were likely to be unreliable, might lose interest and would not, for example, 'see they were eating properly', whereas, some women asserted, 'They'd see to all that at the nurseries.' M-O's surveys were small-scale, but M-O does not appear to have been biased against minders in such a way as to influence replies. In *People in Production*, minding schemes were referred to as 'interesting' and having 'attractions', but though negative as well as positive comments were published about day nurseries, no positive remarks were quoted about minders, with the exception of the woman worker's own mother.[77]

The lack of enthusiasm for minders may have been specific to wartime. As Bevin himself wrote in January 1943: 'owing to the intensity of the call up great difficulties are arising both where there is sickness and where children have to be cared for while their mothers are at work', which meant that it was hard to find a minder and that the choice was limited.[78] Nevertheless by one estimate three-quarters of the children of women war workers were cared for by minders in 1944.[79] In view of the shift in policy during 1941, and the reactions to it described here, one must conclude that this heavy use of minders was not, as it might appear, simply the result of women's choosing, but was heavily influenced by the preferences of the official policy-makers.

Conclusion

The MOH was clearly deeply reluctant to expand the provision of collective child care facilities, in spite of the need for them arising from the wartime mobilisation of women. If women with under-school-age children had been subject to compulsion it would obviously have been easier for the MOL to have insisted on the provision of nurseries. But in view of male reluctance to apply compulsion to any women, it seems likely that such a step could have been taken only if production had reached a dangerously low level, if at all. As it was the MOL desperately needed mothers in industry but had to rely on them entering as volunteers, so its pressure for child care provision was always in danger of rebuttal on the grounds either that in fact such women were not going into paid work, or that they preferred other forms of child care to the nursery. The MOL did score considerable victories in persuading the MOH to alter the rules of premises and staffing under which it provided nurseries, a process which may in fact have led to more appropriate nursery provision, though the MOH saw the relaxation as strictly temporary. And the MOL did manage to secure the establishment of some 1,345 nurseries by July 1943, an enormous expansion from the slender base of 14 nurseries in October 1940.

All the same, the MOL was significantly outflanked by the MOH on the issue of minding, which made sense neither in terms of the supply and stability of women workers, nor in terms of the high standards of premises and staffing which the MOH claimed to be necessary in nurseries to prevent the spread of infectious disease. In spite of these contradictions, the civil servants responsible for policy in the MOH and the MOL combined to put private minding arrangements before collective provisions in the main public statement on child care policy of the war, coinciding with the intensification of mobilisation at the end of 1941. While urging in the name of the collective war effort that 'self help is often the best help', and presenting minding as a new wartime phenomenon, the government was in fact upholding child care practices to which women had traditionally had to resort in the absence of adequate alternatives. In effect MOH policy-makers were resisting the pressure of the wartime mobilisation of women for universal and unconditional collective provision which could, eventually, have contributed to the transformation of child care from an activity which was home-based, full-time, female and private, into a public, collective one, which freed women from a major component of the sexual division of labour both at home and at work. It is, of course, important to ask why this was so.

At a superficial level MOH preference for minders seems to be explained by the facts that minding was cheap for the government, private and also home-based, involving a surrogate mother. But it is difficult to produce a confident explanation for the more general medical prejudice against any form of extra-familial child care, even in wartime, based on the view that 'a mother's place is in the home where she should look after her own children'.[80] It can perhaps be linked to the concern of the medical profession with infant mortality during the early twentieth century, though their equation of working mothers with high levels of mortality was both simplistic and itself based on prejudice.[81] Possibly its roots lie in the establishment of the medical doctor during the nineteenth century as a professional closely enmeshed with the middle-class family, whose authority depended on the displacement of some specifically feminine methods of caring and healing and whose control therefore took a particularly patriarchal form.[82] During the twentieth century the 'sovereignty' of the family doctor spread outwards to the working class largely through the agency of state employees such as the Medical Officers of Health. These suggestions must, however, remain tentative. Suffice to say that although there was a huge expansion in the numbers of nurseries, the weight of MOH prejudice against alternatives to maternal care acted as a major constraint on wartime child care policy.

Notes

1. PRO Lab 26/57, E. Brown MOL to S.F. Wilkinson MOH, 30 April 1940.
2. PRO Lab 26/58, memo by E. Bevin, 16 October 1941.
3. Ibid., ML Circular 128/50, 3 June 1941.
4. PRO Lab 26/57, minute by M. Smieton, 4 November 1940.
5. PRO Lab 26/58, E. Andrews, Labour Party, to Bevin, 26 November 1940; minute by G. Ince, 4 December 1940.
6. PRO MH 55/288. Thanks to Jane Mark-Lawson for this reference.
7. PRO Lab 26/57, MOH to Town Clerks, 18 June 1940.
8. Denise Riley, 'War in the Nursery', *Feminist Review*, 2, 1979.
9. Ibid., p. 87. These themes are further developed in Riley's recent book, *War in the Nursery, Theories of the Child and Mother* (Virago, London, 1983).
10. PRO Lab 26/57, Puxley MOH to Smieton MOL, 3 July 1940.
11. Ibid., MOH to Town Clerks, 18 June 1940.
12. Ibid., MOH memorandum, 28 September 1940.
13. M-OA, Box 276, 'Children, Day Nurseries, 1941-2', interview at Wandsworth Nursery, January 1942.
14. PRO Lab 26/58: ML Circular 128/50 covering MH 2388, 31 May 1941; Replies to inquiry re delays in the provision of nurseries, 7 October 1941.
15. Ibid., 'Day-time War Nurseries'. Critical review by Lady Allen of Hurtwood, June 1942; M-OA, Box 276, report on Cardiff nurseries, 9 February 1942; M. Allen and M. Nicholson, *Memoirs of an Uneducated Lady, Lady Allen of Hurtwood* (Thames and Hudson, London, 1957).
16. PRO Lab 26/58, MOL–MOH correspondence, 7–16 October 1941.
17. PRO Lab 26/57, MOH to Town Clerks, 18 June 1940.
18. PRO Lab 26/58, 'Tottenham Day Nursery, Report on a Visit', 22 March 1941.
19. M-OA, Box 276, 'Coventry Nurseries', November 1941; 'Tottenham Day Nursery', 22 March 1941; 'Municipal Nurseries in Leeds', 4 June 1942.
20. *The Star*, 14 January 1942, 'Red-Tape Threat to War Work "Orphans" '; PRO Lab 26/58: memo on wartime nurseries by Bevin, 16 October 1941; ML Circular 28/397, Appendix, 'War Work in War-Time Nurseries', 18 November 1941; ML Circular 128/74, 9 December 1941. On the shortages of both nurses and teachers see Ferguson and Fitzgerald (1954), p. 329, and P.H.J.H. Gosden, *Education in the Second World War: A Study in Policy and Administration* (Methuen, London, 1976), p. 102. It is perhaps indicative of the limitations of supply that Gosden does not mention the secondment of teachers to nurseries.
21. PRO Lab 26/58: memo on day nurseries by Miss Smieton, 2 January 1941; see note 23 below for examples of those who quoted her view; PRO Lab 26/58, memo from MOH to Select Committee on National Expenditure, August 1943; PRO Lab 26/133, memo on wartime nurseries, 9 April 1943.

22. *Hansard*, 16 October 1941, Vol. 374, No. 109, Col. 1507; PRO Lab 26/58, memo by MOH to Select Committee on National Expenditure, August 1943.

23. MOH, *On the State of the Public Health During Six Years of War: The Report of the Chief Medical Officer of the Ministry of Health 1939-1945* (HMSO, London, 1946). But see Medical Women's Federation, 'The Health of Children in Wartime Day Nurseries', *British Medical Journal*, 17 August 1946, Dr Hilda Menzies in *The Lancet*, 5 October 1946 and examples quoted by Riley (1979), pp. 93-5.

24. PRO Lab 26/57, H.N. Grundy, NW DC to MOL, 14 and 20 May 1941.

25. Ibid., 'Day Nurseries'. Summary of replies received from DCs to Mr Gould's Minute of 29 May 1940.

26. Ibid., 'Position of Day Nurseries for the Children of Munitions Workers', 23 August 1940 and 31 October 1940. Scotland was in fact administered separately by May 1941.

27. PRO Lab 26/58: correspondence between DCs/Divisional Welfare Officers and MOL, April-May 1941.

28. Ibid., NE DC to MOL, 5 May 1941; London and SE DC to MOL, 6 May 1941; replies from DCs to Miss Smieton, January 1941.

29. Ibid., London and SE DC to MOL, 6 May 1941.

30. TUC Pamphlets and Leaflets, 1941/6 and 1942/7 (reports of the eleventh and twelfth annual conferences of unions catering for women workers); PRO Lab 26/58 minutes of meeting between Miss Sutherland, Labour Party and Ince, MOL; *Birmingham Evening Despatch*, 6 January 1942; *Surrey Comet*, 10 January 1942; *Labour Management*, 1941; *Eastbourne Herald*, 24 January 1942; *Worthing Herald*, 23 January 1942; *Picture Post*, October 1941 and June 1942; *Evening Standard*, 20 January 1942; M-OA, 'Diary of a Foreign Correspondent', Glasgow: Report on Glasgow and West of Scotland Women's Parliament, 25 January 1942; *Daily Mirror*, 12 February 1942. On women's parliaments see Chapter 5, N.11.

31. PRO Lab 26/58, London and SE DC to MOL, 1 May 1941.

32. PRO Lab 26/57, 'Notes for an Approach to the Treasury on the Finance of Day Nurseries', February 1941.

33. For example the Secretary of the Nursery School Association said, 'Mothers will use day nurseries as soon as they find out how good they are, so the best plan is to let the nursery speak for itself . . . the main obstacles to the spread of nursery schools are (1) prejudice, (2) lack of premises, (3) lack of staff and (4) lack of equipment. The unwillingness of mothers to send their children is not an appreciable factor.' M-OA, Box 276, interview with Miss Marriott, 4 February 1942.

34. PRO Lab 26/58, correspondence between DCs and MOL April-May 1941.

35. PRO Lab 26/58, ML Circular 128/74, 9 December 1941, and correspondence between mayors and MOL, December 1941.

36. For example in November 1941 the MOH gave a figure of 400 nurseries open and the press publicised this figure, but in Parliament on 22 January 1942 the Minister of Health admitted that only 223 were actually open (93 full-time and 130 part-time) and 267 were in preparation. PRO Lab 26/58, 6 November 1941; *Hansard*, Vol. 377, No. 23, Thursday 22 January 1942.

37. PRO Lab 26/133, memo on wartime nurseries, 9 April 1943 and replies to it from RCs, April 1943.

38. PRO Lab 26/58, memo by MOH to Select Committee on National Expenditure, August 1943. See also D. Riley (1979), pp. 89-93.

39. Hooks (1944), p. 14; Inman (1957), p. 184; Select Committee on National Expenditure, '17th Report, 1940-41, Labour Problems in Filling Factories': 'Workers have to come long distances, sometimes as far as 30 miles and rarely less than three or four.'

40. PRO Lab 26/58, County Borough of Preston, 'Report on the Day Nurseries for the Children of Munitions Workers', January 1941.

41. PRO Lab 26/58, memo by M. Smieton on day nurseries, 2 January 1941.

42. Parker (1957), p. 441, 'The limits were . . . 60 hours a week, and sanction could be given for women to work at night on an eight-hour shift'; *South Wales Echo*, 24 February 1942; PRO Lab 26/57, correspondence between DCs in the North-west, Scotland, Wales, North Midlands and MOL stating a need for night nurseries.

43. PRO Lab 26/57, memo by Z. Puxley on different types of nursery care, 19 September 1940, circulated to all MOL Divisional Welfare Officers, 28 September 1940.

44. PRO Lab 26/58, memo by M. Smieton, 2 January 1941, and Puxley to Smieton, 10 January 1941.

45. Ibid., Puxley to Smieton, 10 January 1941.

46. MOH, *On the State of the Public Health* (HMSO, 1946); M-OA, Box 276, 'Leeds Nurseries', 4 June 1942; *Birmingham Evening Despatch*, 5 January 1942.

47. PRO Lab 26/133, 16 April 1943; M-OA, Box 276, 'Leeds Nurseries', 4 June 1942; TUC Pamphlets and Leaflets, 1941/6, report of the eleventh annual conference of unions catering for women workers.

48. *Daily Mail*, 20 January 1942.

49. PRO Lab 26/57, memo by Z. Puxley, 19 September 1940; minute on Beckenham nursery application, 18 July 1940; the 'fact finding and fact focussing' organisation Political and Economic Planning expressed the view in *Planning*, 254, August 1946, 'Mothers in Jobs', that wartime nurseries had been a service principally for 'wives of servicemen' and 'unmarried mothers'.

50. PRO Lab 26/57, MOH to Town Clerks, 18 June 1940.

51. PRO Lab 26/57, correspondence between DCs and MOL, June–October 1940; PRO Lab 26/58, memo on day nurseries, 2 January 1941.

52. *South Wales Echo*, 24 February 1942; see also: *Eastbourne Herald*, 24 January 1942; M-OA, Box 276, interview with Miss Marriott, 4 February 1942.

53. Nursery provision can be summarised as follows. On 31 July 1943 there were 1,345 day nurseries under the War-Time Nursery Scheme, providing 58,716 places for children up to four years old (PRO Lab 26/58, memo from MOH to Select Committee on National Expenditure, August 1943). Expansion continued to 71,806 places in September 1941, in addition to which there were 6,227 places in nursery schools for two- to four-year-olds, and 131,950 places for three- and four-year-olds in the nursery classes of elementary schools. This meant as far as the total population up to four years old was concerned that there was a nursery place of some sort for only 6.4 per cent. (Ferguson and Fitzgerald (1954), pp. 190–91 and Central Statistical Office (1951), Table 4). As far as the children of women workers were concerned, there appears to be no official total of those under five from which to calculate a percentage, but in the large sample used by the WSS not more than 25 per cent of children under five of working mothers were cared for in nurseries in 1944. The rest were with minders of some sort (WSS (1944), p. 5).

54. M-OA, Box 276: 'St Pancras Nurseries', 23 January 1942; 'Leeds Nurseries', 4 June 1942; 'Wandsworth Nurseries', 23 January 1942. Interview between the author and Mrs S., South Shields, November 1977.

55. PRO Lab 26/58, ML Circular 28/397, 18 November 1941.

56. See, for example, *True Romances*, December 1942, pp. 9–42, and July 1943, pp. 28–9. This was a magazine addressed to working-class women. I should like to thank Pat Allatt for these references.

57. Scott (1944), pp. 127 and 123.

58. M-OA, Box 276: 'Cardiff Nurseries', 9 February 1942 and 10 March 1942;

'Coventry Nurseries', 23 November 1941; 'St Pancras Nurseries', 23 January 1942. See also PRO Lab 26/133 for discussion of waiting lists.

59. PRO Lab 26/57, correspondence between MOL and MOH, June–July 1940. There were some factory crèches. See *Picture Post*, January 1945; Pauline Long, 'Speaking Out on Age', *Spare Rib*, No. 82, May 1979, pp. 14–17 for her memories of using a factory crèche on a 'Truby King ticket' of four-hourly stretches of work punctuated by 20-minute breast-feeds.

60. PRO Lab 26/58, ML Circular 128/74, 9 December 1941.

61. PRO Lab 26/57, memo by Z. Puxley, 19 September 1940.

62. PRO Lab 26/58, memo by M. Smieton, 2 January 1941; ML Circular 128/50, 3 June 1941.

63. T. Blackstone (1971), p. 64; H.C. Dent, *The Education Act, 1944*, Provisions, Regulations, Circulars, Later Acts (University of London, London, 1968), 12–17.

64. PRO Lab 26/57, DC NE to MOL, 3 June 1940.

65. Ibid., DC NW to MOL, 20 May 1940; M-OA, Box 276: cuttings from *Labour Management and Personnel Review* (unspecified date in 1941); *Daily Mail*, 20 January 1942, and others.

66. PRO Lab 26/57, Puxley to MOL, 23 August 1940; Lab 26/58, Puxley to Glover, 24 March 1941.

67. PRO Lab 26/58, ML Circular 128/50, 3 June 1941; MOH, 'On the State of the Public Health' (1946); M-OA, File Report 1151, 'The Demand for Day Nurseries', March 1942.

68. Ibid., ROA 531, MOH to Senior Regional Officers, 3 November 1941.

69. Ibid., ML Circular 128/74, 9 December 1941, covering MH 2535, 5 December 1941.

70. Ibid.

71. Ibid., MOL–MOH correspondence, 17 November 1941; internal MOL correspondence, 27 November 1941; Bevin to various mayors, 9 December 1941.

72. See notes 68 and 69.

73. *Daily Mail*, 20 January 1942; M-OA, Box 276, interview with Miss Marriott, 4 February 1942.

74. TUC Pamphlets and Leaflets, 1942/7, report of the twelfth conference of unions catering for women workers.

75. *News Review*, 22 January 1942.

76. TUC Pamphlets and Leaflets, 1941/6, report of the eleventh annual conference of unions catering for women workers.

77. M-OA, Box 276, 'Leeds Nurseries', 4 June 1942; M-O (1942), pp. 182 and 186.

78. CCA, BEVN 2/4, note dictated by Minister, 2 January 1943.

79. See note 53.

80. PRO Lab 26/58, Assistant RC London and SE to MOL, 9 October 1941.

81. C. Dyhouse, 'Working-class Mothers and Infant Mortality in England 1895–1914', *Journal of Social History*, XII, 2, 1978.

82. B. Ehrenreich and D. English, *For Her Own Good: 150 Years of the Experts' Advice to Women* (Pluto Press, London, 1979).

5 SHOPPING

Shopping was clearly a different type of task from child care. It was one part of a longer process of caring for and feeding people, and it could, at least in theory be combined with industrial work in a way which child care, involving continuous supervision, could not. However, both the Factory and Welfare Advisory Board and the MOL's local officers asserted that shopping ranked with child care as a major impediment to the supply and stability of women's labour during the first years of the war.[1] A Divisional Welfare Officer wrote in February 1941:

> The difficulty or even impossibility of shopping for people working all day seems in the experience of many Employment Exchange officers and Social Workers at least as great an obstacle to the whole-time employment of women with domestic responsibilities as the problem of getting small children looked after.[2]

Survey findings supported this impression. About half the working women in a WSS sample were 'mainly responsible' for shopping, most of whom were married, and 32 per cent of married women workers gave 'shopping difficulties' as the main disadvantage of work. It was the most frequently mentioned problem.[3] M-O's comment on its own investigations of working women was 'the domestic difficulty which they mentioned most often was shopping. Difficulties about children were a subsidiary though considerable concern.'[4]

Shopping, like child care, was a perennial problem for women in paid work, but it was exacerbated in wartime by the long hours required in industry, the shortages of consumer goods and additional problems like the black-out and transport difficulties. Women war workers inevitably absented themselves from work in order to shop, with the result that productivity suffered. In April–May 1941 the Ministry of Supply received numerous complaints like that from Messrs Midland Utilities Ltd, Birmingham, who wrote explaining that they could not maintain supplies of 30,000 guard valves weekly because Messrs Brass Turned Parts could only deliver 100 to 150 gross of nuts per week. The reason is a loss of working hours of about 10 per cent due principally to the very insufficient shopping facilities in their neighbourhood and consequently work people stay away from work or have to be given leave to do their shopping.

Brass Turned Parts confirmed this, adding that in some weeks absenteeism had been up to 17 per cent of the work force.[5] Other engineering and aircraft firms agreed that 'women's need to find time to do their shopping' was the principal cause of their absenteeism and pressed the government to find a solution.[6]

The MOL therefore tried to develop a wartime shopping policy during 1941, in conjunction with the Ministry of Food. The process of policy-making was superficially rather different from the development of child care policy, in that a government-funded institution to do the work of shopping was not under discussion, so government ministries and local authorities were not haggling over the allocation of resources, but at numerous conferences, central and local, they were discussing suggestions for, and actual experiments with, changes in retailing, industrial employment and domestic life, which might solve the shopping problem. The purpose of the negotiations was to agree on official recommendations as to what should be done. Underneath the apparent difference from policy-making on child care, however, a similar process of negotiation was going on. It concerned the extent to which various interest groups were prepared to change customary practices in order to accommodate the mobilisation of women.

Of course government-funded institutions related to the work of shopping and cooking did develop during wartime. Arrangements were made for communal feeding, notably through factory canteens, British Restaurants and school meals, and claims were made that they extensively relieved the shopping and cooking burden.[7] But though the provision of canteens and school meals were greatly expanded compared with before the war and British Restaurants were a wartime innovation (initiated to overcome the dislocation caused by bombing),[8] the figures collected during the war suggest that the service they offered made only a slight difference to the need to purchase food and prepare meals at home. No British Restaurants and very few factory canteens provided workers (male and female) with evening meals. As far as midday meals were concerned, a survey stated in 1942 that 'British Restaurants cater for a very small number of people' and surprisingly low proportions of workers ate their midday meals in factory canteens. Even the highest proportion recorded by the survey was less than half,

47 per cent of dockers. The lowest proportion, 12 per cent were women textile workers, most of whom went home to cook a midday meal, part of a long tradition of combining paid and domestic work.[9] The school meals service, though enormously expanded in wartime and officially presented for the first time as a service with benefits to both rich and poor, provided at its height during the war for not more than one-third of school children.[10]

These figures should not be taken to mean that communal feeding was unpopular. The WSS found that British Restaurants were particularly well liked and, as in the case of nurseries, vociferous demands were made, for instance at women's parliaments and at TUC women's conferences for local authorities to expand the numbers of British Restaurants and also the school meals service, both of which were provided patchily over the country as a whole.[11] There were 2,000 British Restaurants by 1945 compared with 11,800 canteens, a figure which itself needs to be seen in the light of the fact that there were 67,400 undertakings covered by Essential Works Orders in 1944.[12] Canteens belonged within the arena of workplace politics and more ambivalence was expressed about them than about British Restaurants. Issues like their capacity, opening times, the quality and quantity of the food and whether the management was making a profit out of this service to the workers were hot questions on work councils and joint production committees.[13] A speaker at the TUC women's conference in 1943 summed up the varied opinions on canteens with her (impressionistic) judgement that 'for every good canteen there were nine bad ones'.[14]

In explanation of the 'under use' of communal feeding provisions many people, men in particular, said they preferred to eat at home. The sort of things men told the WSS were, 'Do not like the stuff they cook — prefer home meals, wife makes stew for us all.' One woman interviewee explained that for her it was not a matter of simple preference. She had to go home to cook for her children in view of the lack of school meals in her area and in fact changed her job so that she worked near enough home to do so.[15] Another factor was that it could be cheaper for a family to eat together at home than separately at school and work, though against this had to be set the saving in coupons, since canteen and restaurant meals were not rationed. As far as women in general were concerned, the WSS commented: 'Quite a number are afraid that if a wife does not cook her husband's main meal she loses an important function in his life.' The WSS did not support this with direct quotations from women, but M-O collected comments

Figure 5.1: 'If a wife does not cook her husband's main meal she loses an important function in his life,' Wartime Social Survey, *Food* (1943), p. 15. This photograph shows the inside of an East End home in September 1940.

Courtesy of BBC Hulton Picture Library.

indicating that women expected their husbands to want to eat their main meal at home.[16]

In view of the conventional expectation that women would cook the family's principal daily meal, even in wartime, it is not surprising that a reason frequently given by factory women for 'not going to the canteen' themselves was 'the need to shop during the lunch hour'. A journalist on the *News Chronicle* graphically described what this meant for women workers:

Yesterday I joined a stream of women leaving a group of factories at noon for their midday meal break. Many were unfolding paper

carriers and made a dash for a bus to take them to the nearest shopping centre. There they scattered along the street making their
purchases; then several hurried into a tea-shop. Here I managed to
talk to a couple while they ate a hot meal in record time.[17]

Those she spoke to started work at 7.30 before the shops were open,
and finished at 5 p.m. soon after which they closed. Their hour off for
lunch was the only time they could shop. Quite apart from the depriva-
tion of rest and nourishment which this inflicted upon women they
often came up against another problem, which was that many shops
closed at midday, because the Shops Act of 1912 required retailers to
give shop assistants a break at this time. In consequence, at the first
conference on shopping problems held between the MOL, MOF and
retailers' and shop assistants' representatives, the MOL pressed for
changes in retail practices with regard to hours of closing, both in the
middle and at the end of the day.[18] It met, however, with steadfast
resistance, rooted in fears of any change which might reduce retail
profitability.

The suggestion that shopkeepers should stay open in the middle of
the day was rejected on the grounds of staff shortage and the idea that
they should cater for women after work was turned down because the
retailer would be employing staff late to serve a small number of
customers.[19] Retail representatives and the MOF, which acted in many
ways as their mouthpiece in government, were particularly adamant
about this. The MOF refused to be party to the official recommendation that shops should stay open on some nights until 8 or 9 p.m. for
the benefit of working women, even though this amounted to no more
than a return to pre-war arrangements under the Shops (Hours of
Closing) Act of 1928.[20] The MOF stated that retailers refused to consider opening later than 6 p.m., or 7 p.m. on one late night, the times
specified under Defence Regulation 60A designed to ease transport
difficulties in the black-out, even though the Minister of Home
Security, Herbert Morrison, permitted shops to stay open later 'where
it is shown to be specially difficult for workers to do their shopping
before the new closing hours'.[21] The issue of late opening became a
sticking point in the negotiations between the two Ministries, and
indeed between the two interest groups which they broadly represented, industrial and retail. A welfare officer at Rubery Owens Ltd
put the industrial view bluntly: 'He saw no reason why the shopkeeper should complain of inconvenience. After all, the workers in the
factories were putting in all for the War effort,' but shopkeepers

thought that industrialists should change their ways to accommodate the mobilisation of women:

> The representatives of the traders, consumers, Co-operatives and the Trade Unions were strongly resentful that the firms had not adapted themselves to the employment of married women with household duties, and that trouble appeared to them to be thrown back on other sections of the community.[22]

The issue was sufficiently important for the MOF to threaten to withdraw its support from the one official circular of the war on the shopping problems of women workers if the MOL included late opening as one of its recommendations. This was too much for the MOL, which was preparing the circular for release simultaneously with the big recruitment drive of the autumn of 1941, and it conceded defeat, explicitly ruling out late opening in the circular on solutions to shopping problems.[23] Underlying the stubborn response of the retailers was of course the real problem that wartime shortages meant that they would have little to sell late in the day. The few stores which did experiment with late opening, principally Co-operatives, recorded very low levels of turnover, 'We did not take enough to pay for the electric light,' wrote the manager of the Slough Co-op. A MOL official summed up the reasons as follows:

> Women are naturally not prepared to break their homeward journey after a long day's work to do shopping particularly as they know that some of the goods they need will no longer be available. I doubt if it is possible to get reasonable supplies of greengrocery or fish in the evening.[24]

Such a thing would have been possible had a rationing system allocating a proportion of *all* types of foodstuff to every individual been introduced. However such a solution was rejected in the name of freedom. Two kinds of rationing were introduced during the war, the basic ration and the points system. Briefly, the principle behind the first was to allow every individual a small quantity of certain basic foodstuffs which was fixed by the MOF's estimates of how much was nationally available. The customer had to register at a shop for her ration of each foodstuff so that the retailer could obtain from the supplier (ultimately the MOF itself) the exact quantity required and, each time she went shopping, she had to produce her official ration books, so that the coupons could be cancelled. By 1941 the basic ration covered butter, bacon, sugar, meat, tea, preserves and cheese and the entitlement to each was small, e.g. 1s 2d worth of meat, 2 oz butter, 2 oz tea, per person, per week. The MOF believed that for the system to work there would have to be enough for everyone to have a meaningful portion and universal take-up (otherwise there would be waste and under-the-counter trade). In addition the goods had to be non-perishable in order that they would keep until the shopper was ready to come and buy them. Fruit, vegetables and cake were not rationed for this reason, in spite of being basic foodstuffs and in short supply. Bread was rationed only after the war.

The other schemes was the 'points system'. Certain foodstuffs were given a 'points value' in addition to their money value and every civilian was allocated a number of points in coupon form per four-week period. The idea behind this scheme was that demand could be manipulated by moving the points value up or down, but choice of goods consumed and where to buy them would be left with the customer. Thus if demand grew too great for any product, the MOF would raise the points value, but if goods remained too long on the shelves, their points value would be lowered. Again the scheme would not work for perishables, but it avoided confining rationing only to foods universally consumed. Things like canned and dried foods, soap, cereals, sweets and biscuits were put 'on points' during 1941–2.[25]

Rationing proved extremely popular. For instance 91 per cent of a sample of 2,530 'housewives' asked by the WSS in June–July 1942 approved of it and 63 per cent of the sample gave the reason 'everyone gets a fair share'. The Glasgow Women's Parliament demanded an extension of rationing, 'so as to prevent women with leisure standing in queues and buying up everything', and similar demands were made at TUC women's conferences.[26] All the same, even though it may have helped, rationing did not solve the problems of the women worker. For instance there was no cast-iron guarantee that the working woman would always be able to obtain even the basic ration. There were many complaints; for example, one working woman told M-O:

Meat is the most difficult. When I get to the butcher he is always sold out. I just get a bit of joint for the weekend and that's all ... Other people get it that can go early, but there's nothing left when I get there.[27]

A system of registration of all customers with the shopkeepers of

Figure 5.2: Rationing was reputedly popular, even though it involved a considerable amount of paper work. This photograph is of the mother of a large family working on the household accounts.

Courtesy of BBC Hulton Picture Library.

their choice and reservation of all goods would have helped the woman worker and some shopkeepers did reserve both rationed and un-rationed goods for customers who had registered with them for their basic ration. The London Co-op, for example, organised a system of internal rationing into which official schemes were absorbed. It issued 'Family Ration Cards' to every registered family, which entitled them to equal shares of scarce products, e.g. in July 1941 dried fruit, canned fish and tinned milk, as the Society accumulated enough at the ware-houses 'to give each family a supply'. Newcastle, Northampton and possibly many other Co-ops did the same. Managers of individual Co-op stores were advised by their local societies to use their discre-tion as to the goods to include and the quantities to allocate. Women at the TUC women's conference in 1942 discussed such schemes approvingly and a woman representative of the Distributive Workers spoke for many of them when she said, 'Complete registration would do much to solve the difficulty' of shopping.[28]

The MOF, however, regarded such schemes with suspicion, based on a deep-rooted distrust of anything which interfered with the free play of the market. Rationing in general was seen within the MOF in quite a different light from that in which it was seen outside. It was viewed not as a crusade to promote equitable distribution, but as an unfortunate necessity in order to prevent acute shortages. Shopkeepers bewailed the extra work it involved in view of the shortages of shop workers, and the reverse of its actual effect on morale was expected:

> Rationing is . . . essentially inequitable; it provides the same quantity of an article for each person without any consideration of their needs or habits or of their capacity to secure alternatives. It is a restriction of personal liberty, and it tends to undermine the morale of the nation by making people think of the dangers of shortage.[29]

Tampering with the supposedly self-regulating points system by reserving goods on points met with disapproval and the proposal to apply a scheme of universal rationing like that of the Co-ops, nationally, was defeated because it was seen as imposing even greater limits on 'freedom' than already existed under rationing. The MOF view was that 'it would involve far more regimentation of retailer and consumer'.[30] Under MOF influence the MOL circular of November 1941 expressly ruled out registration for all goods at specific shops as a general solution to shop-ping problems even though the MOL had initially pressed for the extension of rationing as a major way of easing them. The MOL wrote:

Any national instructions issued by a Government Department might create an unjustifiable expectation that . . . by shopping with retailers with whom they were officially registered the consumer would be entitled to a supply of certain unrationed foods. This could not be contemplated.[31]

Yet the Co-operatives, which were accustomed to dealing with a 'membership' and committed to the principle of equitable distribution, contemplated such expectations quite happily. Just as official rationing was popular in wartime, the Co-ops which took it further received a good press, especially among women workers.[32] However, this was not echoed in the MOF.

Two concepts of freedom were at stake in the disagreement over the possible ways in which rationing could be used. The 'official' version used by the MOF related to the freedom of the retailer to compete for goods, customers and shopworkers. The alternative, embodied in Co-operative practice, related to the freedom to be derived, through the commitment of the retailer and customer to one another, from the security of knowing that supply and demand were guaranteed.

The system of registration for all types of food and allocation by the retailer of what he or she had in stock, would have lent itself easily to a further step which reduced not just the time it took to shop but also the work involved for the shopper. The shop could receive orders from its customers, pack the goods, and either deliver them or make them available for collection at the convenience of the customer. This, of course, had been a facility offered by some shops before the war, usually, as we saw in Chapter 2, to middle-class customers. During the war many of the Co-operative Societies linked such schemes to their internal rationing systems. In Corby Co-op, for instance, customers were told to leave 'special cards' for unrationed goods with their orders 'so that you may have your fair share'. They collected their order from a special counter where coupons for rationed goods were clipped. In several places other retailers tried ordering schemes, often offering the service selectively, to women war workers only. In Stockton-on-Tees, for example, a factory inspector reported:

The Chamber of Commerce has successfully inaugurated a scheme under which shopkeepers issue special tickets to workers whereby goods required are packed up and set aside for them to be collected later, and in some cases to be delivered to their houses. This system is said to be working very satisfactorily and has been the means of saving working time in the factories of that locality.

The MOL received information on the operation of ordering services which indicated that other traders than just the Co-ops did in fact accept the notion of the fair distribution of goods in short supply. In Bradford and Shipley, for instance, the traders' associations had 'agreed to reserve a fair share of unrationed goods on receipt of a written order' and in Enfield, London, meat distributors 'pledged themselves to save a share of all unrationed goods for the war workers. Orders can be sent by post.'[33] Such schemes struck at least some women workers as being helpful, if not a complete solution, for example, a young London woman told M-O that 'in our factory they gave us pink cards to say we were doing essential war work and couldn't get much time off, so we could give these to the grocer with the order and they make it up for us. That's a help but it's still awkward.'[34]

But although these reports indicate that ordering was working successfully in many areas, such schemes remained a matter of private arrangement, which left the customer vulnerable to the whim of the retailer as to whether and to whom to offer the service.[35] Ordering was not officially recommended, mainly on the grounds that it would be impossible for retailers to find the extra staff to do the work, for all that a recommendation could have included advice on how to organise staff efficiently and, even though ordering was favoured in the MOL and by women at the TUC women's conferences.[36]

Experiments with other solutions were jeopardised by the problem of separating 'essential' from 'less essential' work. Arrangements which could grant assistance with shopping were, like nursery provision, originally intended to benefit munition workers alone. As we have seen some retailers offered ordering facilities on this basis. Others thought that it would be easier for munitions workers to shop in the limited time available, for instance lunch hours, if they were given certificates entitling them to priority service and between May 1941 and September 1942 the MOL received information that such schemes were being tried in a large number of industrial centres.[37] However, there was resentment of what was called the 'propagandist use of munition workers' by other women in full-time paid work and in addition it was felt to be unfair on those 'fully occupied . . . on domestic duties particularly the care of lodgers or other people's children'.[38] Experiments with preference schemes revealed exactly the difficulties anticipated. Shopkeepers withdrew their co-operation when other customers complained that munition workers 'became cheeky and walked to the head of the queue' or took the best of everything.[39]

The problem of deciding who was to have access to assistance with shopping emphasised in the same way as the issue of selection by nurseries that the 'less essential' parts of industry were in fact vital to the functioning of the rest and it was invidious not to offer women working in them the arrangements made for women in 'essential' work. The discussion of shopping privileges emphasised that domestic work had to be included in this totality.

Solutions to the shopping problem which involved changes in retail practice were resisted, whether they involved reorganising reduced numbers of staff or suspending competition by an extension of registration and rationing. Adding to competition, it should be noted, was also unpopular. When it was suggested that factories might run their own shops, along the lines of some pre-war factory stores, the retail interest was unenthusiastic. Individual factory stores, such as British Insulated Cables Staff Guild Stores, Prescot, were nevertheless highly successful during the war. BI developed an efficient and convenient system of making up orders and having the boxes of goods ready for women workers at the factory gates as they left work. The management of the store was sufficiently separate from that of the factory to avoid accusations of 'truck' style exploitation.[40]

Just as some factory stores worked well in spite of lack of official backing, at a local level as we have seen, individual shopkeepers and even groups of traders were prepared to experiment with various solutions. Extended hours of opening and preference schemes did not make sense without the further step of extended registration and rationing and some of those prepared to redeploy their staffs to accommodate women war workers in these ways recognised the benefits of such changes in retail practice for all their customers. These successful experiments emphasise that opposition at national level to changes in retail practice was based not on what was possible in an absolute sense, but on the preferences of powerful sections of the retail interest.

Resistance to solutions requiring changes in retail practice, which would have relieved women of the work of shopping, was frequently cast in terms of the desires and capacities of women workers themselves, just as arguments against collective child care were based on the idea that women did not want and would not use nurseries. For example, it was contended that there was 'no demand' for factory stores[41] and that ordering schemes could not work because working-class women were 'concrete' thinkers unfamiliar with making shopping lists. 'It is not easy for a woman who is accustomed to make up her

mind what she wants and decide what to provide for meals when she
sees what there is in the shops to compose a list in the abstract' wrote
a MOL official and advised welfare supervisors and labour managers
to give women workers 'a little coaching in the art of shopping by
list'.[42] This view flies in the face of abundant evidence collected by
M-O that working-class women were quite used to making shopping
lists.[43] The MOL official did concede that shopping by list was difficult
for anyone when shortages meant that there was no way of knowing
what the shop would have in stock at any particular time. But rather
than looking to the retailer for solutions to this problem, for example
the provision of a list of goods in stock for each registered customer
from which she could make her selection, the officials sought to
'correct' the imagined shortcomings of the woman worker herself.

Taken a little further such thinking made women themselves responsible for the shopping problems which they confronted as a result of
trying to do both industrial and domestic work. Some retailers claimed
that women 'exaggerated' their shopping problems and used them as an
excuse to get time off work, to attend to 'an accumulation of domestic
duties' which were of no concern to the retailer.[44] Women were even
held responsible by some for that symbol of inconvenience of shopping
in wartime, the queue. Many women complained that they had to
queue even for rationed foodstuffs,[45] and some employers deplored the
time this absorbed. For example, the manager of Brass Turned Parts
explained to the MOS that 'when the women go out during the morning
to buy anything, whether it is rationed or not, they have to take their
turn in long queues and are frequently away for two hours at a time,
to make a single purchase'.[46] However, when confronted with such
evidence retailers were reluctant to take any responsibility. Some
claimed that the problem was a figment of press imagination, others
that it existed only at other types of shop than their own[47] and an
important MOF official implied that queues were created simply
because women liked queuing. In a widely circulated memorandum this
official deplored queues as unpatriotic 'hotbeds of discontent' and then
quoted a long extract from the Nazi journal *Das Schwarze Korps* with
no more introduction than that it was 'on the queue problem in
Germany':

> The queue is an ugly creature and a breeder of rumours. As the latter
> it is a political problem; there is no place for rumour in wartime.
> During a war people's energies can be put to better use than stirring
> up trouble by spreading rumours . . . Where there is a queue people

Figure 5.3: Queueing for meat in Palmers Green, North London, March 1940.

Courtesy of Fox Photos Ltd.

imagine there is a scarcity; where scarcity is presumed irrational appetite arises. Scarcity causes more queues, queues increase the urge to get 'just one more' . . . There has, in fact, developed the professional queuer, a malignant and odious breed.[48]

Cause and effect in the queue had been turned round, so that the women in the queue rather than the shortage of the goods they were hoping to purchase became responsible for it. Ways of dealing with queues as such rather than with shortages were seriously mooted in the MOF, for instance that the shopkeeper would dismiss the end of the queue, or more drastically nip it in the bud by refusing to serve the first twelve. But since the objective was to stop queues becoming 'hotbeds of discontent', these were not considered good solutions.[49] All the same, there were suggestions that extreme measures, such as 'action by police for obstruction' to remove whole queues, were being used in 1942, for example extra police were said to be drafted into St Pancras in London on days when queuing was heavy.[50] This was 'queue-taming' like the police surveillance of queues in Nazi Germany described from experience by Katherine Thomas.[51] It is extraordinary that in Britain the system of registration of all customers at all the various types of shop they needed to visit, and thus equitable distribution of goods in stock by the shopkeepers to these customers, should have been rejected in the name of freedom, while these extremely repressive methods of 'solving' the queue problem were seriously considered. Of course they would not have solved it in any case, since they concentrated on the result of the problem rather than its cause. Had they been widely enforced they might have made it impossible for the working woman ever to purchase goods like fruit, vegetables, bread and cake, since, for her, biding her time until the shops were not crowded was not a possibility.

The idea that women created problems for themselves lent itself easily to the idea that women could solve them for themselves. Since what many did was to take time off work in order to shop, a logical solution seemed to be to legitimise this practice. Retailers were keen on this because it made no demand upon themselves, while requiring industrial employers to make changes and leaving the actual work of shopping with women themselves.[52] However, early in the war, industrialists were resistant to the idea. Just as retailers expressed a lack of interest in women's 'accumulated domestic difficulties' of which shopping was a part, many employers regarded themselves as 'too busy getting on with the war effort to think of such things' as the time needed by the women they employed for domestic work.[53] Those who did consider granting shopping time expressed much foreboding about the drop in productivity which would be caused and frequently expected women to make up time they had off, hour for hour, even though the leave was unpaid.[54] Many had scant regard for the impact on women themselves, for instance, employers informed the MOL that they required women to work on Sunday in return for a day off for shopping on Saturday, commenting blithely that this way women still had their rest day, complying with factory regulations.[55] Women themselves often felt that their job meant that they had sold their time to their employer and acquiesced in the idea that they should repay the time taken to shop, or fit in shopping around night shifts as employers expected, in spite of the denial of rest this inflicted upon them.[56] All the same some of them found such arrangements highly unsatisfactory, especially when they were struggling to cope with child care simultaneously. For instance, one woman told M-O:

> It's awkward when you've got a baby, you've got to get a bit of shopping in. They don't do anything for the workers, do they? But they see you get their work done. I haven't had any proper sleep this week. The woman who minds my baby nights has let me down now.[57]

Eventually, however, leave of absence to shop became the officially sanctioned and most widely adopted solution to the shopping problem. The MOL ultimately advocated leave on the reverse of the grounds on which it had previously rejected it, thus in April 1941 leave was seen in the MOL as an interruption to production and therefore contrary to the national interest, but by June 1942 the MOL presented it as essential for the avoidance of absenteeism and thus for long-term productivity: 'It is found that women workers with domestic responsibilities must be given some time off each week to do their shopping.'[58] It was thought at first that 'an extended lunch hour' would be sufficient but, as information came in about the failure of this and other solutions, particularly later opening hours, the shift towards leave grew more definite and it was given official backing as the best solution to shopping problems both in the circular of November 1941 and in the Commons in August 1942.[59] After this sanction had been given, in the context of mounting anxiety about absenteeism, increasing numbers of industrial employers granted leave. By the last part of 1942 satisfaction was being expressed with the effects of leave, for instance, the management of a South London factory said, 'The planned times have not only pleased the women but have contributed to the general smooth running of the factory.'[60] The lesson was that productivity suffered less when the employer controlled absence than when the worked decided for herself when to stay away to do domestic work.

In consequence, even though women sometimes obtained leave schemes as a result of their own organised pressure, employers granted it on terms that would keep it within limits. Some offered no more than the longer midday break or early finish and granted this 'concession' to married women only. In other cases the number of hours of leave per week depended upon the size of a woman's family. A factory inspector commented that such organisation of leave 'has been found preferable to letting women go off for shopping in a haphazard fashion'. Other firms believed that the best way of restricting leave was to require women to request it individually from the foreman, 'as only deserving cases would take the trouble to apply'.[61] Either way, the terms on which leave was offered did nothing to spread responsibility for shopping beyond married women, even though there is evidence that other workers, including men, would have helped if given the opportunity.[62]

In spite of their preference for 'shopping time' compared with spontaneous absenteeism, employers were wary of demands for leave as of right, which raised the possibility of reduced control over their workforces. Thus engineering employers rejected a resolution of the AEU National Committee in 1944 demanding a statutory period off each week for shopping, on the grounds that such arrangements were better made locally, with individual employers, than by statute, and that the need for shopping time was limited to one section of the workforce which was in any case in the factories on only a temporary basis.[63] During the war many employers moved, with the MOL's encouragement, towards alternative ways of organising the working day which avoided the problem presented by such a challenge from organised labour. Shift work, especially the three-shift system, and part-time work often developed directly out of shopping leave schemes, the part-timers taking the place of those on leave. These arrangements dovetailed with official schemes for the reorganisation of women's working hours to promote their recruitment and stability, which we shall investigate in the next chapter. They were said to be 'most successful' in that they 'prevented the machinery worked by married women from standing idle while they were out doing their shopping'.[64]

Employers were described as 'generous' in offering women workers such arrangements, which were said to 'relieve them of some of their domestic responsibilities' and even to 'eliminate difficulties'.[65] But though they may have reduced the problem of time presented by combining paid work and shopping, leave and other arrangements of hours by no means removed that of effort, which the women worker and not her employer had still to expend. Leave, shifts and part-time simply reorganised the times when a woman performed different types of labour, factory work and work for the home. They removed the encroachment of women's domestic work upon industrial productivity and the threat of spontaneous absenteeism to authority relations in the factory. In no way did they 'relieve' women of the work itself.

Leave was one of two solutions to the shopping problem officially advocated by the MOL and MOF in November 1941. The other even more emphatically deposited the work of shopping in the lap of the woman worker herself. This was the recommendation that neighbours' shopping leagues should be formed. The background to the suggestion was that during 1941 MOF officials gave increasing emphasis to the view that working-class women should help each other to shop. A MOF official wrote, 'It should not be beyond the ability of married women war workers to arrange for a neighbour or friend to purchase their food for them. It is an unusual household where such an arrangement cannot be made,' and in October 1941 the MOF claimed that it was a 'custom in many places for neighbours' shopping leagues to be formed'.[66] No one seemed to worry about the ability of women workers to give their neighbours shopping lists, as they had done in the case of orders direct to the shopkeeper. In November 1941 the idea was embodied in the official MOL–MOF circular, 'Workers' Welfare – Shopping Problems', which announced that no national shopping policy was possible and gave pride of place to the neighbours' shopping league:

> Neighbours regularly assist each other on an organised basis with domestic problems, including shopping problems, arising out of the employment of women in industry. Advice on the working of neighbours' shopping leagues can be furnished by the Ministry of Labour.[67]

This statement was issued almost simultaneously with the MOL–MOF circular announcing that private neighbourhood minding was the best way of solving the child care problem.

However, in spite of the confident ministerial assertions about the custom of mutual aid where shopping was concerned there is limited evidence of the existence of shopping leagues. The Women's Voluntary Service, which was closely involved in house-to-house work of a variety of types, was drawn into discussions with the MOL about organising such leagues.[68] However the WVS leadership rejected the proposal, ostensibly on the grounds that it was 'not civil defence work', though in reality because it was not seen as appropriate for WVS members to offer a service to relatively well-paid industrial workers.[69] Working women could no more be turned into objects of charity as far as their shopping needs were concerned than they could on account of their child care needs. Nevertheless, in spite of the official veto, there is evidence that some WVS branches offered help locally, for instance, in Maidenhead and some outer London areas in 1941-2.[70] But the only neighbours' league to which there are references in the MOL files was one in Walsall in June 1941, which was in jeopardy because shop-keepers 'refused to supply scarce goods except to the householder personally' thereby undermining the whole point of the scheme. Factory inspectors reported one example of mutual aid among workers themselves. At Fisher and Ludlow of Plymouth, women chose a proxy shopper from amongst their own ranks to do all their shopping. How she carried it, and what arrangement she made with shopkeepers and her own employers, are not explained. Otherwise some women told M-O that they hoped to find a friend to get in a bit of shopping, but most women asked by M-O about getting help said that it was difficult to delegate the work of shopping: 'It's a problem all this shopping. You can't get anyone to do it, it's too big a thing to ask when it takes so long.'[71]

Even if women did feel that they could ask someone to shop for them, with the obvious advantages that, for instance, a friend would be quick to pick up a bargain and the shopping would be safe with her until the woman worker was ready to collect it, there were real diffi-culties about finding women with any free time. By the end of 1942, 8½ million women between the ages of 19 and 46 had been registered with the MOL and during 1943 those aged 47-50 added a further 1¾ million, the entire age group apart from those in hospital or prison. Women could now be directed into part-time work if they were con-sidered exempt from full-time. Seven and a half million women were said to be in paid employment in 1943, an under-estimate since two part-timers were counted as one full-timer and there were 900,000 part-timers. A further 450,000 were not counted in the statistics of civilian employment since they were in the forces. The rest of those who had registered were exempt from direction on the grounds of essential household work, though many of these were engaged in voluntary work or were caring for evacuees.[72] There was clearly not a wide margin of 'unoccupied' women on which those seeking either proxy shoppers or for that matter child minders could draw.

The real difficulties for women workers of organising neighbourhood shopping leagues did not pass unnoticed, however. Members of the TUC women's conference were emphatic that neither shopping nor child care should be left to private arrangements, stating with reference to shopping, 'neighbours should not be asked to shoulder such responsibilities'.[73] But the implication is that most women workers had no choice but to do their own shopping on top of their factory work, often by taking unpaid leave, in spite of all the suggestions for spreading the work of shopping from the individual woman to the industrial employer, the government or the retail organisation.

Conclusion

In conclusion, the search for a shopping policy in 1941-2 and the ultimate failure to find one reveal that neither of the government departments concerned, nor the retailers or industrial employers whom they broadly represented, were willing to accept responsibility for women's shopping problems. Each of the latter felt that the other group should change its practices to accommodate them and, though there was change within both, it was partial and constrained.

The ranks of the retailers were split between those wedded to a definition of freedom as competition and those to whom it meant co-operation. The latter did go some way towards relieving women of the work of shopping, pointing to potential change in the way that shopping as one aspect of domestic work could be conducted. But the entrenchment of the conventional view of retailing freedom in the MOF ensured that sanction was not given to a general change on these lines even for the duration of the war. Only a handful of industrial employers involved themselves in the work of shopping and expectations prevalent among employers, male workers and women workers themselves about home-based eating, coupled with inadequate provision, meant that wartime communal feeding went only a little way towards relieving women of the burdens of shopping and cooking. In granting women 'leave' or arranging hours of work so that they had time to shop, employers were cautious about changing their practice and reluctant to make any arrangements that would lessen their control of their workforces. In doing so they did nothing to alter either the nature of shopping or its gender identification.

Even though the 'private' family function of shopping had been made 'public' under wartime pressure, the favoured solution was to return it, like child care, to the private sphere of the woman herself and her family and neighbourhood. Were shopping and child care, then, 'returned' during the war unaltered? Child care perhaps showed more signs of change than shopping. Alternatives to mother-based child rearing, whether nurseries or private minders, were widely used. They had to be, in view of the demand for women's labour power and the incompatibility of child care with modern forms of capitalist production, though in the light of the figure of 43 per cent of three- to five-year-olds attending nursery classes in 1901, one cannot say with confidence that they were more widely used than ever before. Even the pressure of wartime mobilisation, however, did not topple the notion that shopping could be done in addition to industrial work, together with a chain of other types of domestic work. Of course, such an addition meant squeezing higher productivity from the woman in industry by elongating her working day at the expense of her rest and nourishment, as well, no doubt, as her personal enjoyment of what she was doing. There was no wartime shopping scheme equivalent to the wartime nursery, which in spite of conflict and constraint and its temporary status did emerge and became a symbol of collective provision for women's benefit, wrought by the pressure of wartime production. The history of shopping in wartime emphasises that the idea of a long list of such 'concessions' is wishful thinking indeed. In the absence of official pressure to force retailers to change their practices or to involve employers in shopping, ideas for changing its nature, and through this the extent of women's responsibility for it, could not be realised.

Notes

1. PRO Lab 26/57, minutes of first meeting with FWAB, 10 June 1940.
2. PRO Lab 26/60, Divisional Welfare Officers' monthly reports, London Division, February 1941. Several others made the same point.
3. WSS, 'Workers and the War', a collection of short reports on inquiries made by the regional organisation of the Wartime Social Survey, May–October 1942, pp. 2–5 and 13–17; WSS, 'Women at Work' (June 1944), p. 22.
4. M-O (1942), p. 179.
5. PRO Lab 26/60, correspondence between Messrs Midlands Utilities, Messrs Brass Turned Parts and MOS, 3–16 May 1941.

6. PRO Lab 26/60, correspondence between MOS Area Officers and MOL and MOL Welfare Officers and MOL, February–April 1941; Lab 26/61, 'Report of Visit to Short Brothers, Strood, Kent', 17 October 1941.

7. Hooks (1944), p. 8. According to her they 'saved the double job of a long day in the plant followed by preparing meals and otherwise caring for the family'.

8. George Hodgkinson, *Sent to Coventry* (Maxwell, London, 1970), pp. 160 ff.

9. WSS, 'Food', April–July 1942, pp. 35, 39.

10. D. Fraser, *Evolution of the Welfare State* (Macmillan, London, 1973), pp. 195–6. See also PRO Lab 26/58, reports to MOL from DCs, April 1941.

11. WSS, 'Food', April–July 1942, p. 35. 'There is a great demand among workpeople for British Restaurants . . . The food is generally thought to be good, the service pleasant and efficient.' They received a favourable mention at the TUC women's conferences, e.g. TUC 1943/16, 'British Restaurants could serve up a good dish for about 8d.' See also M-OA, 'Diary of a Foreign Correspondent', 25 January 1942; report on Glasgow and West of Scotland Women's Parliament. These parliaments were held around the country in 1941–3 to urge maximum production. They were at least originally organised by the Communist Party and for this reason they incurred Labour Party suspicion and were proscribed by the General Council of the TUC in January 1943. See CCA BEVN 2/12, Labour Party, General Purpose Committee, 'Working Women's Organisations', 9 December 1943. They nevertheless provided a platform of a range of industrial, political, co-operative and housewives' groups. See also *World News and Views*, 9 January 1943 and other issues in 1941–3. Thanks to James Hinton for this reference.

12. G. Williams, *Women and Work* (Nicholson and Watson, London, 1945), p. 101; Parker (1957), pp. 417–19 and Table XI, p. 499. See also CCA, BEVN 2/3, Sir A.W. Garrett to Ernest Bevin, June 1942.

13. WSS, 'Food', June 1943, p. 15; Les Moss, *Live and Learn: A Life and Struggle for Progress* (QueenSpark Books, Brighton 1979), pp. 44 ff; Enfield Rolling Mills Works Council Minute Books, 5 January 1944, 7 June 1944, 11 June 1945. Bevin, aware of these problems, would have preferred canteens to be provided by a non-profit-making organisation. See CCA, BEVN 3/3, E.B. to Lord Woolton, 13 November 1942.

14. TUC Pamphlets and Leaflets, 1943/16.

15. WSS, 'Food', April–July 1942, p. 39; interview with Mrs S., South Shields, 17 November 1977.

16. WSS, 'Food', June 1943, p. 15; M-O (1942), p. 179.

17. *News Chronicle*, 16 July 1941.

18. PRO Lab 26/61, minutes of a meeting of the Retailers' Association and the Shop Assistants' and Distributive Workers' Unions with the MOL and the MOF, April 1941.

19. PRO Lab 26/61, RWO Birmingham to MOL, 28 August 1941; correspondence October 1941.

20. PRO Lab 26/60, ML Circular 128/20, 'Workers' Welfare: Hours of Closing of Shops', June 1940.

21. PRO Lab 26/61, correspondence between J.J. Taylor MOL and Bankes Amery MOF, October 1941; Herbert Morrison, Home Office, to Waldron Smithers MP, 22 October 1941.

22. PRO Lab 26/61, report by Cllr J. Whiston, Walsall, 9 September 1941; Lab 26/60, notes on Ealing and Acton Food Executive Committee, 2 September 1941.

23. PRO Lab 26/61, MOL to Bankes Amery, MOF, 18 October 1941; ML Circular 128/70, 19 November 1941.

24. PRO Lab 26/61, MOL to Bankes Amery, MOF, 18 October 1941; correspondence with MOF May–June 1942; *Co-operative News*, 31 January 1942.

25. This summary is drawn from R.J. Hammond, *Food, Vol. 1, The Growth of Policy* (HMSO, London, 1951). See especially Chapters 8, 15, 27 and 29 and Fig. ii, p. 402.

26. WSS, 'Food', May 1942–January 1943, pp. 15–16; M-OA, 'Diary of a Foreign Correspondent', Glasgow, 25 January 1942; TUC Pamphlets and Leaflets, 1942/7.

27. M-O (1942), p. 227; See also M-OA, Replies to Directive, March 1944.

28. PRO Lab 26/61, copy of circular from London Co-operative Society to grocery branch managers and utility food shop manageresses, 21 July 1941; TUC Pamphlets and Leaflets, 1942/7.

29. Hammond (1951), p. 125, quoting MOF memorandum to Cabinet.

30. Ibid., p. 199. See p. 306 on MOF views on the points system.

31. PRO Lab 26/61, ML Circular 128/70, 19 November 1941.

32. M-OA: Replies to Directive, March 1944; Topic Collection No. 4, 'Shopping', Box 3, 'Shops Survey, Ealing, Bolton, Chester, 1942'.

33. PRO Lab 26/61, reports from Inspectors of Factories, 18 September 1942.

34. M-O (1942), p. 229.

35. Ibid., p. 228, for the comments of a woman worker from whom the service was suddenly withdrawn.

36. PRO Lab 26/60, correspondence 18 April 1941; Lab 26/61, note on shopping difficulties, August 1941; correspondence 15 October 1941; TUC Pamphlets and Leaflets, 1942/7.

37. PRO Lab 26/61, FWB(42)10, Arrangements made to meet the shopping difficulties of women employed on war work, 30 May 1942; communications received 30 May 1941, 9 September 1941, 30 May 1942, 18 September 1942.

38. PRO Lab 26/60, notes on Ealing and Acton Food Executive Committee, 2 September 1941; Miss Smieton, MOL to MOS, March 1941.

39. PRO Lab 26/61, H.W. Bonner, Wednesbury, to Cllr J. Whiston, Walsall, 30 May 1941, and report on shopping schemes used by local firms, by Cllr J. Whiston, 9 September 1941. See also Select Committee on National Expenditure, 'Third Report, 1942–3', 17 December 1942, para. 45.

40. PRO Lab 26/60, B1 Staff Guild Stores Ltd to MOS, Manchester, 7 April 1941.

41. PRO Lab 26/61, J.J. Taylor, MOL to MOP, 6 June 1942.

42. Ibid., circular to welfare supervisors or labour managers, 3 November 1941.

43. M-OA, Topic Collection No. 4, 'Shopping', Box 3.

44. PRO Lab 26/61, minutes of a meeting of the Retailers' Associations and the Shop Assistants' and Distributive Workers' Unions with the MOL and MOF, 18 September 1941. The allegation was repeated many times, e.g. PRO Lab 26/61: conference of Regional Welfare Officers, October 1941; Bankes Amery MOF to Taylor MOL, 15 October 1941.

45. M-OA, Diaries, July–August 1942: 'Office Worker, London'; 'Civil Servant, Morecambe, Lancs'; 'Secretary, Gateshead, Durham'; 'Housewife, Barrow'; Replies to Directive, March 1944, 'Poultry Farmer's Wife'.

46. PRO Lab 26/60, Southern Area Board, MOS, note on solutions to shopping problem, 16 April 1941.

47. PRO Lab 26/61, minutes of a meeting, 18 September 1941.

48. Ibid., note on shopping difficulties by Bankes Amery, MOF, 27 August 1941.

49. Ibid., see also correspondence between Glasgow food officers and MOF, October 1941 and minutes of a meeting, 18 September 1941.

50. M-O (1942), p. 229.

51. Katherine Thomas, *Women in Nazi Germany* (Gollancz, London, 1943), p. 40.

52. PRO Lab 26/61, minutes of meetings, April and September 1941.

53. M-OA, Town Box, Coventry, File 3708, report from Coventry, 26 January 1942.

54. PRO Lab 26/61, report by Cllr J. Whiston, 9 September 1941; reports from Inspectors, 18 September 1942.

55. Ibid., Southern Area Board, MOS, to MOL, 16 April 1941.

56. M-O (1942), p. 231; PRO Lab 26/61, reports from Inspectors, 18 September 1942.

57. M-O (1942), p. 231.

58. PRO Lab 26/61, minutes of a meeting, April 1941; MOL to MOF, 6 June 1942.

59. PRO Lab 26/61, ML Circular 128/70, 19 November 1941; *Evening News*, 6 August 1942.

60. Ibid., reports of Inspectors, 18 September 1942; for the effect of leave on absenteeism see PRO Lab 26/4, reports on absence from work, June–September 1943 and October 1943–April 1944.

61. Ibid., 'Passes Out' were often issued to ensure that only the 'right' women got out of the factory.

62. WSS, 'Workers and the War', October 1942, p. 14; PRO Lab 26/60, Eastern Area Officer MOS to MOL, 8 April 1941, quoting a case of men paid early absenting themselves to shop.

63. AEU, *Report of the Proceedings of the 26th National Committee and 6th Rules Revision Meeting*, 4 June–14 July 1945.

64. PRO Lab 26/60, NW Area Officer MOS to MOL, 8 April 1941; Lab 26/61, FWB (42) 10, 30 May 1942; reports of Inspectors, 18 September 1942.

65. PRO Lab 26/61, MOL to MOP, 6 June 1942; reports of Inspectors, 18 September 1942; Lab 26/4, report on absence from work, September 1943.

66. PRO Lab 26/61: Bankes Amery MOL to J.J. Taylor, 15 October 1941; correspondence with Glasgow Food Officers, October 1941; MOF, note on shopping difficulties, October 1941.

67. Ibid., ML Circular 128/70, 'Workers' Welfare: Shopping Problems', 19 November 1941, cf. PRO Lab 26/58, ML Circular 128/74, 'The Care of Young Children of Women Workers', 9 December 1941.

68. PRO Lab 26/60, WVS correspondence with MOL, 30 May and 12 June 1941. On the work of the WVS generally see Charles Graves, *Women in Green: The Story of the WVS* (Heinemann, London, 1948).

69. PRO Lab 26/60, WVS Industrial Liaison Officer to MOL, 30 July 1941.

70. Ibid., M-O (1942), p. 230.

71. PRO Lab 26/60, Regional Welfare Officer, Birmingham, to MOL, 5 June 1941: Lab 26/61, reports from Inspectors of Factories, 18 September 1942; M-O (1942), p. 228. There was frequent mention of reliance for help with shopping, child care and housework on older school children, e.g. M-O (1942), p. 180.

72. Bullock (1967), pp. 172 and 255.

73. TUC Pamphlets and Leaflets, 1942/7.

6 WORKING HOURS

We have seen that the belief that women's conventional family roles and responsibilities should not be displaced by wartime mobilisation had a major impact on the shaping of official policy on recruitment, child care and shopping. The compromises struck between these expectations and the need to mobilise women led, inevitably, to problems both for government ministries and for women themselves, concerning the question of how women were to allocate their time between the two types of work they were urged to do. As far as women were concerned, the time required in order to shop, cook, wash, care for children, etc., or arrange for others to do these things for them, encroached upon their hours of paid work and led to fatigue and tension. As far as the MOL was concerned, the official decision not to subject married women with children under 14 to legally binding compulsion, and to exempt from it many women with conventional household responsibilities, significantly increased the difficulty of maintaining and enlarging the workforce. These decisions meant that the Ministry was trying to control a voluntary workforce and they gave rise to two main issues. Firstly, there was the problem of the intrusion upon industrial production of time-consuming domestic work. Official reluctance to collectivise domestic work meant that, in the majority of cases, women workers still bore the main responsibility for it, but the MOL's efforts to recruit women and maintain their productivity were in vain if women's domestic responsibilities caused them to be absent or late or to quit after a short time. Secondly, there was the problem of balancing stability and recruitment. For example, the Ministry might lose from full-time work women who had volunteered, if employers offered alternative arrangements of hours, more attractive to women struggling to cope with a double burden, such as part-time work, but if they did not offer such arrangements they might get no new recruits. And they might lose volunteer women altogether if they tried to lengthen their hours for any reason, for instance to compensate for reduction in the numbers of women in 'non-essential' industries, such as boot and shoe manufacture, when those subject to direction into 'essential work' were removed.

As a result it was not just the normally private realm of domestic life which became a public concern in wartime. The government had to

123

go further and concern itself with correcting the negative consequences for production of its own attempts to leave the burdens of home on the shoulders of women workers. In so doing it entered another realm where, as in the home, decision-making was normally private, even though the parameters were set by Factory Acts which stated, with many exemptions, when and for how long women's labour power should be used.

In character with its approach to child care and shopping, the Ministry of Labour did not intervene directly on the issue of the distribution of women's time between paid work and home work. Rather it identified key problems such as absenteeism, bad time-keeping and high rates of turnover, and initiated fact-finding and discussion of causes. Others concerned with maximising war production, especially Mass-Observation, also took an interest in these problems and did their own research into them, which often supported and sometimes amplified the findings of the MOL. In particular M-O collected evidence of women's own, often painful, experiences of trying to achieve a balance between home and work.

Absenteeism and other problems of labour time did not affect women alone. Concern about the recruitment and productivity of men as well as women during 1942 led the MOL to urge employers to keep records of absenteeism in September 1942 so that they could deal with it in their own workplaces.[1] The Lord President's Committee, the principal executive organ of the Cabinet, however, did not consider this to go far enough and ordered an official inquiry to start in January 1943. The problem of particular concern to the MOL was that loss of production due to absenteeism caused employers to demand more labour from a dwindling supply, but the LPC was more directly worried about productivity *per se*. Although it had risen during 1942 in all industries except mining, the increase was 'less than it otherwise might be' because of absenteeism. The LPC said that the objective of the survey was to identify the causes of absenteeisn 'e.g. health, transport difficulties, indifference, etc.' so as to 'enable attention to be concentrated where it is most needed'.[2] Eight hundred firms had agreed to participate in the inquiry by June 1943 and, in 1945, 640 were still submitting reports. At its peak the survey covered 14 per cent of those working in munitions. Thus the MOL was monitoring absenteeism in depth on a regular basis during the last three years of the war.

The inquiry found that within an overall increase of absenteeism during the war there were variations according to the season and in the proportions of so-called 'avoidable' absence. However two features were constant: women's absenteeism was twice that of men and the absenteeism of married women was 'significantly higher' than that of single women.[3] Other bodies found exactly the same thing and made some additional points, for instance the Industrial Health Research Board stated that married women's absenteeism was three times that of single women[4] and M-O said that it was particularly high among women in unskilled work.[5] All three surveys noted that averages concealed wide differences between individual women and individual factories but all presented an overall picture of women losing 10–15 per cent of their hours in this way as compared with a loss by men of 6–8 per cent of their hours in wartime and about 5 per cent before the war. The causes of women's absenteeism in wartime thus became the focus of attention.

The MOL found that sickness was the reason most frequently given for absence by members of both sexes and the absence of women for this cause was about half as heavy again as that of men.[6] But sickness even when genuine was not in itself an explanation of absence but demanded further interpretation. The MOL pointed to fatigue and a commentator suggested that this fatigue was the result of long hours and difficulties in dealing with domestic problems which led to 'a general deterioration in health among women' especially in ROFs.[7] Fatigue and the frequency of short periods of sickness noted by the Wartime Social Survey related also to the poorer eating habits of women than men. Women filled up on milk, puddings, cakes and biscuits whereas men ate more meat.[8] These habits were themselves products of the pressures under which the double burden placed women. As we have seen, many simply did not have time to eat a proper midday meal. Numerous women experienced anaemia and nervous disorders during the war, especially when working at night, and of course wartime pressures were interacting with a generally low level of health among working-class women before the war.

On the other hand, sickness might be an excuse for absence caused by other factors. There was a good deal of discussion about this in the MOL and in the Lord President's Committee. Members of both bodies suggested that sickness was an ostensible rather than the real reason for women's absence and would be reduced by measures of 'detection'. One such measure was to enforce the requirement that a doctor's certificate be produced for all absence due to sickness. However, this did not reduce the overall amount of women's absence, but simply shifted the emphasis from uncertified to certified sickness amid numerous objections, for instance workers complained about the fees charged for certificates, doctors that it was difficult to refuse one even when they could not certify an illness and employers that the certificates did not tell them if the illness was genuine.[9] The Lord President's Committee mirrored the employers' suspicions and revealed a preference for putting the needs of production before the workers' welfare, when in September 1943 it questioned 'gastritis' and 'colds' as definitions of illness and urged that workers should go to work even when they were 'feeling seedy' and visit the doctor or nurse at work.[10]

If sickness was not genuine, what was the real reason for absence? Two causes were considered in some depth and solutions were sought. On the one hand, 'boredom' with the job and 'lack of conviction of its importance and urgency' were identified as making a significant contribution to absenteeism. On the other, a sense of prior commitment to the home was held responsible.[11]

As far as the first cause was concerned, the MOL hoped that a combination of education and group pressure would persuade absentees to mend their ways. Education concentrated on instructing workers about the 'part their particular job plays in the final product' by, for example, mounting exhibitions demonstrating the use of the parts produced in the factory or arranging visits from servicemen who actually handled the equipment in combat.[12] More profoundly, the MOL advocated altered styles of management to reduce absenteeism. In this they were supported by the Industrial Health Research Board which concluded that a cause of absenteeism was 'lack of good feeling and co-operation between the management and the workers and between all groups in the factory'. The MOL offered as a solution a strong statement in favour of what came to be known as 'human factor' management:

> The adaptation of the industrial machine to meet the reasonable requirements of the human beings who operate that machine is essential if the optimum national output is to be maintained and anything approaching war weariness is to be discouraged.[13]

To this end two steps were taken. One was to urge unions and employers' organisations in essential industries to make agreements to set up joint production committees, composed of representatives of management and workers, and the other was to enforce an order that employers engaged on government work should appoint special staff to supervise the health and welfare of their factory workers.[14]

The MOL explicitly expected the joint production committees to act as a form of shop floor management to discipline absentees:

> The workers' representatives have a special responsibility for convincing the thoughtless minority of their fellow workers that absence from work, whether during normal or overtime hours, except for unavoidable reasons, not only interferes with the nation's war effort but is grossly unfair to the great majority, who do their part with diligence and enthusiasm in spite of the long hours and domestic inconvenience involved.[15]

After mid-1941 the Communist-led Shop Stewards' National Council urged workers' representatives in similar terms to the MOL 'to set an example of devotion and discipline'.[16] In some cases JPC members were not averse to chastising their fellow workers, particularly when the representatives were men and the absentees were women. For example, Arthur Exell, a shop steward at Morris Motors, Cowley, describes how union representatives on the 'Joint Works Production Committee' made a deal with management, promising to 'see to it that people came to work' in return for permission to unionise them. The particular targets were women in the Radiator section, who, rather to Exell's surprise, joined the union readily, whereupon the JPC exercised just the kind of control the MOL wanted: 'we had to come down a bit hard on these females'.[17]

There was some resentment among women themselves about the behaviour of what the MOL called the 'thoughtless minority'. For example an ex-domestic servant told M-O:

> I'm fed up with my job. I'm a fast worker but a lot of girls take liberties . . . It's shocking what the girls do, coming late and going off to the pictures in the afternoons. I get paid on a flat rate like the rest and I have to make up for what the others don't do, because somebody's got to do it.

But in other factories, such as Ekco near Malmesbury and Tube Investments Ltd, in Aston, Birmingham, M-O observed that there was little or no group pressure against taking time off, rather it was encouraged even when enmeshed in a web of lies.[18] Of course hold-ups to production, about which there were frequent complaints accompanied by allegations of poor management, made it hard for women, or any workers, to feel a sense of 'devotion and discipline'.[19] And was the

MOL right to identify absentees as a 'thoughtless *minority*'? A study of two war plants showed that the habit of taking time off occasionally was very widespread among the women workers:

> In a six-week period, 88 per cent of the married women in one plant and 76 per cent of those in the other plant were absent at some time, compared to 82 and 63 per cent, respectively, of the single women.[20]

Some women workers responded in a positive way to the extra attention to their 'health and welfare' which resulted from 'human factor' management. M-O noted that speeches by management in the canteen congratulating the women for their hard work went down well, and concluded, 'Girls of the machine shop type are far more influenced by personality than they are by any number of abstract appeals to patriotism or by impersonal regulations and penalties.' But women's own comments suggest that even in a factory self-styled 'progressive' in this respect the attention could be very superficial, amounting to no more than an infrequent tour of inspection by the works manager and the occasional solicitous question.[21] Welfare officers (restyled personnel managers after the war) were sometimes liked when they appeared to be acting for the workers, but were often regarded as nosy-parkers who had to be strung along, particularly when they were older women of a higher social class who put discipline before 'good feeling and co-operation', like 'Grandmother Marflett' at a welding factory in Huddersfield, who was described in the letters of women working there as routing them out of the lavatories, breaking up chats and disapproving of make-up and boyfriends.[22]

It is difficult to determine whether 'human factor' management had any effect on absenteeism. None of the surveys attempted to evaluate it as a solution. However, even at Ekco, a factory run on 'progressive' principles, indifference to work was seen by M-O as the overwhelming cause of absenteeism, which though lower than at other factories in the district was still about 10 per cent.[23] M-O's report *People in Production* was almost evangelical in its advocacy of human factor management, yet its findings pointed to deeper causes of boredom and indifference than management styles alone. The sheer length of time which workers were required to spend at work, as well as its intrinsic tedium, provoked the desire for a break.[24] At Ekco the normal working day was twelve hours, and 'almost everyone feels that the hours are too long'. Some women felt that the factory was robbing them of part of their lives, for instance one woman said: ' "When you're in there the time goes so slow you think it will never be eight o'clock but somehow when you look back the weeks seem to fly by. I've been here two years, but I sometimes feel I've only been here a few weeks. It gives me quite a nasty sort of feeling, like it's running away with my life." '[25] Seizing control of time by opting out of work was obviously an attractive alternative to such a nightmare. It manifested itself not just in taking time off, but in bad timekeeping, time wasting and clock-watching, which M-O thought as harmful to productivity as absenteeism.[26] M-O put it down to 'apathy about the factory and everything to do with it', but another interpretation is that it was caused by the lack of opportunities for control over and satisfaction in the work women were given to do and their subordination within the factory. As we have seen, fears that factory work would be like this discouraged some women from volunteering. We shall explore further the nature of women's war work and their place at work in the next chapter.

M-O's data suggested a complex relationship between women's hours of work and their sense of satisfaction or otherwise with their work, but the solutions to absenteeism proposed in the MOL did not engage with such horrors as the factory 'running away' with life. The MOL interpretation was that indifference was the product of indiscipline and, as we have seen, it saw its task as finding ways of instilling in workers application to work. The JPC solution covered working hours and the MOL, backed by the Lord President's Committee, also sought to organise the limited leisure time of workers, particularly younger ones, in the hope that such activities might have a positive effect upon the workers' attitude to work, a social control argument worthy of the pioneers of Sunday schools in the late eighteenth century.[27]

As a reason for absence MOL officials treated domestic work with more respect than they did 'indifference'. As we have seen in the context of child care, concern to protect the family home during wartime competed in the MOL with the desire to subordinate it to the dictates of production, but the former triumphed over the latter at least in the MOL's public presentation of its views on the absenteeism of married women. The writers of an official pamphlet 'The Problem of Absenteeism', released in September 1942, quoted a report by two 'senior women Factory Inspectors' on absence due to domestic responsibilities, which gave enormous emphasis to the importance of 'home life'. It was depicted as 'a person's own very private business and . . . the ultimate object and reward of his labour'. The war had caused 'what amounts to a destruction' of the home life of a large proportion of workers, who were consistently presented as male. The heroic achievement of married women workers was to stand in the way of this destruction and this explained and justified their absenteeism.

> A married woman with a house, a husband and children, already has a full-time job which it is difficult to carry out in these days. Yet thousands of them are working long hours in factories. They are trying to do two full-time jobs. If they can carry on with a mere half-day per week off the ordinary factory hours they are achieving something marvellous.[28]

Though welcome as recognition of the real work of running a home, this construction of 'home life' had its limitations. It followed the definition of 'home' used in mobilisation, seeing it as male-dominated and placing it wholly within the confines of a marital and child-rearing framework. In particular it took no account of the relationship of single women to their homes, in spite of the fact that many bore considerable domestic responsibilities without help. Forty-five per cent of single women and 62 per cent of married women in a group interviewed by M-O gave reasons other than sickness as their excuse for absence, among which ties of home, shopping, children, husband or other relative on leave featured prominently. In contrast only one in a hundred of the men asked by M-O gave domestic reasons for absence.[29]

The pamphlet 'The Problem of Absenteeism' received a hostile response from some employers, indicative of their attitudes to the encroachment of domesticity on their women workers. For instance a leader writer in the *Engineer* dubbed the pamphlet 'an apologia for the absentees'. The writer scorned the suggestion that 'the planned hours of working of individuals or sets of workers should be arranged with some regard to their personal convenience', and ridiculed 'the modern view that the factory is an establishment primarily designed for the convenience and sustenance of labour'.[30] Such views informed a preference for traditional disciplinary measures rather than any other solutions, such as changed management styles or changes in hours. The removal of the disciplinary sanction of the sack, by the Essential Work Order, which outlawed dismissal without the consent of the local National Service Officer, was lamented.[31] NSOs could prosecute persistent absentees, but, in keeping with Bevin's approach to managing labour through consent rather than coercion, they were reluctant to do so. In March 1942 Factory Inspectors pressed on employers' behalf for absenteeism to be made a direct offence under the EWO, but even so prosecution was used in only a small proportion of cases.[32]

In defence of women's absence for domestic reasons, M-O commented approvingly that 'many women . . . cannot contemplate without horror a speck of dust in their homes'. This in fact ludicrously understated the problem of trying to cope with the two full-time jobs of home and factory, as a description by an observer of a 50-year-old woman worker shows. She cared for her husband, who also worked in a factory, her two school-age children and a married daughter and son-in-law. She was caught by the investigator rushing home from the factory at lunchtime:

When I arrived with her, the whole house was in a complete mess. Two days' washing up is piled high in the sink; a great bundle of washed but unironed clothes lie on the floor beside the sink; odd shoes and socks belonging to the children are scattered about on chairs; and the table is a mass of crumbs and dirty crockery. Mrs B. seems to be at a complete loss where to begin.

Mrs B. was described as making various attempts to get the housework done, but there was not enough time to make much impact before she had to rush back to the factory, whereupon she said:

'It's no good, I can't keep up with it. I thought I'd like to do a bit and bring in some money, but I can't keep up with it. If I could just have a couple of days to get straight, then it would be all right, you could keep it under, but I can't manage like this.'[33]

As well as feeling overwhelmed by the double burden, many women workers, married and single, felt deprived of the emotional compensations of domestic life. Long hours which meant that they never saw their children except asleep, or which caused them to be excluded from the daily decision-making and conviviality of home life, were resented. For instance, one Ekco worker was told by her sister not to interfere with decisions about taking in evacuees: ' "You leave it to Mum and me . . . it don't matter to you who we have and who we don't, you're never there," ' to which the girl's hurt comment was, ' "Just as if it wasn't my home as much as hers." ' She and others felt like billetees, though women living in uncongenial billets absented themselves frequently to visit their own homes, regardless of lost wages and travel costs.[34]

Not surprisingly, if tension between home as a place either of labour or of emotional support, or both, and war work became more than could be resolved through absenteeism, women left. Factories employing mainly women were said to have a turnover of nearly 100 per cent in 1940–41, compared with 36 per cent before the war.[35] The introduction of the EWO in March 1941 made a difference to the wastage rates of men and women taken together. However, even in 1943, when conditions were supposed to have improved, the proportion of women workers leaving the munitions industries was 0.92 per cent per week, which meant that a firm had to recruit half of its total female labour force a year to maintain the current level of employment.[36] Single women were said to leave without permission if they felt like it, flouting the Direction Order. Married women frequently worked in establishments which were not scheduled under the EWO and many could not in any case be directed because they had children under 14 at home.[37] Absenteeism remained obdurately at 12–15 per cent for women until 1945 when it rose slightly.[38] The heroic picture drawn by many publicists of women war workers bearing the wartime double burden stoically, without complaint, was wrong.[39] They took time off consistently to make it possible to do their two jobs and left work when the burden became too great.

It seems that a reduction in the hours of work would have been helpful both to women workers and to those trying to manage them in the work place. Working hours in wartime were governed by regulations which 'relaxed' the provisions of the 1937 Factory Act laying down a 48-hour week for women, restrictions on overtime and a ban on night work. For example, in August 1940 an Emergency Order covering munitions and engineering permitted authorisation of the employment of women up to 60 hours per week. After some initial hesitation among policy-makers, amid opposition from the unions, women were permitted to work at night, on Sundays and on continual seven-day rotas. The emphasis in the first two years of war was on extending the hours for which women could work. From 1941 onwards, however, it was argued in the MOL that such hours were too long and in 1942 an order made it possible for a district inspector to impose 55 hours on any industry in the area.[40] Nevertheless, even a 55-hour week represented ten hours on weekdays and five at the weekend and overtime was often required in addition. It was common practice for women to be expected to work from 7.30 in the morning to 7 at night on several days of the week, or to 'make up' six hours' overtime on Saturday afternoons.[41] Travelling time, often considerable if a woman was working at a remote 'green field' factory, and given the petrol shortage and transport difficulties of wartime, obviously added to the length of the working day. Discussions of child care assumed that women would be away from home for at least twelve hours a day. Even after the first tentative efforts had been made in the summer of 1942 to reduce hours, 28 of the 42 ROFs engaged in engineering required women to work a basic week of over 55 hours, including two which extracted 66 hours from women, and M-O reported in 1942 that 10 per cent of the women in 'war industries' whom it interviewed were working over ten hours a day.[42]

These facts, and the pressure which the TUC's Women's Advisory Committee was still applying in the cause of shorter hours in 1944, suggest that the MOL had an uphill struggle to achieve its professed aim of reducing hours after 1941. When couched in terms of human factor management its advocacy seemed to carry little weight, such was employers' dismissal of the idea that it was appropriate for them to consider their workers' 'convenience'. However, one might expect the argument that shorter hours realised higher productivity to have made a deeper impression upon them.

This argument was of course not new. Apart from Marx's theories about absolute and relative increases in surplus value, it was repeatedly urged that the First World War had proved that the productivity of any worker, man or woman, dropped after an optimum number of hours, so simply lengthening a worker's hours did not increase output in a direct ratio. On the contrary, striking examples of reductions in hours resulting in increases in productivity were quoted from the Report of the Health of Munition Workers Committee of 1918 and from issues of the journal *Industrial Welfare* published between the wars. For instance, it was claimed that the productivity of women turning aluminium fuses on capstan lathes rose by 13 per cent when the actual hours they worked were reduced from 66 to 48.[43] M-O commented that 'to an extraordinary extent' such findings had been 'neglected' in the years 1939-42.[44] What had been noticed by official sources in 1940-41 was an immediate increase in production when hours were lengthened after the fall of Dunkirk, followed by a sharp fall. M-O drew the conclusion that 'emotional drive' could produce such results, but that they were impossible to sustain. The M-O investigator at Ekco in 1943 was convinced that in the absence of such drive women workers there spread eight or nine hours' work over the twelve required of them.[45]

In spite of the evidence about the relationship between hours and productivity, some of the biggest employers, notably government departments, refused to shorten hours. The Ministry of Supply was a case in point. It flatly refused to allow managers of the ROFs which it controlled to drop Sunday work or reduce weekly hours and was repeatedly criticised by the Select Committee on National Expenditure as a result. For instance, in September 1943 the management of ROF Aycliffe wanted to drop Saturday working, because 50–60 per cent of its 9,200 women workers absented themselves on Saturdays. But the MOS refused them permission to do so.[46] In the same month, however, the Ministers of Supply and of Aircraft Production finally came round to the idea which the MOL had been pushing since 1941 that 55 hours was 'the maximum number of hours per week which could be worked without a disproportionate increase in absenteeism'.[47]

One of the most common arguments offered by employers against reducing hours was that male workers would not stand for it because it would mean a drop in earnings, especially overtime earnings. Managers in the Midlands munition industries complained in 1941–2, 'Generally little could be done by individuals to reduce hours. Reduced hours meant reduced incomes. There was Income Tax to be paid on last year's big earnings.' Shipbuilding firms in the North-east claimed that union opposition to any reduction in high earnings would make it impossible to reduce overtime, a point confirmed by the report of the Engineering and Allied Trades Shop Stewards in October 1941 which insisted that 'No Cuts in Earnings' was an essential condition for increased production. Union opposition to reduction of overtime on Tyneside and a demonstration in March 1942 by 1,000 workers at a south-west town against a proposal to reduce weekend work in three factories seemed to indicate that opposition to reductions in hours was general.[48]

M-O thought that the result of dependence on overtime for the worker was that ' if a rest was required he could take it on Monday or some other day when only half the same money was paid'.[49] But as this statement suggests, the preoccupation with overtime earnings applied more to men than to women. It is possible to over-emphasise the idea that women were not motivated by financial incentives in the same way that men were and Richard Croucher has criticised me for doing so in an earlier publication.[50] All the same, Croucher's contrary argument that the desire to increase their earnings was important to women, based on evidence that women frequently complained about the size of their wages and that Irish women were working to send money home, does not fully deal with the issue of the different approaches to earning of men and women. In particular it ignores the evidence of women's specially high rates of absenteeism at weekends, when the highest rates were paid and men made a point of going to work. Women's absenteeism on Saturdays and Sundays was often double the weekday level and four times that of men. In isolated ROFs weekend absenteeism could affect over half the women workers. Relatively high wages, piece rates or overtime bonuses made no difference, especially when transport was difficult and the distance from the shops was great. In contrast to the male reactions to threats to overtime mentioned above there were virtually no complaints from women at Ekco when Saturday afternoon overtime was removed, even though M-O recorded that as many as 20 per cent of the women were 'dissatisfied' with the size of their earnings.[51]

M-O's evidence suggests that women workers, single and married, felt that they needed Saturdays and Sundays to shop, to do domestic chores and to attend to their own welfare and to that of their children, if they had any. This explanation of women's willingness to swap factory for domestic work at the weekend should not be understood to mean that women worked for 'pin money' while men were the 'real' breadwinners. On the contrary, there is plenty of evidence to add to Croucher's that money was important to women, for instance women told the WSS and other surveys that the financial gain was the most important reason for working and women trade unionists were emphatic that women, like men, worked through economic necessity.[52] Nevertheless, the pattern of women's wartime absenteeism supports Scott and Tilly's interpretation of married women's approach to earning, which was that they saw their wage as subsidising the domestic economy which they themselves managed and which perforce demanded in addition their labour.[53] In a sense women, whether married and caring for a family, single and contributing to such care, or single and caring solely for themselves, were more literally 'bread winners' than men, typically, cared for by their 'dependants'. Since the 'winning' and providing of bread requires not only purchasing power, but in addition the transformation of purchased products into things that can be consumed, the same motive that propelled women into paid work also pushed them out, when the hours of paid labour threatened to make it impossible for them to perform the socially necessary domestic labour for which, as women, they were expected to take responsibility, in addition, of course, to restoring their own capacity for work. As we have seen in the context of mobilisation, child care and shopping policies, and as we shall see further in the context of approaches to women's place in the workforce, their wartime participation in paid labour did virtually nothing to change but rather reinforced this logic of women's double burden.

It comes as no surprise that none of the women asked by M-O said that hours were too short and, when asked about what improvements they would like to see in their own job, 14 per cent of women spontaneously mentioned changes or reductions in hours, compared with only 3 per cent of men. Some women felt a strong grievance against wartime hours of work and the intransigence of employers about cutting them down. In 1943 a Mass-Observer overheard two women saying:

'They've no right to keep us here these hours . . .'
'They ought to be made to cut them down. They will too. I saw in the paper they're going to put all the factories on shift work, eight hours a day, and no one will be allowed to work twelve hours like we do.'[54]

Contrary to this woman's hope and expectation, however, there were some official attempts to lengthen rather than to reduce hours.

It was the 'non-essential' industries which had been subject to concentration, such as cotton, hosiery, the pottery industry and boot and shoe manufacture that were the targets of such efforts. As we have seen, these industries suffered a labour shortage when men and directable women were released for 'essential' work in the forces and munitions. To compensate for these withdrawals, the MOL tried to obtain agreements that longer hours would be worked by the immobile women left behind. By January 1942 it had been successful as far as cotton, hosiery and the potteries were concerned. Only the boot and shoe industry rejected the demand to lengthen hours.[55] Its unusual resistance highlighted the contradictions in the MOL's efforts to boost industrial production through using married women's labour power, without either exerting compulsion over them or collectivising domestic work.

The employment of women, including married women, had been increasing numerically and as a proportion of those employed between the wars, in both the North Midlands and south-west centres of boot production. Employment practices had developed to accommodate the need for time for domestic concerns, for instance it was said that in Leicestershire before the war women were not expected to keep strictly to starting times and often had an extra hour at lunchtime,

flexibility which was possible in an industry organised on a piece-
work basis. Women were loath to give up such practices in wartime,
in particular they dug their heels in where overtime work was concerned. MOL local officials noted that, if pressurised to work late,
women in the 'Household R' category simply left.[56]

This was the context in which Bevin wrote to the Federation of
Boot Manufacturers and the National Union of Boot and Shoe Operatives in the autumn of 1941, suggesting that women in the boot and
shoe industry should work for 54 hours a week instead of 48 in the
interests of releasing more labour 'for the Forces and for vital war
production'.[57] The idea met with opposition from an impressive
array of interests, namely the MOL Regional Controllers, the
employers and the union.

Both management and union defended the practice of women working no more than 48 hours on the grounds that any extension would
be bad for both the home and the production process. As far as the
home was concerned:

> It is considered quite impracticable to expect women operatives,
> with homes and children to provide for – and frequently with
> evacuated women and children in their homes – to maintain their
> attendance and to sustain their out-put over a 54 hour week, especi-
> ally with the onset of winter.

The production process would suffer, because women staffed the key
department in a boot and shoe factory, the 'closing department' where
uppers and soles were joined. If the industry was required to work
longer hours there would be a high level of absenteeism here, leading
to congestion of work as uppers and soles produced in other departments piled up waiting to be joined. Thus there were fears that output
per operative would actually decrease if a 54-hour week were enforced.[58]

However the District Factory Inspectors were unsympathetic, ques-
tioning the real motives of women in resisting an extension of hours, in
rather the same way that other officials tried to cast doubt on the 'real'
reasons for absenteeism, or queues, or the 'real' demand for canteens,
factory stores, ordering facilities or nurseries. For instance the North
Midlands District Inspector argued that married women in the boot and
shoe industry were claiming too much time for home:

> Many married women have domestic obligations which demand

careful consideration but I cannot subscribe to the contention that in all cases, or even in a very high proportion of them, these obligations are actually so inflexible as to be incapable of modification . . . There are now many married women in other industries in this District working substantially more than 54 hours per week with equal domestic responsibilities.[59]

'Selfish' motives were imputed to women, such as trying to avoid the high rate of income tax incurred on overtime earnings or being 'unreasonably' devoted to leisure. The District Inspector did not acknowledge that overtime did mean a lot of work and not much financial gain for a married woman once the family tax bill had been paid, nor that there was precious little 'leisure' left after even the 'short' week of 48 hours, which meant nine hours a day plus three on Saturday. He was flatly condemnatory: 'Motives of this nature for unwillingness to work a few hours longer each week are bad and merit ruthless treatment.' He and others, including a woman inspector in Leicester, accused women boot and shoe workers of indulging themselves in the relatively pleasant conditions of the industry, while ignoring 'the urgency of maximum effort by the whole population of the country'.[60]

The MOL's other local officers, the Regional Controllers, who were more closely concerned with labour supply and stability than the inspectors, did not support their views. The North Midlands RC pointed out that rates of absenteeism and turnover were so high at factories working long hours that employers were currently, during 1942, being forced to reduce hours. Doubt was cast not on women's motives but on whether facilities for domestic work such as nurseries, school meals, shopping arrangements and so on were adequate to permit women to work longer hours.[61] Prompted to investigate, one of the inspectors discovered that such provisions barely existed in the boot and shoe areas of the North Midlands. For instance she found only one shop, in Corby, operating an ordering scheme, few nurseries anywhere except Nottingham, only three poor quality British Restaurants in Northampton and employer resistance to establishing canteens. In addition, the area was suffering severe transport difficulties. Employers and unionists replied that even if the facilities had been functioning properly nine hours a day was long enough, but in view of their inadequacy longer hours were unconscionable.[62]

To this argument, the RC in the North Midlands added a telling thrust against the proposal to make women work longer hours in the boot and shoe industry. Such a step would, he argued, be self defeating.

Of 25,000 women in the industry, 15,000 were married and most of these were volunteers from the 'Household R' class:

> There is reason to be thankful that we have not the problem of persuading the 15,000 into industry. Having got this number where the great majority can best serve the national interests it would appear to be sensible to interfere as little as possible with their comfort.[63]

His statement neatly expresses the central dilemma of MOL labour supply policy: the attempt to raise war production while simultaneously perpetuating women's role at home.

The boot and shoe industry did not succumb to the pressure of the central MOL and local inspectorate to extend its hours. In seeking an explanation, it is tempting to see the RC's argument as decisive; however, it applied equally to the cotton, hosiery and pottery industries where hours were extended, albeit with the possibility of exemptions. No doubt the stand taken on behalf of women by the RCs, employers and the union was important in persuading the MOL to give up the search for an agreement on longer hours. However the Ministry was in a sense let off the hook after the middle of 1942, as a result of a reduction in the leather supply leading to tighter Board of Trade restrictions on production, which made it rather irrelevant to require boot and shoe workers to work longer hours.[64]

The unwillingness of the boot and shoe employers to lengthen hours was unusual. Most employers were loath to reduce much longer working weeks. However, during 1942-3, in view of the high levels of absenteeism and turnover, the MOL did persuade some employers to experiment with reorganisation of hours. The new arrangements fall into three categories, leave, shifts and part-time work, all of which were used, as we have already seen, by some employers to cope with the specific problem of absenteeism due to the need to shop. Inevitably it was suggested that they should be more widely applied in order to achieve a balance between domestic and industrial work.

To recap, provided the granting of leave remained at the management's discretion, it was a popular solution with employers for the sporadic absenteeism caused by shopping. The MOL suggested in a pamphlet of March 1941 that it should be granted for other domestic commitments, as well, giving the example of times when a husband came home on leave.[65] However managements disliked the fact that such reasons tended to escalate, for example, married women took leave for sons as well as husbands and single women for brothers and boyfriends. Some of them claimed in 1942 that they were losing 10 per cent production as a result. But M-O, which reported this information, defended absence of this sort, in terms of what it saw as a necessary equation between the family and the labour process:

> While winning the war is the only big consideration, if the bonds of family and continuity are weakened beyond a certain point, the morale, unity and work effort of the country is weakened.[66]

Such views may have prevailed with employers, or they may simply have bowed their heads to the inevitable. Either way the MOL survey into absenteeism indicated that during 1943 managements became increasingly willing to grant leave. In the period January–April 1943 10 per cent of women's absence was said to be due to leave, whereas in June–September 1943 20 per cent was attributed to this cause. The effect of this on figures of absenteeism, of course, was simply to transfer numbers from the 'avoidable' to the 'unavoidable' category, not to reduce it as such. Thus by September 1943 slightly less of women's than men's absenteeism was classified as avoidable, but their overall absence rates were as high as ever.[67] As this reclassification suggests, the practice of married women taking time off for domestic work was becoming legitimised in the second half of the war. For instance, C.R. Parsons, an engineering firm on Tyneside, experienced 20 per cent absence of married women in the gun shop during 1942-3, 'but though the management consider the problem serious they believe the absenteeism is legitimate because of the women's domestic circumstances'.[68]

The growth of tolerance was accompanied by a gradual change of attitude towards older women. In place of the prejudice characteristic of 1940–41, managers started to refer to the 'keenness' of older women and the way they carried over their 'household pride' into their work. 'They are more absentee but there are several reasons for that, and they certainly try harder,' said one manager comparing married women with conscripted men. Similar comments were made about ex-domestic servants, suggesting that domestic labour produced the right mentality, in the eyes of management, for work in industry. It was widely observed, by other workers as well as employers, that older married women were among the most diligent when they were actually at work.[69]

In some cases, employers introduced shift work in order to reap the benefits to productivity which accrued from just that 'tenderness for the workers' convenience' which the leader in the *Engineer* had scorned in October 1942. They could recruit older married women whom they regarded as hard working and they could keep their machinery running for 24 hours without high rates of absenteeism. Three eight-hour shifts, often introduced for women alone, were thought to be the most effective arrangement, though there were variations, including a 24-hour shift at one factory, during which women slept for six hours in air-raid shelters at work. Shifts were supposed to be a 'Godsend to women with any domestic cares', but in practice this must have depended on whether domestic arrangements for child care, shopping, feeding, etc. dovetailed with shift times and whether women managed to get any rest between shifts.[70] Women frequently complained about the 'night shift nightmare' which played havoc with their sleep, for instance Doris White, working nights on 'major repairs' to aircraft, wrote, 'Sleep was punctuated with all the sounds of life of people who slept at the proper time. But when the time came to sleep at night, then I could not sleep in peace.' Some welfare officers became concerned that married women 'on nights' barely slept at all, since they got themselves up early in the day to shop, cook, do the washing, fetch children from school and so on.[71]

Part-time work developed as a variation on shift work. At the beginning of the war, 'part-time' was so hazily defined that women working an hour or two below the full-time minimum of 48 hours could be classified as part-time workers, with the advantage for the employer, though not necessarily for the worker, of exemption from MOL controls. In the last three years of the war, however, when part-time schemes were developed on a large scale, 30 hours a week was the normal length of time required.[72]

In introducing the idea of part-time work to employers, the MOL stated that it represented a capitulation of the industrial labour process to the home. 'When a firm decides to employ part-time labour it has in fact decided to modify the organisation of the factory to suit the convenience of the workers who have domestic responsibilities.'[73] This makes it sound as though the purpose of part-time arrangements was to accommodate women with domestic commitments who were already working in industry. However, the MOL did not in fact see it in this way. The labour shortage was so acute in 1943 that its aim was to keep as many women as possible in full-time work and to offer part-time arrangements only to those whose age and home circumstances exempted them from any form of compulsion or direction and who were not otherwise expected to participate in war work. The MOL's dilemma was summed up by the Regional Controller in the North Midlands in September 1941:

> Many married women would prefer part-time employment. This is not undesirable if it means attracting women who would not otherwise be in industry, but the danger particularly in localities where there are large demands for female labour on essential war work is that it creates a tendency for women who can undertake full-time work to take part-time employment merely because it is less irksome.[74]

The official position was that, whatever their domestic difficulties, married women exempt from direction should, if possible, be prevented from slipping out of full-time work and must definitely not depart from work altogether. Part-time war work was seen not as a solution to the domestic crisis of women at work, but as a solution to the crisis of labour supply. This preoccupation was reflected in the Control of Engagement (Directed Persons) Order, introduced in April 1943, which made it possible to direct women in the 'Household R' category, apart from those with children under 14 at home, into part-time work.[75] As well as giving the muscle of compulsion to the long-standing official attempts to recruit 'Household R' women as volunteers, the order had two types of breakwater effect. Firstly, it was supposed to prevent overburdened women who were trying to opt out of full-time work from drifting right out of work and, secondly, it was a step to prevent women slipping into a new government scheme, the organisation of engineering outwork.

Outwork was to take place in local centres or a woman's own home and involved work as diverse as the assembly of four-cylinder air-cooled engines and the sorting of small aircraft parts muddled during an air raid.[76] As with part-time work, it was not the intention to ease the tension between work and home experienced by women already working in factories, in this case by allowing them to work at home. Rather outwork was to be supplied to women in rural areas whose domestic responsibilities and location caused them to be regarded as 'immobile', but not so fully occupied that they could not assemble a few aero-engines from time to time. The direction of women into part-time work would make it difficult for them to desert factory work for the new scheme. Nevertheless these attempts to get as much as possible out of every woman who could be found were regarded with as much trepidation by some MOL officials as the proposal to extend boot and shoe hours had been. They thought that women disliked 'being caught up in the official machine' and that 'any attempt to impose control may lead to workers withdrawing from the labour market altogether'.[77] This indeed was the dilemma in which the MOL was placed by its initial decision, heavily influenced by the Women's Consultative Committee, to respect the domestic role of married women as just cause for exemption from direction to war work and by its failure to persuade other government ministries to take radical steps to relieve women of domestic work.

Some employers resisted part-time arrangements, complaining that their foremen did not like them because they made the production line more complicated to organise or that part-timers had a disturbing effect on full-time workers because of their different starting and finishing times.[78] Underlying these complaints was a continuing assumption that factory organisation should bear no relationship to 'workers' convenience'. For instance one labour manager wrote:

I interviewed four young women sent by the Labour Exchange as volunteer workers after Saturday's recruiting drive. Each wanted half-time work only, some mornings, some afternoons. Wanted to feel that time off now and then for their family's sake would be allowed. Didn't fancy working until 6.30 p.m. or until 4.0 p.m. on Saturdays. Had to point out that a factory isn't a place where you can drop in for a spot of work just when you feel like it.[79]

The order of 1943 helped Labour Exchange managers to pressurise employers to use part-timers, as did the standardisation of arrangements into a 'split shift' system, whereby two groups of women took half of a full-length shift each. Eventually employers started to express satisfaction, for instance one said, 'The machinery is kept running twenty-four hours and everyone has sufficient time for their shopping and home duties.'[80]

Indeed the employment of part-timers increasingly took on the appearance of being not only tolerable, but positively advantageous to employers. Firstly, part-time workers were thought to be more productive than full-timers, for instance it was said that 'two part-time women might produce as much as 50 per cent greater output than one full-time woman . . . suffering from the effect of fatigue' and it was claimed that they had a stimulating rather than a disruptive effect on full-timers by setting 'a new pace' in the workshop. In addition part-timers

Figure 6.1: Outworker inserting glass in instrument covers in her own home. The original caption commented on the enthusiasm of such outworkers some of whom, 'at their own expense, supply cleaning materials to remove putty smears from the glass'.

showed only half the rate of absenteeism of full-timers and were better time-keepers.[81] Secondly, the least popular work on the shop floor was rapidly identified as the most suitable work for part-time organisation. For instance, the MOL recommended 'all jobs where the onset of fatigue or boredom is relatively early' and 'work which is carried out in unpleasant surroundings caused by noise, dirt, smell or heat, e.g. in smiths' shops, paint-spraying shops, hot press shops, etc.' It was said that 'acclimatisation can in time overcome much of the initial revolt and nausea produced by unpleasant conditions'. In other words, employers were encouraged to dump the most boring and unpleasant work upon part-timers because of the difficulty of persuading anyone to overcome their 'revolt and nausea' sufficiently to do it efficiently for full-length hours. This was not conducive to overcoming the 'prejudice against the roughness and undesirability of factory life' which had inhibited the voluntary recruitment of 'Household R' women, but the need to do so was greatly reduced by the Order of 1943.[82]

In addition to the benefits to employers of part-timers' productivity on unpopular work, there was a third economic advantage. The wage to part-timers represented a double saving in that all women received lower wages than men anyway and part-time women received none of the supplements paid to full-timers, such as bonus and overtime rates and unemployment and accident insurance contributions.[83] Of course such savings to the wages bill had not gone unnoticed before the war, when in conditions of labour surplus employers had frequently employed workers on 'short-time'. Though part-time and outwork were presented as new wartime developments and justified in terms of labour shortage and war aims, both contained shadows of unscrupulous employment practices of earlier years. The type of work and of worker were different, but the principle remained the same: part-time and outwork were cheap and efficient ways of getting work done.

The 1944 TUC women's conference heard that part-time work for women was not altogether popular with husbands because they 'saw a lot of their comforts disappearing',[84] but, in spite of the exploitative aspects discussed above, one would expect that it was quite popular with women themselves. Seven hundred thousand women did part-time work in 1943 and 900,000 in 1944. Evidence of their feelings is, as so often, skimpy. When the WSS asked part-timers whether they wanted to continue with it after the war, 31 per cent said they did, 7 per cent wanted to opt for full-time work and 27 per cent were unsure. The comments of a 40-year-old housewife, recorded by Mass-Observation, are more explicitly indicative of enthusiasm, rooted in her perception of the importance for women of working outside the home:

> I thoroughly enjoy my four hours working here in the afternoon.
> I'm all agog to get here. After all, for a housewife who's been a
> cabbage for fifteen years – you feel you've got out of the cage and
> you're free. Quite a lot of the part-timers feel like that – to get out
> and see some new faces – it's all so different, such a change from
> dusting. I think the war has made a lot of difference to housewives.
> I don't think they'll want to go back to the old narrow life. Another
> thing, they enjoy earning a little money for themselves, of their very
> own, even if it all goes to the children.[85]

Conclusion

The development of part-time work for women during the war was
curiously two-faced. In a sense it was a victory for the recognition of
human needs over the demands of production. This was certainly how
the MOL presented it. Yet the identification of the needs it catered for
as exclusively female had two effects. One was to confirm, through
the type of work organised on a part-time basis, the picture of women
as the least skilled workers doing the lowest status jobs at the lowest
rates in the workplace, a stereotype which we shall consider more
closely in the next chapter. The other was to do nothing to change the
centrality of women to the home. It was not, after all, women's own
specific needs which required them to be there, but the needs of men,
children and others who could not or would not look after themselves.
It might be argued that the absence of one-third of the male workforce
in the armed forces made it unlikely that women's centrality to the
home could have been displaced in wartime. But the government did
have an alternative to its compromises with the women-centred home,
which would have greatly reduced the MOL's difficulties in managing
women as a source of labour. It could have gone so far in collectivising
domestic work that it would have been possible to recruit married and
single women on the same basis as men. All would have benefited from
a shorter working day than the typical nine or ten hours and absenteeism caused by the impossibility of combining full-time industrial and
domestic work would have disappeared. However, such a prospect was
ruled out, as we have seen, by the vested interests of many groups in
women's domestic role and particularly by the government's inhibi-
tions about forcibly removing women from the home, especially from

their role as child rearers within it, into war work. It is, however, important to note that the British government took the conscription and direction of women further than any of the other governments involved in the war,[86] which reflects both the relative severity of the labour shortage in Britain and the strength of patriarchy in the other combatant countries.

Notes

1. PRO Lab 26/131, MOL Pamphlet, 'The Problem of Absenteeism', September 1942.

2. Ibid., LP 42, 9 October 1942.

3. PRO Lab 26/4, reports of the 'Enquiry into Absence from Work', January–April 1943–4.

4. Reported in *MOL Gazette*, April 1944; PRO Lab 26/131, RC Northern Region, September 1943, said the same of his area.

5. M-O (1942), p. 235.

6. PRO Lab 26/132, 'Enquiry into Absence from Work'. Papers submitted to FWAB, 13 June 1944; PRO Lab 26/131, circular to all Regional Controllers, 10 November 1943.

7. PRO Lab 26/131, March–April 1944; J.M. Hooks (1944), p. 10.

8. WSS 'Food', April–July 1942, pp. 34 and 4; June 1943, p. 11.

9. PRO Lab 26/131, RC Northern Region, 1 December 1943; PRO Lab 26/132, 8 June 1943.

10. PRO Lab 26/4, discussion of conclusions of Lord President's Committee, 10 September 1943. Inez Holden (1941), pp. 101–2, suggested that such facilities did not always exist.

11. PRO Lab 26/131, 'The Problem of Absenteeism', September 1942; reported in *MOL Gazette*, April 1944.

12. M-O (1943), p. 43; Williams Ellis (1943), pp. 31–2.

13. Reported in *MOL Gazette*, April 1944; PRO Lab 26/131, MOL Pamphlet, 'The Problem of Absenteeism', September 1942.

14. On joint production committees see Inman (1957), pp. 376–92; Engineering and Allied Employers' National Federation, memorandum of agreement with AEU, NUFW and Confederation of Shipbuilding and Engineering Unions on constitution of Joint Production Consultative and Advisory Committees, 18 March 1942. On welfare officers see Factory (Welfare and Medical Services) Order, SR and O 1325, 16 July 1940. The Select Committee on National Expenditure discovered resistance to the employment of welfare officers, especially among firms with no tradition of employing women. See 'Third Report 1942–3', 17 December 1942, para. 37.

15. PRO Lab 26/131, 'The Problem of Absenteeism', September 1942.

16. *Arms and the Men*, full conference report of the Engineering and Allied Trades Shop Stewards' National Council, London, 19 October 1941, p. 21.

17. Arthur Exell, 'Morris Motors in the 1940s', *History Workshop*, 9, 1980, pp. 93–5.

18. M-O (1942), p. 195; M-O (1943), pp. 118–19; M-OA, Topic Collection, 'Industry', 1941–7, Box 140, Report on Tube Investments Ltd, Aston, Birmingham, 1942. (Hereafter Tube Report.)

19. M-O (1942), p. 128 ff; M-OA, Topic Collection, 'Industry', 1941–7, Box

140, Tube Report, pp. 44–5; M-OA, Topic Collection, 'Women in Wartime', Box 3, File F, letters from women welders, 1942, especially those from Jenny, Helena, Dorothy, Agnes and Amy.

20. J.M. Hooks (1944), p. 10.

21. M-O (1943), pp. 69, 68.

22. M-OA: Topic Collection, 'Women in Wartime', Box 3, File F, letters from women welders, 1942, especially Enid, Amy, Agnes; Topic Collection, 'Industry', 1941–7, Box 140, Tube Report, pp. 87–97.

23. M-O (1943), p. 118.

24. M-O (1942), pp. 244–5.

25. M-O (1943), pp. 52, 42–3.

26. Ibid., pp. 27–8 for vivid descriptions of 'lavatory mongering' and clock watching, which is also described by Inez Holden (1941), pp. 17–18.

27. PRO Lab 26/4, discussion of conclusions of Lord President's Committee, 10 September 1943.

28. PRO Lab 26/131, 'The Problem of Absenteeism', September 1942.

29. M-O (1942), pp. 167 and 241. On the domestic responsibilities of single women see Scott (1944), pp. 123 and 111, and on the extent to which those living at home could rely on their mothers to look after them see M-O (1943), pp. 32, 87, and M-O (1942), p. 195.

30. *Engineer*, 30 October 1942.

31. M-O (1942), pp. 249–50, 105; M-OA, Replies to Directive, March 1944, production engineer, Wallington, Surrey.

32. M-O (1942), pp. 249–50; PRO Lab 26/131, report on Regional Controllers' Conference, 11 March 1942; SR and O 1942, No. 583, Essential Work (General Provision) Amendment Order 1942, 25 March 1942; Inman (1957), pp. 284–5 (on the frequency of prosecution).

33. M-O (1942), p. 232. There are many other examples of women coping more or less adequately with the double burden. See, for example, M-OA, Topic Collection, 'Industry', 1941–7, Box 140, Tube Report, 1942. A woman worker in her thirties, who did not look well, said one evening, 'I'm going home to do an evening's scrubbing. First I've got to do my bit of shopping on my way home. I have to queue for it, because they make no allowance for me being in the factory all day. My two little boys are in school all day. They have their dinners there and the teacher keeps them till 6 o'clock when I call for them. But I have to get them home and wash them and put them to bed. Then I have to get a meal ready, and there's always some washing and mending to be done every night. I never get to bed before 12. I wish I had a daughter about 14 years old. My friend's got a girl of 14, and she is such a help.'

34. M-O (1943), pp. 34–5, 86, 85, 96 ff.

35. *Occupational Psychology*, No. 2, 1941, quoted by M-O (1942), p. 98. The Industrial Health Research Board reported 84 per cent turnover at a factory with over 5,000 women employees in 1940–41. Chorley and Euxton ROFs in the North-west were cases in point.

36. Inman (1957), p. 209.

37. M-O (1942), pp. 108, 100.

38. PRO Lab 26/4, Conclusions, May 1943, and Lab 26/131, report on absenteeism for ILO, 13 February 1945.

39. See, for example, Scott (1944), p. 8: 'Only women however know what it has cost them to do the double job of working for the country and their families. They never grumble about it, but in considering these women who are doing men's jobs the background of the home must be remembered.'

40. For the details of pre-war restrictions on hours see Royal Commission on Equal Pay, *Report* (1946), p. 109 para. 352 and note; p. 110 note. For wartime

relaxation see Hooks (1944), pp. 3–4; *Industrial Welfare and Personnel Management*, xxii, No. 261, August 1940. For union opposition see TUC Pamphlets and Leaflets, 1944/18.

41. PRO Lab 26/51, report on Short Brothers, 17 October 1941.
42. PRO Lab 26/58, memorandum on day nurseries, 2 January 1941; J.M. Hooks (1944), p. 3; M-O (1942), p. 192.
43. See K. Marx, *Capital* (1887), Vol. 1, Chapters xvi and xvii; M-O (1942), p. 190; *Industrial Welfare*, December 1939, quoted in M-O (1942), p. 221.
44. M-O (1942), pp. 148–9. Others also commented on this. See G.M. Young, *Sunday Times*, 15 February 1942; Williams Ellis (1945), p. 24.
45. Select Committee on National Expenditure, '21st Report 1940–1, Output of Labour', 6 August 1941; M-O (1942), p. 191; M-O (1943), p. 114.
46. Select Committee on National Expenditure, '51st Report 1941–42', 16 July 1942; PRO Lab 26/131, report from RC Northern Region, September 1943.
47. PRO Lab 26/4, meeting of Lord President's Committee, 10 September 1943.
48. M-O (1942), p. 191; *Arms and the Men*, 19 October 1941, p. 21; PRO Lab 26/131, report from RC Northern Region, September 1943; M-O (1942), p. 211.
49. M-O (1942), p. 210.
50. R. Croucher, *Engineers at War* (Merlin, London, 1982), p. 256; P. Summerfield, 'Women Workers in the Second World War', *Capital and Class*, 1, Spring 1977, pp. 38–9.
51. M-O (1942), p. 220; Hooks (1944), p. 10. See also PRO Lab 26/133, correspondence on closure of nurseries, April 1943, where women's weekend absenteeism was stressed. Ibid., RC NW to MOL, April 1943; Lab 26/131, report from RC Northern Region, September 1943; M-O (1942), p. 239; M-O (1943), p. 119.
52. WSS (1944), pp. 20–21; RCEP, *Minutes of Evidence*, 27 July 1945, para. 3066 ff.
53. J.W. Scott and Louise A. Tilly, 'Women's Work and the Family in Nineteenth Century Europe', *Comparative Studies in Society and History*, 17, 1975.
54. M-O (1942), p. 194; M-O (1943), p. 61.
55. PRO Lab 8/108, Gould to Stevens, 16 January 1942. The pottery industry agreed to a 53-hour week, the spinning section of cotton to four hours overtime per week and the hosiery industry to 54 hours. (In the case of the potteries, however, the MOL was forced to exempt youths under 16 from the extension of hours.)
56. On the growing numbers of women in the boot and shoe industry see Census of England and Wales, *Occupation Tables* (HMSO, 1924, and HMSO, 1934). On workplace practices see PRO Lab 8/479, RC North Midlands to Gould, MOL, 23 September 1941; PRO Lab 8/108, RC South-west, 3 December 1941; PRO Lab 8/108, HM District Inspector, 6 December 1941.
57. Ibid., Bevin to Federation of Boot Manufacturers and National Union of Boot and Shoe Operatives, 30 October 1941.
58. Ibid., Chester, NUBSO, and Colvin, FBM, to Bevin, 20 November 1941; see also RC South-west, reporting a very similar statement by the British Boot and Shoe Advisory Committee, 3 December 1941.
59. Ibid., HM District Inspector of Factories, Northampton, 2 February 1942.
60. Ibid., HM District Inspector of Factories, Northampton, 28 January 1942, 2 February 1942; Miss Keeley, Inspectorate, East Midlands Division, 3 February 1942.
61. Ibid., RC North Midlands, 30 January and 9 February 1942.
62. Ibid., Miss Keeley, Inspectorate, Leicester, 3 February 1942; minute of a meeting between Bevin, Colvin and Chester, 23 March 1942.

63. Ibid., RC North Midlands, 30 January 1942. He repeated the argument in a letter of 9 February 1942.

64. Ibid., MOL to BOT, 28 April 1942; minutes of a meeting of Northampton Boot and Shoe Advisory Committee, 7 May 1942.

65. MOL, *The Employment of Women. Suggestions to Employers* (HMSO, London, 24 March 1941).

66. M-O (1942), p. 168.

67. PRO Lab 26/4, reports on the 'Enquiry into Absence from Work', 1943–4.

68. PRO Lab 26/131, report from RC Northern Region, September 1943.

69. M-O (1942), p. 166; M-OA, File Report 1238, 'Appeals to Women', May 1942; see also M-O (1943), pp. 26, 41, 44; M. Goldsmith, *Women at War* (Lindsay Drummond, London, 1943), p. 199; M-OA, Topic Collection, 'Industry', 1941–47, Box 140, Tube Report, pp. 11–12.

70. PRO Lab 26/61, FWB (42) 10, 30 May 1942; M-O (1942), pp. 213–14.

71. TUC Pamphlets and Leaflets, 1942/7; Doris White, *D for Doris, V for Victory* (Oakleaf Books, Milton Keynes, 1981), p. 51; PRO Lab 26/60, FWAB, October 1941.

72. PRO Lab 8/634, RC South-west, 24 October 1942; Hooks (1944), pp. 5–6. See also PRO Lab 8/623, 1942–3, consultation with TUC and BEF re part-time work for women.

73. PRO Lab 8/634, 'Labour Supply Memorandum', No. 6, January 1943.

74. PRO Lab 8/479, RC North Midlands, 23 September 1941.

75. Parker (1957), p. 289; TUC Pamphlets and Leaflets, 1943/10, 'Part-time Women Workers: The Law Explained'.

76. Hooks (1944), p. 6; Scott (1944), p. 101.

77. PRO Lab 8/703, minutes of discussions, January–March 1943.

78. PRO Lab 8/634, correspondence, 8 October and 4 November 1942.

79. M-O (1942), p. 177. See also p. 95 and M-OA, Town Box, Coventry, File 3708, 'War Work, Coventry, 1941', where it was reported 'most firms will still not touch it'.

80. PRO Lab 26/61, FWB (42) 10, 30 May 1942.

81. PRO Lab 8/634, RC South-west, October–November 1942; Correspondence with industrial firms and employment exchanges, October–November 1942; Hooks (1944), p. 5.

82. PRO Lab 8/634, 'Labour Supply Memorandum', No. 6, January 1943; RC South-west, 4 November 1942.

83. PRO Lab 8/634, RC SW 24 October 1942. Protests were voiced at the TUC women's conferences; see TUC Pamphlets and Leaflets, 1942/7 and 1943/16.

84. TUC Pamphlets and Leaflets, 1944/18.

85. WSS (1944), pp. 4 and 15. M-OA, File Report 1970, 'Women in Pubs', January 1944, p. 2. See also M-O, *The Journey Home* (1944), pp. 57–8.

86. Milward (1977), p. 219.

7 DILUTION

The discussion so far has concentrated on the interaction of the mobilisation of women with the conventional expectation that women's
first responsibility was to the home. Mobilisation also inevitably disturbed the distribution of men and women in the workforce. Just as
the changes called for by the recruitment of women in the areas of
domestic work examined above were encouraged by some and resisted
by others, so those demanded in the workforce were matters of intense
negotiation.

Sexual divisions between industries were breached by mobilisation,
as the figures quoted at the beginning of Chapter 3 indicate. To recap,
by 1943 women formed significant proportions of the workforce in
industries where relatively few women had been employed before the
war, e.g. 52 per cent of the workers in chemicals, 46 per cent in metals
and 34 per cent in engineering, compared with 27 per cent, 32 per cent
and 10 per cent respectively in 1939. (see Table B8.) These were, of
course, overall figures, concealing wide variations. For example in
engineering women never formed more than 16 per cent of the workers
in the marine branch of the industry, whereas by 1944 they formed
over 60 per cent of the workers in electrical engineering. But there was
no section of the industry in which the sexual composition was un-
affected by the wartime mobilisation of women.[1] Further, whereas
the entry of women to the 'essential' industries before the war was
characterised by segregation involving women's confinement to work
considered less skilled and valuable than that done by men, integration
was now urged by the dilution policy, under which agreements on the
relaxation of restrictive practices were made between unions and
employers, in order to enlarge workforces and release men for service
in the armed forces.

It was widely believed at the time that these changes caused the
complete reversal of women's pre-war position in the workplace. From
now on 'it was the job that mattered and not the sex of the worker',
claimed Caroline Haslett, Honorary Secretary of the Women's Engineering Society in 1941, and the editor of the *Economist* wrote in November of that year that as a result of dilution, 'The women have the
whiphand.'[2] Authors like Peggy Scott liked to quote the spectacular
'men's jobs' which women were doing in the forces and in industry,

such as crane driving, stud welding and acetylene burning, stressing the extremes to prove that 'women have always known that they were capable of greater things than tradition put into their hands'. Male authors were fascinated by women doing exceptionally heavy work, for instance Bernard Darwin wrote that the Southern Railway sleeper works at Redbridge was 'in possession of the Amazons', describing with relish the 'robust matrons' who lifted large wooden sleepers there.[3] Such images fed the idea that in general the division between male and female employment within industries was disappearing under the effects of wartime dilution, an idea which was given authoritative backing. For instance the *Report* of the Royal Commission on Equal Pay published in 1946 stated that 'conventions limiting the field for the employment of women have been crumbling fairly fast in recent years', and women's war work 'has exerted and will continue to exert a lasting influence in breaking down whatever element of the old fashioned or the irrational remains in the public's estimation of the capabilities of women'.[4]

A few dissentient voices, however, cast doubt on the idea that the war had put women on an equal footing with men, let alone allowed them to get the 'whiphand'. For example, an ATS mechanic wrote that the women's services were being used 'to do the very many "lesser" jobs in almost the same way as a white man can find employment for native servants', and Janet Hooks concluded her survey of British methods of employing women in wartime, 'though considerable in-creases occurred in the numbers of women at work, still it could not be said that the main industries of the country were carried on chiefly by women'.[5] The official historian of labour in the munitions industries was convinced that women were still segregated in terms of skill: 'No overall figures at all exist to show the degree of skill possessed by the women dilutees, but it can be said that many were employed as semi-skilled workers and only a very small proportion in the highly skilled grades.' Though nearly half of all engineering workers were 'paid at skilled rates' in 1944, few of them were women.[6]

There were, in short, two views of the process of dilution in war-time. It was seen by the majority to promote women's entry into the male sphere and break down segregation, but others believed that, on the contrary, it operated to perpetuate gender divisions. The question of its effects is an important one for women. The optimistic inter-pretation that dilution promoted integration has the depressing consequence that since women's employment position in the recent past has been characterised by a high degree of segregation within and between industries,[7] women must have lost their wartime gains. On the other hand, the view that women's wartime employment remained highly differentiated from that of men requires explanation, since the dilution agreements were supposed to permit the employment of women on 'men's work'.

It seems that the argument should be resolved by discovering the nature of the work women did during the war. Though skill was commonly depicted as an attribute of individual workers or the work they did, such factors were less relevant to the category of work in which and the rate at which they were employed than the workers' collective degree of control over work, particularly over its classification in terms of skill and gender. The answer to the question about the effects of dilution must in fact be pursued through the workplace struggles over women's status and remuneration which were conducted mainly by men and which continued throughout the war.

Under the auspices of the Ministry of Labour, though not its direct intervention, dilution agreements were made between employers' organisations and unions in numerous industries. By 1944 these included engineering, shipbuilding, chemicals, vehicles, the electrical trades, metals, foundry work, iron and steel, railway work, transport, gas, building, textiles, clothing, tailoring, hosiery, entertainments, printing, and the manufacture of boots and shoes, food, tobacco, soap, and boxes.[8] Some of these agreements were made nationally between all the unions in the industry and the employers' organisation, as in the case of engineering, but others were more specific in character, applying only to certain workers in particular areas, as in the case of an agreement between the Scottish Association of Master Bakers and the Transport and General Workers' Union, in respect of van drivers in Dundee.[9] The list of agreements is in itself an indicator of the widespread nature of occupational segregation, since their purpose was to enable employers to use women on work formerly done only by men. At the same time, the agreements were supposed to protect the male worker from the dangers of undercutting: if women were paid a lower rate on the same jobs, men might be permanently displaced from that work.

The basic formula of the agreements was that women doing men's work would start on the women's rate, move to a proportion of the men's rate and work their way towards the full male rate over several periods of weeks, eventually attaining it if they could do the work without 'special assistance, guidance or supervision'. Women would be employed on a temporary wartime basis. Since, as we saw in Chapter 2, many of these industries already contained a sector where women were employed, there was, in addition, often a clause stating that women doing work designated 'work commonly performed by women in the industry' did not come under the agreement.[10]

The following discussion of the implementation of the dilution agreements will concentrate on the engineering industry, though it was very probably one among a number of similar cases in and out of 'essential' work. Engineering merits attention because its various branches embraced most munitions work and national agreements on the extended employment of women in engineering were negotiated with the Engineering and Allied Employers' National Federation by the three main unions in the industry, the Amalgamated Engineering Union, the Transport and General Workers' Union and the General and Municipal Workers' Union.[11]

The AEU, which signed its agreement on 22 May 1940 (see Appendix A), was a craft union of, essentially, skilled men, which excluded women from membership until 1943. Its leaders saw the agreement quite unambiguously as an arrangement for men. A few months before it was made, in February 1940, Fred A. Smith, General Secretary of the AEU, said, 'the AEU was and always had been opposed to the introduction of women into the industry . . . Not with the consent of the union would women be brought in, in normal times.'[12] Evidence about skilled engineers' behaviour towards women dilutees in the first three years of the war suggests that this view was not uncommon in the ranks of the engineers. In spite of the protection which the dilution agreement was supposed to afford them, the entry of women frequently provoked suspicion and sometimes hostility. For instance, J.T. Murphy, a radical shop steward, described men's reactions to the influx of women at a railway engineering factory in 1940–41 thus: 'Steadily their numbers increased. In they came, brunettes and blondes and gingers, quiet women and cheeky ones. The men watched them with curious eyes, wondering whose jobs they were going to take.'[13] The same question was in the minds of workers in a factory manufacturing steel tubes, who stated categorically, ' "It's not women's work here" . . . "There's no job in this place fit for a woman." '[14] Beneath their overt desire to protect women from hot, dirty and heavy work was the traditional concern to protect 'their' jobs against what they saw as competition from a rival workforce. Some of the men at this factory, particularly the skilled workers, were prepared to go to the lengths of sabotage to express their opposition. For example, when a woman was put on a particular lathe in the turning department during the day, the skilled men who used it at night responded by loosening the nuts on the machine so that they would fly off if it was started without read-justment. A man on the day staff explained to the woman worker, who was understandably upset, 'They don't like you to be working on this machine. They say, "Here's one woman doing it — they'll be getting other women in and then we'll be out of jobs and sent in the army".'[15]

Both skilled and semi-skilled men frequently expressed their sus-picion of women dilutees in less dramatic but nevertheless obstructive ways. Government reports and other sources reveal numerous strikes or threatened strikes, which were illegal under Order 1305 of 18 July 1940, in opposition to substitution, in engineering and indeed more widely.[16] For instance in spite of Clause 2 of the engineering agreement requiring that a record was kept of every substitution of a man by a woman and the promise of the 'Restoration of Pre-war Practices' at the end of the war,[17] skilled men in Murphy's railway engineering works blocked proposals for the relaxation of restrictive practices on the grounds that 'a job once lost by dilution was never recovered'.[18] Men in the shipyards were also obstructive. The success of their opposition is reflected in the relatively low proportions of women in these sections of industry. In 1941 women comprised only 10 per cent of the workers in railway engineering and 5 per cent in marine engineering (though there was expansion subsequently). In shipbuilding and repairing, with their own particularly craft-minded unions, women dilutees never formed more than 6 per cent and 4 per cent of the workforces at any point during the war.[19]

When dilution did take place skilled men could still offer passive resistance by refusing to teach women all the parts of a job and by using those they were supposed to train as 'assistants or labourers'.[20] This was sufficiently common for the Shop Stewards' National Council to issue a stern reprimand to 'fellow workers' in October 1941. It was no use applauding films of Russian women working on munitions for the Red Army, unless 'we now accept our own direct responsibility for teaching women how to do the most skilled jobs and drop all our prejudices and fears about the introduction and training of women for industry'.[21] Such prejudices were not, however, easily shed. Even when they did not overtly oppose women, skilled men often treated them with amused condescension as 'scatterbrained little nitwits who can't do anything right'.[22] These patronising attitudes could co-exist with superficially pleasant relations on the shop floor. For example, at Tube Investments Ltd men and women sat together during breaks when 'some good natured teasing goes on and the air is sometimes full of flying pieces of paper or rope that they throw at each other'.[23] But teasing could merge into forms of harassment which even the toughest found hard to bear, like Doris White who had to run the gauntlet of the 'caterwauls' of an all-male shop every time she was sent from her repair shop to the stores.[24] The other side of the coin was that women sometimes exploited feminine stereotypes to avoid punishment for lateness or mistakes.[25] Men professed to like women workers individually, frequently referring to their good looks and their youth, but they complained 'together they're more nuisance than they're worth', and beneath the surface there was often deep-rooted hostility to women's presence in the workplace. For example, a tool setter at Vickers Armstrong, Newcastle-upon-Tyne, described the women he set up for there as 'selfish, avaricious and willing to bribe and deceive' because they adopted strategies to earn more money such as including scrap in finished work, speeding up their machines and offering the setters cigarettes and hints of other favours for the 'cream of the work'. He recorded with glee, however, the subterfuges by which men concealed scrap and boosted their own earnings. This man eventually took demotion to a job on a machine to get away from women.[26]

Women could not put a foot right as far as men who believed that they had no place in the industry were concerned. They were blamed on the one hand for inefficiency and bringing down the take-home pay of male co-workers and on the other for super-efficiency and bringing down piece rates. Thus some machine setters complained about loss to their piece-rate earnings incurred by the need to attend to women machinists' problems[27] and one skilled man blamed his 'useless woman mate' for earnings in the region of £3 and told her that 'in five years she will be as incapable as she is now'.[28] In contrast, other setters were afraid of women 'busting the rate', expressing themselves either jokingly, 'Don't work too hard, now — remember, it's against the rules to sweat at the job,' or more viciously. M-O quoted several examples 'of girls being discharged or repressed for over-ability or over-enthusiasm', for instance 'a girl who had been through a technical engineering course in a Government Centre was sent to a factory and discharged at the end of the first day because her work was so much better than the men's and the manager foresaw serious labour trouble'.[29]

Anxiety about piece rates was only one component of this hostility, which was also the product of a feeling that it was essentially wrong for a woman to earn as much or more than a man or to be given the label skilled worker. This could lead to irrational behaviour by men, neglectful of even that degree of protection offered them by the dilution agreement, and conducive to exploitation of both men and women. For instance at one factory in 1942, the men were so adamant that they did not want women on skilled jobs that the firm adopted a policy 'whereby on no account will women be allowed to do jobs at men's rates . . . merely to keep the peace' and, at another, Rootes in Coventry, the shop stewards and the management made a secret agreement that women dilutees would never be paid the full male rate, but would be kept at the most at 75 per cent of it.[30] This, of course, could have made men vulnerable to undercutting and job loss. But they had the guarantee that women were coming into engineering temporarily to fall back on and presumably believed that they had the shopfloor strength to enforce it.

In view of the attitudes outlined here, it is perhaps not surprising that in the first three years of the war there were relatively few AEU claims for the full male rate for women under the Extended Employment of Women agreement. However, 1943 marked a turning point. It was the year in which the AEU finally decided to admit women to membership. The background to the decision lay in the fact that technical changes creating new types of work were taking place very rapidly in wartime and were enabling employers to take on women without reference to the dilution agreements. The general unions, the TGWU and NUGMW, which had traditionally recruited unskilled and semi-skilled workers in engineering, were expanding rapidly as the influx of women (and non-skilled men) swelled their ranks. If the process went on unchecked the AEU's claim to be the only legitimate engineering union would be undermined and its control in the industry would be seriously weakened. To emphasise that the admission of women was a step taken to protect men, the rights of women within the union were circumscribed. They held special white membership cards labelled 'Section V (Temporary Relaxation Agreement)' and the AEU did not appoint any women's officers to represent them nationally. Delegates to the AEU's National Committee from the annual AEU women's conferences were entitled only to advise on women's questions and had no voting rights. Women could be elected shop stewards, but even this concession was not free from patriarchal constraint. Men decided that in order to preserve the 'dignity of negotiations within the industry' women stewards should be over 21.[31]

In spite of their inferior status within the AEU, women joined in large numbers. By the end of 1943 there were, according to Richard Croucher's study, *Engineers at War*, 138,717 women AEU members.[32] Some were cajoled by men who felt that a craft union was not really the place for women, especially those they saw as frivolous young girls, but that if they joined they could at least be made to behave themselves, like 'Mr King a lay preacher and union boss' who was described by Doris White bullying young women working on glider frames to sign up.[33] Other women were keen to enrol and hopeful that their pay would be raised, though one saw pitifully clearly why women had been admitted:

> If they hadn't let us in and didn't make a fuss to raise our wages we'd be as skilled as the men by the end of the war and yet working for smaller wages. See? And the boss would want to keep us on after the war instead of taking the men back. If we get into the union and get the men's pay, the boss will prefer to take on the men after the war. There wouldn't be a proper reason to keep us on, now would there?[34]

This women loved her work as a mechanic and did not want to return to her pre-war job in a food store. But if she felt any resentment about the personal consequences of the union position, it was not admitted by the author of the book in which she was quoted.

In view of the indifference of the AEU towards women before 1943 and the self interest which lay behind its attentiveness in that year, it is galling to read numerous wartime statements to the effect that women were apathetic towards trade unionism and ignorant of its principles.[35] In fact when women were directly represented on works councils and by women shop stewards they developed a close concern with workplace politics[36] and, as we shall see shortly, there were cases of women workers taking militant action. But why should women take an interest in trade unionism if they were invisible in its theory and derogated by its practice? George Gibson, Chairman of the TUC in 1941, told the TUC women's conference of that year that the purpose of trade unionism was 'to build a better Britain' for 'two generations . . . the boys coming back and their fathers who remembered the last war and its outcome',[37] but however well disposed a woman might feel towards men, what had such a vision to offer her, as a working woman? Even women trade union leaders were not free from the habit of berating women for their lack of involvement in traditional trade unionism, particularly on occasions when women's total union membership was being considered. Although there had been a tremendous expansion, at the height of mobilisation in 1943 not more than one-quarter of women workers belonged to unions (2 million out of about 8 million women). Florence Hancock, National Woman Officer of the TGWU, demanded that 'women must more and more develop a Trade Union consciousness and must shoulder more responsibility, working alongside their men colleagues in a spirit of mutual co-operation'.[38] But would the co-operation in fact be mutual, or were trade unions so imbued with patriarchy that they would always sacrifice the interests of women to those of men?

With this question in mind, let us look first at the activities of the AEU and secondly at those of the general unions, on behalf of their women members. After 1943 the number of claims advanced by the AEU for the full male rate for women under the Extended Employment of Women agreement rose[39] and during 1944 the union managed to secure agreements with some employers such as the Ministry of Supply to institute a regular review procedure to 'ascertain whether the best of the women employed under this Agreement have achieved that degree of experience and versatility which would justify their being placed on the appropriate men's rate'.[40] There was, however, considerable resistance from employers to granting equal pay. Croucher reports that a shop stewards' survey of 30,643 women in 58 engineering factories in 1945 found that 6,010 women had replaced men and 6,475 were on the same work as men, but only 2,050 were actually receiving the full man's rate.[41] The employers' defence was that few women on the same work as men in engineering 'carry out that work by the same method and with no more supervision or assistance' than a man and therefore 'only a minority of the women are able to qualify for the full time-rate'.[42] Such claims provoked a replay of the acrimonious First World War dialogues between employers and unions. The AEU's riposte was that employers used the smallest alteration to a machine to claim that methods had changed and imposed unwanted supervision. 'The not infrequent result is that women capable of setting their machines are forbidden to do so, or that the woman's day is not complete unless a foreman or chargehand addresses a few words of good cheer to her, thereby knocking 20 per cent off her pay packet each week.'[43]

Even though the AEU was more committed to obtaining the men's rates for women after 1943 and spoke about women in increasingly sympathetic terms, skilled men remained determined to remove women from engineering at the end of the war. The employers backed them in this. Sir Alexander Ramsay, Director of the Engineering and Allied Employers' National Federation, said in 1945, 'The Relaxation Agreement is as it were a label tied round the neck of those women who came in to replace men, for the purpose of getting them out when the war is over.'[44] Employers clearly had no interest in keeping on women at men's rates of pay if they had a supply of male labour and if women presented a threat to workplace stability.

True to form, the AEU was active in the last year of the war in getting women out of engineering. After D-Day, as production was gradually re-oriented towards peacetime needs, AEU shop stewards told women they would have to leave when redundancies were declared. Disputes occured not over whether or not women should go, but over which women should go first — 'mobile' usually single women or 'immobile' married women — which could be seen as a classic divide-and-rule tactic.[45] Obviously male workers had no desire for women receiving a man's rate to stay longer than absolutely necessary. They were probably even more anxious for women who had not been granted equal pay to leave, because if they were kept on they would undercut and might permanently displace the men. The energy which engineering shop stewards put into persuading employers to honour Clause 1 of the 1940 agreement must have been further stimulated by the fact that the AEU discovered from a survey it conducted in 1944–5 that 66 per cent of women engineering workers, three-quarters of whom had entered the industry during the war, wanted to remain in engineering after the war.[46] What could women do, in the face of such treatment by their own union? They had, after all, their white union cards to remind them that they were only the temporary guardians of men's jobs. Most historians subscribe to the view that women made little fuss about the loss of their jobs in engineering at the end of the war.[47] Some protests have come to light, however, and further research may reveal more. Cases of women's unwillingness to leave their wartime jobs may have been overlooked both at the time and since, in order to construct a comfortable myth about women's quiescent acceptance of the 'return to the home' at the end of the war, in the same way that evidence of women's other wartime preferences, for instance for nurseries, rationing, or ordering schemes, was ignored· or misread.

There were several protests over the closure of factories where large numbers of women worked, such as Vickers Armstrong in Blackpool and Manchester and Shorts aircraft factory in Rochester,[48] and the official historian refers to 'a mass demonstration by workers experiencing redundancy' in the neighbourhood of one ROF. She attributes the non-participation of ROF 'representatives' to the careful handling of job loss by labour managers at the factory, who were assiduously notifying women of vacancies elsewhere as well as attending to individual problems concerning unemployment benefit and reinstatement.[49]

The issue of re-employment in other paid work may have caused as much grievance as displacement from munitions work, as it did in the United States,[50] but both job loss and reinstatement are notoriously difficult issues for workers to exercise collective muscle over, especially when they are divided. All the same, in May 1945 women working at a Ferranti factory in the North-west protested about leaving engineering to re-enter textiles, where wages and conditions were inferior and there was no guarantee that they would be re-employed at their previous levels of pay and skill, and there are other references to the reluctance of ex-textile workers to swap new engineering factories 'for some of the old mills from which they had come'.[51] There is no evidence that they received any help from the engineering unions, however, though at a Renold Chain factory in Manchester women appealed to the general union for help against the AEU policy of ensuring that women dilutees were sacked first. Richard Croucher writes that the NUGMW protested on their behalf, but that the AEU's monopoly of the key shop stewards' positions rendered the general union powerless to defend women.[52]

Throughout Croucher's account, the general unions are depicted as acting in women's interests over the issues of their status and remuneration during the war, in contrast with the skilled unions, which he represents as defending themselves in the traditional way against competition from a rival workforce, which in this case was women, but had in earlier times been unskilled men. What was the relationship between the general unions and women workers? If the evidence suggests that, in contrast to Croucher's view, they too were trying to promote the privileges of men at the expense of women, one must conclude that divisions in the workplace were not just between skilled and unskilled workers, but were more profoundly rooted in gender differences. If this was the case, it is unlikely that the process of dilution could genuinely have integrated women and men at work.

In engineering, the Transport and General Workers' Union both recruited women and negotiated their pay and status under an Extended Employment of Women agreement which, in conjunction with the National Union of General and Municipal Workers, it signed with the Engineering Employers' Federation in May 1940.[53] The general unions' view of the agreement was outlined by Jack Jones, TGWU negotiator in Coventry, who said in 1940 that it must be operated

> so that the men will be appeased and the women too will feel that they are not being used against the interest of the men. They are not there to cheapen the industry or to take the jobs of the men for

the whole of the future, but just for the duration of the war.[54]

In other words, the general as well as the skilled unions negotiated the agreement in order to protect men from undercutting and permanent displacement by women.

But the TGWU faced a different problem from the AEU. The latter, at any rate at the beginning of the war, was defending work defined as skilled in terms of apprenticeship requirements, which was universally acknowledged as 'men's work'.[55] The dividing line between men's and women's work in the semi-skilled and unskilled categories with which the general unions dealt was far less clear. But it was vital to them that women war workers should be classified as dilutees temporarily guarding men's jobs and should be paid at men's rates, since the alternative was that they would, in Jones' words, 'cheapen' these jobs and take them for the 'whole of the future'. However, the TGWU rapidly came up against the claim by employers that women war workers on unskilled or semi-skilled work were doing work which had been 'commonly performed by women in the industry' before the war. Such women had been written out of the agreement in Clause 3, under which the unions had no power to insist on payment of the man's rate or that these women were temporary. Clearly, if the employers' claim was not challenged, ever-increasing areas of work could be reclassified as 'women's work' and given to women at women's rates. Men would lose the rate they had negotiated and access to the jobs themselves and women would be denied the remuneration employers had been paying to men.

Not surprisingly in view of the threat to male workers embodied in Clause 3, its interpretation was the subject of close local negotiations from the start. One place in which discussions took place was Coventry, where conferences were held between the local branches of the TGWU and the Engineering Employers' Federation in 1940 and 1942 on the subject of the appropriate gender label for various unskilled and semi-skilled jobs. They included jobs as diverse as machine-shop labouring, store-keeping, inspection, work on capstan lathes, Lister truck driving and making body cores in the foundry. The main issue was whether or not these jobs were commonly performed by women in the industry and in the course of negotiations the employers put forward two criteria, the national picture and women's competence, to establish whether this was so.[56]

An example of one of the non-skilled types of work under dispute was machine-shop labouring. The job involved cleaning the floor and the base of the machines in the workshop, including collecting swarf, that is greasy grindings and metal shavings. Using the criterion of the national picture, the union contributed the view that 'scrubbing the floors is a man's job normally' but that 'you might find in Scotland . . . or here and there at small firms, a female on the same class of work . . . but we do submit it is not a common practice in the industry'. One of the employers' representatives promptly retreated from the principle of the national picture. 'It is very difficult to specify and say that a particular job is not commonly performed by women in the industry . . . all these cases have to be considered on the facts of the individual job.' Confusion reigned at the conference as other employers threw in 'the facts of the individual job' of scrubbing floors in their own factories. 'Personally, I should say that is a man's job all right', said the Chairman. 'We use men for office cleaning,' contributed another employer, but for that work the Chairman said, 'We have always used women, just in the same way as charwomen.' 'We have women attached to various sections, who sweep up and clean the place generally,' said a third employer, speaking of the machine shops as well as the offices. Employment practice was obviously so varied that there was no clear local picture, let alone a national one. The union representatives complained that this confusion led to some gross injustices. For instance, it was alleged that some Coventry employers initially assumed that, because of practice in their own factory, a job like sweeping up was a man's job and put women substitutes on the full male rates. Then, on discovering that in other factories it was regarded as women's work, they shifted to the women's rate, despite the fact that this meant a reduction in pay for the women.[57]

The union men believed that the employers were learning fast how to paint the 'national picture' to suit themselves. For example, although they admitted that women were not employed on foundry work like core-making in Coventry, they stated that 'it is quite common practice up and down the country to employ women core-makers', so the substitution was not subject to Clause 6 of the dilution agreement under which it would have been paid at the male rate.[58] The TGWU grievance was that whenever the union applied for the operation of Clause 6 in the case of a woman replacing a man on a job in Coventry, 'we are simply told it is common in the industry' for a woman to do that job and consequently the agreement appeared to them 'a mere scrap of paper' offering no protection to men. Union concern at the local conferences, it should be noted, was not primarily about justice to women, but that the union strength through which women had been excluded

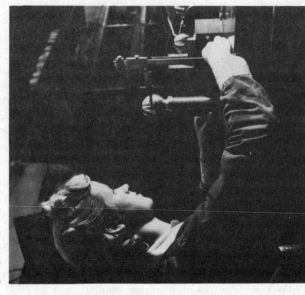

Figure 7.1: Welder at LNER Lowestoft Works, April 1942. Note the supervision.

Figure 7.2: Inspector examining high-precision machine parts with a Vernier height gauge and a Johanssen slip gauge.

Figure 7.3: Capstan operator producing primers for 25-pounder shells. Note the swarf all over the machine. It was the job of the machine shop labourer to clean this up.

Courtesy of the Imperial War Museum.

Figure 7.4: Making large cores for a diesel crank case.

Courtesy of the Imperial War Museum.

from certain jobs in Coventry would be undermined by employers using the principle of the 'national picture' to take advantage of union weakness elsewhere for the purpose of reclassifying work.[59] Clause 3b of the agreement supposedly prevented such a development, since it stipulated that a record should be kept of women on work nationally regarded as women's work, in factories where it had not been 'commonly performed' by women before the war and that they should be regarded as temporary. But the Coventry conferences indicate that this was seen as devoid of any power of protecting men.

Figures 7.1, 7.2, 7.3 and 7.4 illustrate types of work whose gender identity was disputed. Employers claimed that it was 'commonly performed by women in the industry' and trade unionists that it was 'men's work'.

When the principle of women's competence was applied, some trade unionists felt even more strongly that employers manipulated the evidence to suit themselves. A typical case discussed at one of the Coventry conferences was that of inspection. In trying to draw a line between men's and women's inspection work, one trade unionist, Gibson, stated, 'You can get work that is difficult although it is light.' 'Yes, I know,' replied the Chairman calmly, 'You have cases where you put men on.' To employers it was axiomatic that women would be given nothing but the simplest as well as the lightest of jobs. Gibson, however, disputed that this was happening. Women were being used on 'very important work', 'on which Verniers are used and depth and height gauges', and were being paid the woman's rate. The reply was that 'it has always been the practice to use women inspectors on work coming within their competence'.[60]

Union negotiator Jones saw the danger to men in this line of thinking, according to which women were basically incompetent, so that any work coming within their competence must be inferior to that done by men and should therefore be classified as women's work. Jones argued that the nature of the work and the ability of the worker were no use as criteria for the sexual division of labour. Thus the argument of his fellow trade unionist that work like sweeping up 'round broaching machines, for instance where there is oil on the floor . . . is hard work for a man, let alone a woman' was irrelevant to the question of whether it was men's or women's work.

Even the question of hard work does not arise. We might not classify some of the jobs the men were on, sweeping up the floors and all the rest of it, as hard jobs, but they were definitely men's jobs. Again we can confuse the capacity of a woman to do a job and what is common practice in the industry.

Jones wanted a general agreement between union and management on the classification of work by gender, based on the union view of what was customary, which was that 'it is not a common practice generally speaking for women to be employed in aircraft and engineering except on work of a very light kind, and we would like that to be kind of generally agreed on both sides'.[61]

Of course the employers would agree to no such sweeping statement, insisting that it was common practice to employ women in diverse ways in engineering. All the same most employers adhered stubbornly to the idea that none of the work women did in engineering demanded more than limited competence. When women were doing semi-skilled work which was indisputably commonly performed by men, such as driving Lister trucks, they resorted to the idea that women were less versatile than men to justify not raising their pay to the full male rate. In the case of driving it was claimed that by virtue of being women they could not do as much maintenance on the vehicle as men could. When this kind of argument was inappropriate employers could always fall back on the idea that women needed 'special assistance'. For example, one firm refused to pay women foundry workers as much as men on the grounds that the firm 'had to procure very much smaller wheelbarrows than the men use' to enable the women to carry two-hundredweight loads. They claimed that this proved that women could not wheel as much as men, though of course it ignored the fact that women simply made more journeys with their smaller barrows. In such cases the TGWU protested that men's competence was being unrealistically appraised. The good all-round man capable of doing any maintenance and lifting any weights alone was 'only to be found in heaven'. The employers however continued to deny that the average woman could be as good as the average man and insisted that women belonged in an inferior category of workers.[62]

Women's forte was seen, as always, to be simple repetitive work 'which necessitated no acquired skill, but rather a capacity for doing the same job, day in, day out'. It was of course assumed that women's limited capabilities rendered them tolerant of boredom and made them ideally suited to such work, rather than that changes in the production process made work boring and that women did it for economic reasons. 'Light fingering work' was often bracketed with repetition work as if it, too, 'came naturally' to women and demanded no skill.[63] For example, women were supposed to make natural welders because it was 'like knitting' at which all women were presumed to excel (though the letters of women welders collected by M-O show that welding was rather more dangerous than knitting). Women were also meant to be good at using precision instruments, at stamping and at electrical engineering, because they all required a delicate touch, though these jobs were practically never regarded as skilled when women did them.[64] This angered some women trade unionists, such as Florence Hancock, who observed the vicious circle in which women were trapped. Fine engineering work was given to them because they were better at it than men, but it was placed outside the male skill categories and was paid at less than the male labourer's rate, since, because women did it, it was classified as 'women's work'.[65]

The struggle over classification contined throughout the war, with the employers trying hard to classify the work women did as women's work and the general unions doing their best to ensure that as many categories of work as possible were paid as men's work. The official historian writes that the unions had some success, but nevertheless in September 1942 three-quarters of the women workers in engineering 'came under the women's schedule as performing women's work'.[66]

Since it was in employer's interests to reinforce the idea of women's incompetence and inferiority as workers, it was in general seen as pointless to give women more than superficial training. The MOL led the way in June 1940:

> We are not contemplating any large scale government training of women for munition work since they will be employed in the main on repetition work and such training can be given better by employers than in special institutes run by the Government.[67]

Many employers agreed, and there were complaints in the *Engineer* that the government was wasting time and money when early in 1941 the MOL decided to reverse its policy and admit women to its training centres, in the interests of recruitment.[68] However, there was nothing to compel employers to deploy trained women appropriately and extrainees often complained that they were given dead-end jobs in the works for which their training was irrelevant.[69] Others complained that the training was not worthy of the name, especially after January 1942 when the government courses were cut from 16 to 8 weeks and the number of centres was reduced. The emphasis henceforth was on introducing women to a 'time-table life' and making them 'machine conscious' but the purpose of training was overtly not 'to make these people into engineers'.[70] The astounded praise heaped upon those rare women who did beat their way through prejudice and restriction to become skilled toolsetters or fitters (who were possibly more common in the women's services than in industry) emphasised that they were the exceptions who proved the rule.[71]

The unhelpful attitude of many skilled men, who as we have seen were often disinclined to give women adequate shop-floor training, coupled with expectations that women would not be competent and the monotonous work they were frequently given to do, must have made it difficult for women not to behave in such a way as to confirm the stereotype being used to disadvantage them. Many detailed descriptions of wartime workplaces portray women workers as cheeky, lazy, carefree 'girls' flirting with chargehands and foremen and exploiting every opportunity to avoid working.[72] The image is stronger, however, the less complex and interesting the work. For example, at one factory, women repeating a single operation at noisy machines on separate benches were more 'irresponsible' than women working together on the more exacting task of assembly.[73] At another, women who had been slack when 'dogging up', which involved repeatedly guiding long steel tubes through a vice, were transformed into enthusiastic and efficient workers in 'Gowshall's department' where they worked as a team, threading concentric tubes together.[74] This suggests that it was not gender but the labour process that determined women's responses to work, which were themselves, of course, human responses and therefore not homogeneous.

Employment practice, however, ignored these distinctions. It was economically convenient to assume that the patterns of behaviour women displayed on the most simplified work were intrinsic to the sex as a whole and hence that women were innately suited to unskilled work alone. It justified the separate 'women's schedule' of wages agreed between the Engineering Employers' Federation and the general unions, under which women's work was paid at a national minimum time-rate which was, throughout the war, significantly lower than the male labourer's rate. In May 1940 it was 35s compared with the male minimum rate of 57s and, though the women's rate rose during the war to 56s in 1944, it was still well behind the 75s 6d minimum now paid to men.[75] The convergence of women's low minimum rates with two other factors discussed earlier, namely that three-quarters of women were classified as doing women's work and that women had to budget their time differently from men, because of the unbreached convention that they alone were responsible for domestic work, ensured that women's average industrial earnings rose at the most to 53 per cent of men's during the war. (See Table B9.)

The evidence reviewed here suggests that the economic convenience to employers of describing the work women did as non-skilled, women's work was fused to the assumption that women were inherently lacking in skill, in such a way as to create a powerful set of ideas about work and gender that was hostile to the interests of workers of both sexes, since men lost out by the downgrading of work and women suffered from the low rates of pay. However, the male leaders of the general unions were so enmeshed in patriarchy, with its advantages to them of a relatively privileged position at work and a dependent domestic worker at home, that they reacted defensively. They devoted their efforts to attaching the label 'men's work' to the work women did, so that it would come under the dilution agreement by which they did it on a temporary basis and would not slip into the category 'women's work', out of men's reach. This is not to say that the general unions did not deliver substantial wage increases to women. Reclassification of the work a woman was doing as men's work involved a sizeable increment and the general unions were under pressure from their women members to raise the women's basic rate too. Nevertheless they consistently negotiated separate rises for men and women which perpetuated the gender-based differential.[76] Most importantly they did not tackle the fundamental question of the justice and wisdom of a separate category of work for women paid on the basis of a women's wages schedule.[77]

The dual classification not only divided men from women. It divided women from each other, since those on 'women's work' earned less than others in the same workplace whose work was deemed 'men's work'. The patent injustice when women worked the same hours side by side at similar machines led to bitter and confused comparisons of wage packets among women themselves.[78] To avoid the unrest to which this gave rise, the management of Royal Ordnance Factories gave up trying to classify different types of work by gender and operated the so-called 'group system' which in effect meant that rates of pay were related to the wages schedule of whichever sex was in the majority in the factory. This itself emphasises the artificiality of gender labels. As Robinson, an administrator of ROFs, explained to the Royal Commission on Equal Pay in 1945, 'they found this business of sorting out men's work from women's work quite impossible'. Patriarchy was by no means undermined of course, since the system meant that whole factories were sex-typed and in addition the minority of men within those deemed to be on women's work were not expected to work at women's rates. Robinson made the point succinctly: 'The men in the filling factories get the men's rate; you could not put them down.'[79]

There were, however, some occasions when women collectively refused to be classified as inferior workers and tried to insist on their rights to the same remuneration as men. Strikes or threats of strikes occurred for example at a Bristol engineering factory, at the Rolls-Royce Merlin engine plant at Hillington near Glasgow in 1943 and at other factories on Clydeside subsequently. They had in common the fact that women replaced men and received lower rates for the same work. Women at the Bristol engineering factory threatened to strike because they were so 'incensed' by the employers' refusal to pay them the men's rates. The employers justified themselves on the grounds that 'in other parts of the country women had been working these machines for many years before the war'. The TGWU negotiated a settlement for the women, but the result was not parity with men. The employers would not put anything in writing and all that the union managed to extract was an 'understanding' that the women would get 1d, then 2d, then 3d an hour above the women's rate after a certain number of weeks. Women were not admitted to the men's rate and the principle that this work was 'commonly performed by women in the industry' was not breached.[80]

The case of the Rolls-Royce plant at Hillington, near Glasgow, has become something of a cause célèbre and is often, erroneously, seen as a victory for the 'rate for the job'.[81] Women working there objected to receiving the women's rate when unskilled male workers who were as lacking in experience as they were and as newly recruited to the factory, which itself was brand new, received the male rate. The injustice became more glaring when, over time, many of these men were called up and their jobs were taken over by women, who were still paid the women's rate. Negotiations were complicated by the fact that the general unions and the AEU, which admitted women to its ranks in the course of the dispute, were competing over the recruitment of women and there was in addition both a strong Communist and a strong Catholic presence in the factory. During a year of inconclusive bargaining, frustration built up among the women and a strike was threatened in July 1943.[82] Following this a Court of Inquiry was set up, at which the AEU evoked the 'national picture' to claim that the greater part of the work done by women at Hillington was performed by men before the war. The employers' counter-claim was that in this case the national picture was irrelevant, because the machinery at Hillington had been purpose-built for the specific process of the production of Merlin engines and none like it existed elsewhere or had existed before the war, so there was no national picture by which to be guided. They used the idea that women had limited competence to justify applying the women's rate, claiming that the machinery had been 'specially simplified for operation by women'. This did not of course explain why men on it received the men's rate. The Court of Inquiry, under Lord Wark, recommended a system of grading for this new work. Rates of pay in the higher grades were to be related to skilled men's rates and at the bottom of women's rates.[83] The unions negotiated a settlement for Hillington on this basis. The women, however, were not satisfied because they believed that 80 per cent of them would still be on the lowest women's rate. They struck in October 1943 for a week, taking out with them most of the men in the plant.[84]

Eventually an agreement was reached in which each machine was mentioned by name. However, it was not, as has sometimes been proclaimed, a victory for the removal of sex discrimination in remuneration. The rate for the job on each machine was classified in relation to the sex-related grades proposed by the Wark Inquiry.[85] The support of men for the Hillington women was not free from patriarchal concern either. There was much wavering by AEU and TGWU shop stewards and even women's most stalwart supporters, members of the Clyde Workers' Committee, who actually called the workers out, concluded their broadsheet on the strike, entitled 'A Message to All Clydeside Workers', with the words, 'Rolls Royce workers are determined to achieve their demands and in doing so realise that they are defending the wages of their husbands, brothers and sweethearts and other workers in the armed forces.'[86] Women's right as fellow workers to equal pay was not on the male agenda.

Further research will probably reveal more occasions on which women workers tried to insist on parity with men, especially in view of authoritative wartime statements to the effect that 'Disputes relating exclusively to the wages of women and girls are proportionately more prone to result in strike action than where men are concerned.' The explanation offered by the MOL official who wrote this was that women had 'less experience of trade unionism and factory discipline' than men. In fact the weekly reports of industrial commissioners to the MOL Industrial Relations Department suggest that women were goaded into action by the numerous mysterious inequalities they experienced in things like merit allowances, output bonuses and holiday pay, as well as basic wages.[87] Their dependence on the male-dominated unions to negotiate for them or support strike action, however, made their chances of removing anomalies slim.

The Hillington strike did, however, mark a new stage of union activity on the remuneration of men and women. Women in the movement increased their pressure on the male leadership. Between them the TUC women's conferences held in 1944 and 1945 passed ten resolutions demanding 'equal pay for equal work' and higher rates for 'women's work', compared with just one in 1943.[88] Throughout 1945 the general unions pushed for the application of a grading scheme to the engineering industry nationally and persuaded the AEU to drop the opposition it had previously maintained and to consider grading sympathetically. The unions were still not united, however, and the reasons for their differences on the subject of grading are indicative of their preoccupation with protecting men and of the very limited sense in which they espoused women's equality at work.

The general unions, which had for a long time accepted a separate category of women's work and which continued to do so, pushed for a scheme in which some grades were related to women's rates and others to men's, like the Wark proposal.[89] Under this scheme, therefore, the sex of the worker determined the grades of work which he or she might do, though within this division the skill possessed by the worker determined the grade of work actually allocated. Such a scheme did not remove the danger to the unions embodied in the principle that some work was 'commonly performed' by women, which as we have seen gave employers the opportunity to redefine work done by men as women's work and attach to it lower rates of pay. However, as long as the unions maintained control through collective bargaining of job evaluation and decisions about the allocation of grades, they could maintain their resistance to downgrading. In addition their scheme was popular because it had immediate material advantages for both men and women. It would protect men in the higher grades of work from female competition and peg them to higher rates than they were currently receiving and it would bring some women immediate pay rises, since, instead of a single category 'women's work' tied to the women's wages schedule, there were several women's grades, between which there were pay differentials. The engineering employers provisionally agreed such a scheme with the general unions as early as December 1942, but they would not implement it without the AEU's support.[90]

The skilled union, however, rejected it because the gender division tied some grades to what it described as a 'discriminating level' (i.e. the woman's rate). The engineering shop stewards' newspaper, *New Propeller*, commented, 'It would appear that grading is now being pressed for by the employer, not because it helps to fix wage standards but because it helps to degrade skilled work and thus lowers wage rates.'[91] The AEU argued that a national grading scheme for engineering work must be tied to the men's rate alone, so from 1945 they included in their plans for a new wages structure the demand for a minimum for women not lower than the male labourer's basic rate. However, the employers rejected the abolition of the distinction between men's and women's rates and maintained their opposition to such a change throughout the 1940s and 1950s as if confirming the suspicions voiced in *New Propellor*.[92]

At face value it looks as though the AEU had at last come round to the wisdom of abolishing gender divisions at work and of admitting women to an equal place with men in engineering. However, the context in which the AEU first put forward the proposals is important. During the year 1944-5 AEU shop stewards were, as we have seen, actively enforcing the temporary status of women under the dilution agreement. In addition, Jack Tanner, President of the union, was predicting at the AEU women's conference that there would be few jobs for men after the war, let alone for women, and Alexander Ramsay, President of the British Employers' Confederation, was asserting on the Royal Commission on Equal Pay that no employer would take on a woman if he had to pay her the same as a man.[93]

The Royal Commission on Equal Pay, to which several references have already been made, was set up in 1944 after the defeat of the Coalition government on an amendment to the Education Bill which would have given equal pay to teachers, had it not been overturned when voted on again as an issue of confidence in the government. Even though the Commission was authorised only to 'examine', 'consider' and 'report' on the remuneration of men and women and not to make recommendations it constituted an opportunity for a thorough airing of the views of both employers and trade unionists.[94] The opinions of three of the four women on the panel of the Commission are also important. Though not self-declared feminists, Anne Loughlin, leader of the Tailors' and Garment-Makers' Union, Miss L.F. Nettlefold, a lawyer, and Janet Vaughan, a doctor of medicine, chose to make a stand against the majority of the Commission in the name of equality for women and submitted a Memorandum of Dissent to the *Report* of the Commission, published in 1946.

When giving evidence, both the AEU and the Trades Union Congress, which spoke for the unions as a whole, used egalitarian terms. The AEU argued that the classification of some work as women's work 'is a very unsatisfactory and almost meaningless definition, open to unlimited abuse', and claimed for women 'the right of every human being to a living wage, the right to a decent standard of living, the right to fair remuneration for highly productive and profitable labour'.[95] The TUC's position was that basic wage rates should be equal and the value of the work done should be the sole determinant of earnings. There was nothing to prove that in general women were less efficient than men and anyway new techniques were raising productivity regardless of sex. The recently introduced family allowance made it unnecessary to negotiate a 'breadwinner element' in men's wages and, if full employment was achieved after the war, as Labour promised, there would be jobs for all: 'We are asking for equal pay not for prohibitions,' said George Woodcock, head of the TUC's research department.[96]

The trade union evidence is suggestive of a shift towards the principle of equality between the sexes, at least as far as the union leadership was concerned. However, there were reservations in the union position, which, set in the context of union activity in the last years of the war and the current disagreements over grading, cast doubt on the idea of a sudden *volte face*.

Jack Tanner, President of the AEU, was uncertain, when pressed, about whether the union would really drop from negotiations the claim that men should be paid a 'breadwinner's wage' large enough to support a family. The AEU had no wish to lose the leverage in wage negotiations which was to be derived from the conventional expectation that men were, or were about to become, heads of households. Rather than dealing with the issue, Tanner insisted that women's wage rates should be as high as men's, on the grounds that this represented justice to women and that it would prevent women being employed at a lower rate in preference to men.[97] Though the emphasis given to the first point was new, the second had a long history inseparable from the union's hostility to the presence of women in engineering. The TUC, on the other hand, submitted a statement to the effect that women's work, defined as recognised areas in which women were 'superior' workers to men, should retain its gender label, in spite of the AEU objection to the term and all the dangers revealed during the war of agreeing that there were categories of work 'commonly performed' by women. The enduring patriarchalism in TUC thinking is also reflected in its justification of equal compensation for war injuries (achieved in 1943 by the persistence of parliamentary feminists). Rather than arguing for this as of right, the TUC put forward the view that, since a woman's chances of marriage or remarriage would be reduced by her injury, she could not be treated as a dependant in the award of compensation.[98]

The employers' representatives were adamant both that equal pay was undeserved by women and that it would be economically ruinous. They argued with as much conviction as at the end of the First World War that women had 'disabilities' which had 'to be taken into account in fixing the occupational rates for women as compared with those of men'.[99] In spite of contrary evidence from those women who had done skilled work during the war, women's competence was still deemed to be less than men's, both in terms of their physical capabilities and their versatility and ability to meet emergencies. These were seen as inherent characteristics, but environmental factors were viewed as equally immutable. They included women's limited training and experience, the restrictions on their working hours and duties, especially on night work, and their high rates of absenteeism, all of which were said to make them less valuable to employ. Above all, employers depicted women as having of necessity a prior orientation to marriage and the family which on the one hand meant that women were merely temporary workers in paid employment and on the other justified paying men more than women, since it was confidently asserted that men expected to assume a patriarchal role in a family within which wives and daughters were dependants.[100]

The *Report* of the Commission put forward the view that the value of men and women to employers was being equalised through factors such as technical changes, the constraints on men's availability as a result of collective bargaining and steps which reduced women's absenteeism, among which it named the 'provision of home help, industrial nurseries and other social services'.[101] But nevertheless on the whole the *Report* reflected the employers' opinion that at present the wage differential was justified. For example, it adopted the *prima facie* position that women must be less efficient, otherwise employers would not use men on the same processes when they had to pay them more.[102] Most importantly, the *Report* was emphatic that paid employment was but an incidental stage in women's lives because of their natural relationship to marriage, family and the home. It quoted the view of an economist, R.F. Harrod, that society required the level of women's wages to be lower than men's, 'to secure that motherhood as a vocation is not too unattractive financially compared with work in the professions, industry or trade'. And it was emphatic that the patriarchal duties of men required them to be paid more than women. Men had to 'prepare for and to assume the moral responsibility backed as that is by the sanction of the law, for founding and maintaining a family group'.[103]

The women dissenters objected to some of the *Report*'s main points. They argued that its *prima facie* position on efficiency ignored other factors which determined the distribution of women in the workforce, notably protectionist union behaviour, and they were scathing about Harrod's statement on the relative financial attractions of motherhood and paid work. They commented that, since elsewhere the Commission suggested that equal pay would have the effect of excluding women from work, the *Report* ought to advocate it in order that all women would be driven into matrimony.[104] However the three dissenters did not make a radical attack on the Report's assumptions about women as a sex and in fact subscribed to the views that women as a group were less efficient and adaptable than men and that women's lives were and would continue to be dominated by the 'natural and traditional sphere of women's work, housekeeping and the care of children'.[105] Their defence was of those women whose life histories were different from the majority. This minority did not marry, they stayed at work throughout their lives, they wished to acquire training and promotion, they were not absentee and they had to support themselves and often dependent relatives. The thrust of the arguments of the 'dissenters' was that these women should not be penalised by the behaviour of the majority. Though not directly representing any one women's interest group, they reflected the views, essentially, of the single women who had spearheaded the pre-war campaign for equal pay in the civil service, local government and teaching. Their arguments could not encompass women whose relationship to work and to home gave rise to characteristics which conformed to the employers' image of the 'disabled' woman worker, but as a result they failed to attack the validity of gender differences as a whole and overlooked the permanent wartime changes in women's work patterns: paid work would no longer be a mere 'incidental stage' in women's lives now that an increasingly large proportion of women both married and returned to work after marriage, remaining there into their fifties.[106]

The *Report* of the Royal Commission did imply, however, that it would be appropriate for women in the 'common classes' of the civil service to receive the same rate as men on the same work.[107] Even though the 'dissenters' demanded a wider application of equal pay, the interests they represented were appeased by this endorsement of a

long-standing demand and following the war the TUC Women's
Advisory Committee devoted considerable efforts to securing its implementation. It was however rebuffed by the Labour government of
1945–50, whose members asserted that equal pay would have in-
flationary tendencies. The Women's Advisory Committee on which sat
Anne Loughlin, one of the 'dissenters', succumbed in 1948 to the
pressure of the TUC General Council, on which sat George Woodcock,
to give up insistence of equal pay and endorse the government's wage
freeze.[108]

The dominance of the interests of the 'committed' single woman
worker in the women's trade union movement is indicated by the
WAC's plan for 'post-war resettlement', put before the TUC women's
conference in 1942. Married women were to be encouraged to leave
work by the offer of compensation, in the form of their wartime
national insurance contributions. If they wished 'to continue in gainful
employment' they might apply to a tribunal 'to substantiate their claim
to employment', but women working before the war were to have
priority in job reinstatement.[109] However, this plan was rejected by the
conference, a sign both of a shift within trade union membership and of
the determination of many women, married as well as single, to remain
in paid work after the war. The WAC was forced to send out a special
memorandum reassuring women that it supported the right to employment of women who had not worked before the war, but who wanted
to continue to do so after the war. In 1943 it put a revised plan before
the conference, emphasising that 'there must be no discrimination'
between women, but still insisting that 'women who were wage earners
in the pre-war period and who were transferred, directed, conscripted
or who volunteered for any form of war service, should, when released,
be given the first opportunity of employment'. Further, it retained a
paragraph suggesting that women 'who do not desire to remain in, or
resume, gainful employment' should be compensated from the Unemployment Insurance Fund, though there was now no reference
specifically to married women or to the need for a special justification of their wish to work. The memorandum said of women in general
that, 'By having shared equally with men the tremendous task of producing for the needs of the war, they have an equal right to employment after the war', but the WAC was not prepared to make radical
proposals for the expansion of women's employment, referring only
to some very traditional women's occupations such as nursing, child
care, canteen work, public domestic service, and (its most adventurous
proposal) the development and production of articles for domestic use.

Though in its final form the memorandum asserted that 'the sex of the worker should not be a factor in determining payment which should be based on the work performed',[110] like the Memorandum of Dissent to the Royal Commision on Equal Pay, it did not address the issue of more fundamental relevance to women's remuneration, the patriarchal underpinnings of the segregation of women in industry.

Conclusion

The influx of women to war industries inevitably disturbed the division between men's and women's work. Women were allocated to all sorts of jobs, in and out of engineering, which had conventionally been done by men. They were admitted, however, under agreements which were operated to control and contain the change. In the interests of perpetuating a 'cheap' workforce, employers insisted that women could only receive a male rate if they did 'men's work' unaided, while in the interests of retaining relatively privileged jobs trade unionists demanded that women dilutees should be temporary and that the work they had done should be restored to men after the war. Employers tried to expand the areas of sex-stereotyped work created by the process of substitution which had been taking place between the wars and trade unionists tried to resist this reclassification. Underlying the conflict between the opposed interests of employers and trade unionists over the place of women at work was a fundamental assumption made explicit in the case of employers but common to both: women were first and foremost the wives, mothers and dependants of men and women did not therefore have the same rights of remuneration for or access to work as men.

The war did little to shake this conviction, though it did expose to male trade unionists its contradictions as far as they were concerned. The presence of women in the workforce at lower rates than men constituted an irresistible temptation to employers seeking economies in their wages bills to label any work women could do 'women's work', allegedly inferior to men's work and thereby effectively debarred to men. Under such conditions women would always constitute a 'danger' to men unless they were removed entirely from the workforce, as many AEU shop stewards would have liked them to have been removed from engineering. Such a disappearance was accomplished almost completely at the end of the war in certain sectors where the skilled unions were extremely strong, for instance in shipbuilding, foundry work, printing, sheet-metal work and toolmaking. But it was highly unlikely to occur throughout industry. Women like men were constrained for reasons of survival to enter the labour market. Not all women succumbed to the magnetic force of marriage and, if they did, in general the wages paid to men, which also varied hugely between grades of skill and occupations, may not, even at the end of the war, and even with the addition of the Family Allowance for second and subsequent childrenn, have added up on average to a 'family wage'. Employers were only too keen to employ women especially on processes which had undergone technical change, wherever the unions permitted it, in the conditions of 'production drive' and continued labour shortage after the war. In the absence of a grading agreement in engineering, the wartime dilution agreements remained in force, so the same process of 'gender restructuring' which had been taking place during the war could continue after it. In short, even in the 1940s men in general did not earn enough to keep a dependent unpaid domestic servant at home, but by refusing her equal rights to skill, status and remuneration at work, both she and men themselves suffered, women from double exploitation as workers and as women, and men, ultimately, from job loss.

The arguments of union leaders at the Royal Commission on Equal Pay betoken some recognition of what was in essence a contradiction between capitalism and patriarchy. Yet the solutions proposed, such as the rival grading schemes of the skilled and general unions, followed by the ready capitulation of the trade union leadership, including women leaders, to the pressures of the Labour government on the issue of equal pay, in the context of the behaviour of men on the shop-floor towards dilutees at the end of the war, do not suggest that recognition led to anything more profound than new strategies by which to live with the contradictions.

Notes

1. Inman (1957), p. 80.
2. *Engineer*, 25 April 1941; *Economist*, 29 November 1941.
3. Scott (1944), pp. 7–8; Bernard Darwin, *War on the Line: The Story of the Southern Railway in War-Time* (The Southern Railway Co., London, 1946), p. 180.
4. RCEP, *Report* (1946), p. 192.
5. Sergeant Theresa Wallace, quoted by Scott (1944), pp. 38–9; Hooks (1944), p. 24.
6. Inman (1957), p. 80.
7. See C. Hakim, 'Sexual Divisions Within the Labour Force: Occupational Segregation', *Department of Employment Gazette*, November 1978.

8. TUC Pamphlets and Leaflets, 1942/7 and 1944/18; Hooks (1944), p. 29; RCEP (1946), p. 194; Darwin (1946), p. 173.

9. TUC Pamphlets and Leaflets, 1944/18, Appendix 1.

10. *Engineer*, 31 May 1940; Inman (1957), pp. 441-2.

11. Bullock (1967), pp. 27-9.

12. *Engineer*, 2 February 1940.

13. J.T. Murphy, *Victory Production! A Personal Account of Seventeen Months Spent as a Worker in an Engineering and an Aircraft Factory; with a Criticism of Our Present Methods of Production and a Plan for Its Reorganisation* (John Lane, The Bodley Head, London, 1942), p. 45.

14. M-OA, Topic Collection, 'Industry', 1941-7, Box 140, Tube Report, p. 15.

15. Ibid., p. 18.

16. For example the AEU demanded the removal of all women workers from skilled work in Coventry in June–July 1940 (E. and R. Frow, *Engineering Struggles* (Working Class Movement Library, Manchester, 1982), p. 155); the NUR objected to women becoming porters in Februrary 1941 (PRO Lab 10/367); skilled workers in a Southport tank and munitions factory objected to the introduction of women in August 1941, (M-OA, Topic Collection, 'Industry', 1941-7, Box 120); as did shipyard workers, boilermakers and steel tube manufacturers in Scotland, May–December 1942 (PRO Lab 10/363).

17. The Restoration of Pre-War Trade Practices Bill became law in February 1942. Its purpose was to return industry to pre-war 'rules, practices and customs' with regard to 'the classes of persons to be or not to be employed' and the 'conditions of employment, hours of work or working conditions' of any type of work. It was to apply 18 months after the end of the war unless unions and employers agreed to the modification of any of the practices concerned. CCA, BEVN 2/3, memo by E. Bevin, 3 February 1942.

18. Murphy (1942), p. 16.

19. Inman (1957), p. 80; Bullock (1967), pp. 61-2. See *Engineer*, 19 December 1941 and 11 September 1942 for classification of women's work in shipbuilding.

20. M-O (1942), pp. 167 and 123.

21. *Arms and the Men*, 19 October 1941, p. 7.

22. M-O (1943), p. 63.

23. M-OA, Topic Collection, 'Industry', 1941-7, Box 140, Tube Report, pp. 16-17.

24. White (1982), p. 16.

25. M-O (1943), pp. 63-73, and see discussion in P. Summerfield, 'Women Workers in the Second World War', *Capital and Class*, 1, 1977.

26. M-OA, Topic Collection, 'Industry', 1941-7, Box 140, Tube Report, p. 17; J.W. Williamson, *Recollections 1930-1945* (unpublished typescript, 1975), p. 85.

27. M-OA, Topic Collection, 'Industry', 1941-7, Box 140, Tube Report, p. 17; Select Committee on National Expenditure, 'Ninth Report', May 1942, para. 21.

28. M-OA, 'Diary of a Housewife', Bedford, 1942.

29. M-OA, Topic Collection, 'Industry', 1941-7, Box 140, Tube Report, p. 16; M-O (1942), p. 121.

30. M-O (1942), p. 123; MRC, MSS 66/1/1/2, 28 August 1940.

31. Croucher (1982), p. 298.

32. Ibid., p. 274, but Lewenhak (1977), gives a figure of 132,010 (p. 240).

33. White (1982), pp. 70-2; Murphy (1942), pp. 44-5. Some of the women interviewed by the author said they were more or less 'dragooned' into the union, e.g. Mrs MacD., Newcastle-upon-Tyne.

34. Goldsmith (1943), pp. 204-5.

35. E.g. Murphy (1942), p. 41; the women were 'abysmally ignorant of politics and trade unionism'; M-OA, Topic Collection, 'Industry', 1938–42, Box 143, Tirrell Report – English Electric, Bradford: the women 'are absolutely disinterested in any form of organisation or unionism'.

36. Contradicting the statement quoted in note 35, the Tirrell Report goes on to say that women at English Electric participated vigorously in works committees to get, for example, a redistribution of overtime hours. 'They will really vote for a delegate and really delegate their representative to ask for specific things.' Croucher suggests that issues linked to workplace conditions, such as ventilation, drew women into trade unionism since they were 'matters of specific interest to women' (p. 266). However, he himself does not quote any convincing evidence to suggest that such issues were more important to women than hours and pay, or that they were in fact specific to women rather than of general concern.

37. TUC Pamphlets and Leaflets, 1941/6.

38. TUC Pamphlets and Leaflets, 1943/16 and 1944/18.

39. Croucher (1982), pp. 280–1; P. Inman (1957), p. 357.

40. PRO Lab 10/475, 'Women Employed on Skilled Engineering Work', Ministry of Supply memo SS 5/342, 14 June 1944.

41. Croucher (1982), p. 279.

42. RCEP, Appendices to the *Minutes of Evidence* (1945), VI, Memorandum of Evidence by British Employers' Confederation, para. 19.

43. RCEP, Appendices to the *Minutes of Evidence* (1945), VIII, Memorandum of Evidence by AEU, para. 27.

44. RCEP, *Minutes of Evidence*, BEC, 20 July 1945, para. 2679.

45. Croucher (1982), p. 299.

46. RCEP, Appendices to the *Minutes of Evidence* (1945), VIII, Memorandum of Evidence by AEU, para. 33 and Appendix 6.

47. E.g. Croucher (1982), p. 297; Calder (1971), p. 658.

48. Frow (1982), pp. 195–6.

49. Inman (1957), pp. 270–1.

50. Sheila Tobias and Lisa Anderson, *What Really Happened to Rosie the Riveter? Demobilization and the Female Labour Force, 1944–47* (MSS Modular Publications Inc., Module 9, New York, 1973).

51. Croucher (1982), p. 297; Inman (1957), p. 201.

52. Croucher (1982), p. 299.

53. Inman (1957), p. 58.

54. MRC, MSS 66/1/1/2, proceedings in local conference between Coventry and District Engineering Employers' Association and Transport and General Workers' Union. 'Interpretation of Relaxation Agreement Relating to the Extended Employment of Women in the Engineering Industry', 28 August 1940.

55. Inman (1957), p. 356.

56. See note 54 and MRC MSS 66/1/1/6, proceedings in local conference between Coventry and District Engineering Employers' Association and Transport and General Workers' Union, 18 August 1942.

57. MRC MSS 66/1/1/2, 28 August 1940.

58. MRC MSS 66/1/1/6, 18 August 1942.

59. MRC MSS 66/1/1/2, 28 August 1940.

60. Ibid.

61. Ibid.

62. Ibid., and MSS 66/1/1/6.

63. *Engineer*, 7 and 14 July 1944.

64. Scott (1944), pp. 123, 39, 49; PRO Lab 26/61, 'Report on Short Brothers, Strood, Kent' by Miss Renny-Tailyour, Technical Officer, 17 October 1941;

M-OA, Topic Collection, 'Women in Wartime', Box 3, File F, letters from women welders, 1942. See also M.D. Cox, *British Women at War* (John Murray, London, 1941), pp. 63–5.

65. RCEP, *Minutes of Evidence*, 27 July 1945, paras. 2937–45.

66. Inman (1957), p. 354.

67. PRO Lab 26/59, Tribe to Riddelsdel, 11 June 1940.

68. Parker (1957), p. 285; *Engineer*, 3 January 1941, 28 March 1941, 4 April 1941. For MOL's reply see *Engineer*, 15 August 1941, summarising MOL leaflet, PL 92/1941.

69. Murphy (1942), p. 61; M-OA, Topic Collection, 'Women in Wartime', Box 3, File F, letters from women welders, 1942, especially Jenny and Amy.

70. M-OA, 'Diary of a Foreign Correspondent', Glasgow, 25 January 1942; M-O (1942), p. 114; *Engineer*, 24 April 1944.

71. E.g. *Engineer*, 24 April 1942.

72. See M-O (1943); Holden (1941); J.B. Priestley, *Daylight on Saturday* (Heinemann, London, 1943).

73. M-O (1943), pp. 26 and 56.

74. M-OA, Topic Collection, 'Industry', 1941–7, Box 140, Tube Report, pp. 3–4, 8 and 41.

75. Inman (1957), p. 354.

76. See Frow (1982), pp. 185–7 and Inman (1957), p. 354.

77. The MOS observed very explicitly that this was the case during the war in its evidence to the RCEP. See Inman (1957), p. 353, note 1.

78. Inman (1957), p. 358; M-OA, Topic Collection, 'Industry', 1941–7, Box 140, Tube Report, p. 46; Williamson (1975), p. 87.

79. RCEP, *Minutes of Evidence*, 27 July 1945, para. 3107. See Inman (1957), p. 359, on the group system.

80. RCEP, *Minutes of Evidence*, 27 July 1945, para. 2907 ff.

81. See Calder (1971), p. 466; Frow (1982), p. 189; R. Davies, *Women and Work* (Arrow, London, 1975), p. 96.

81. Croucher (1982), pp. 285–95.

83. 'Report by a Court of Inquiry Concerning a Dispute at an Engineering Undertaking in Scotland, 1943', Cmd. 6474.

84. Croucher (1982), p. 288.

85. Inman (1957), p. 366.

86. PRO Lab 10/281, pamphlet on Hillington Strike, 2 November 1943.

87. PRO Lab 10/281, 'Causes of Industrial Unrest' by H. Emerson, 3 November 1943; See, for example, PRO Lab 10/363, DCIC Scotland, weekly reports to MOL Industrial Relations Department.

88. TUC Pamphlets and Leaflets, 1944/1, 1944/18 and 1945/1.

89. Inman (1957), p. 364; Frow (1982), p. 187.

90. Inman (1957), pp. 363–4.

91. Quoted by Frow (1982), p. 187.

92. Inman (1957), pp. 366–7.

93. Tanner is quoted by Croucher (1982), p. 277; for Ramsay see RCEP, *Minutes of Evidence*, 20 July 1945, paras. 2858–9. See also AEU, report of the proceedings of the National Committee, 4 June–14 July 1945, p. 55, para. 27, where it is reported, 'Where there is necessity to reduce personnel . . . the employers accept the principle that the names of dilutees should first be submitted to the National Service Officer for removal.'

94. Smith (1981), pp. 670–1.

95. RCEP, *Minutes of Evidence*, Appendix xiii, Memorandum of Evidence submitted by the AEU, paras. 15 and 2.

96. RCEP, *Minutes of Evidence*, 27 July 1945, para. 2930.

97. RCEP, *Minutes of Evidence*, 3 August 1945, paras. 3406–12 and 3380.

98. RCEP, *Minutes of Evidence*, 27 July 1945, paras. 2985, 3119–20 and Appendix vii, para. 41; Lewenhak (1977), p. 238.

99. RCEP, *Minutes of Evidence*, 20 July 1945, paras. 2874 ff.

100. Ibid., see especially paras. 2806 and 2858–9.

101. RCEP, *Report* (1946), pp. 113–14, para. 352.

102. Ibid., p. 111, para. 345.

103. Ibid., p. 119, para. 366, and p. 117, para. 362.

104. RCEP, *Report*, Memorandum of Dissent, p. 189, para. 9.

105. Ibid., p. 188, para. 6.

106. For documentation of these trends, see Social Survey, 'Women and Industry' by Geoffrey Thomas, March 1948, pp. 6–7.

107. RCEP, *Report*, pp. 22, 143. For a fuller treatment of the evidence presented to the Commission and its *Report*, see P. Summerfield, 'Women Workers in the Second World War' (University of Sussex D.Phil., 1982), pp. 320–52.

108. Lewenhak (1977), pp. 249–50.

109. TUC Pamphlets and Leaflets, 1942/7, Appendix 1, para. 5.

110. TUC Pamphlets and Leaflets, 1943/16, Appendix 1, 'Memorandum on Post-war Reconstruction − Women and Young Persons', especially paras. 7 and 4. See also TUC Pamphlets and Leaflets, 1944/1, Appendix III, on 'The Use of Redundant Woman Labour for Post-war Housing and in the Development of Articles for Domestic Use'.

8 CONCLUSION

It was suggested at the outset that entrenched assumptions about women's role profoundly constrained the extent of the change in it actually achieved during the Second World War in response to the demands of mobilisation. The five areas we have looked at, the process of mobilisation, the facilities for child care and for shopping, the adjustment of hours to counter the negative effects upon productivity of the double burden and the issue of dilution lead to the conclusion that the implementation of official policy during the war did little to alter but rather reinforced the unequal position of women in society.

This is quite contrary to the standard interpretation, by men, of the role of the Second World War in the social history of women.[1] Historians have been misled in part by claims made at the time and in part by the way that domesticity did become, so exceptionally, a public issue. Ideas for its reorganisation were canvassed and some collective provisions for it were made, wherein lay potential for profound change. Notably, the Minister with the main responsibility for mobilisation, Ernest Bevin, consistently favoured the collective management of domestic work both as a temporary method of coping with wartime exigencies and as a model for permanent change in the future. For instance, in January 1943 he stated his 'anxiety' about the effects of the intensity of the call-up of women on the 'standard of domestic life' and thus on morale and proposed a state-backed 'collective service' to 'ease the problem . . . by getting women from the unoccupied classes organised into groups to assist in homes where the mothers go out to work'. This he thought might become the germ of the 'post-war organisation of a proper domestic service'. But this initiative, which could have led to the socialisation of housework, was deflected. Instead of applying themselves to the creation in wartime of this kind of service, civil servants set up a committee to inquire into the post-war status of domestic service.[2] The potential of ideas such as Bevin's, which was, in a sense, a logical extension of capitalist pressures on the home, has attracted attention. Their containment by the forces of patriarchy has been less closely observed. Above all, what has been overlooked is that the great bulk of wartime domestic work was thrown back to the private sphere of a woman's own resources and those of her family, friends and neighbourhood, albeit parcelled in the rhetoric of the war effort.

This was particularly so of shopping, where the 'solutions' of leave and leagues clearly left the work with women themselves and 'collective feeding' made small inroads on the practice of women cooking 'the main meal of the day' for their families. It was also largely so of child care, in so far as the majority of women had to find their own private minders. But it would be wrong to see the situation as a 'frozen' one, in which the influences shaping women's lives stood in 1945 exactly as they had done in 1939. In retailing there was development of the non-competitive concept, in the expansion of the Co-operative Societies and changed practices within some other shops, even though the main-stream remained committed to individualistic notions of retailing 'free-dom' and even though the introduction of self-service in the 1950s represented a move by retailers to hand more of the work of shopping to the shopper.

Developments were also taking place in child care, though not in the direction usually assumed. Within the provision of wartime collec-tive child care, there were two opposing trends. One was towards universalisation and the other towards selectivity. Neither unambig-uously represented the opening or the closing of opportunities for permanent provision of nurseries. The first could be located firmly within the war effort as it was by most of those in the MOL and thus nurseries could be seen, even by those who wanted them to be univer-sally available, as impermanent. The second trend could be located in a longer history of the provision of day and residential nurseries for the poor, the sinful and the inadequate, which was now linked, partly in the light of the 'revelations' of evacuation about the health and behaviour of city children, to a movement for permanent nursery institutions to compensate for what was seen as the inadequate or mis-taken child rearing taking place in many more homes than just the poorest and most deprived. The latter trend (represented for instance by the Women's Group on Public Welfare, authors of *Our Towns*, 1943) found its way into the 1944 Education Act, with Churchill's blessing, where it connected with those representing the first trend (towards universality) who were arguing for permanent provision of nurseries.

Just what happened to the two trends after the war is a separate area of research. Nevertheless the post-war circumstances of production drive and labour shortage in some areas, of concern to raise the birth rate, and of measures to compensate for poverty (family allowances, free secondary education for all, social insurance, the National Health Service) ensured that there was not an immediate and complete defeat of collective child care provision. However, from the variety of wartime arrangements for collective child care, the model selected for development was not the all-hours, all-meals, all-comers day nursery. This was returned to the laps of the local authorities as a safety net for the children of the unfortunate and inadequate. It was the part-time, two- or three- to five-year-old nursery school which local education authorities now had the duty to provide 'to meet the needs of the population of their area'. The collection and interpretation of evidence of these needs was at the mercy of their discretion.[3] While the numbers of day nurseries shrank rapidly after the war, those of nursery schools remained stable but did not expand to keep pace with the rising birth rate and they were not as we have seen by any means tailored to the needs of women going out to work.[4]

Women were not expelled from paid work after the war. They were drawn into it along lines which followed the pre-war pattern. Thus decline continued in textiles and clothing and domestic service, but increased numbers of both men and women were employed in food, drink and tobacco, distribution, miscellaneous manufacturing, chemicals and other expanding industries. The number of women continued to increase, not just absolutely but also proportionately, in industries like engineering, vehicles, metals, gas, water and electricity and transport. Even though there was a fall from the high wartime proportions of women in these industries, women formed a larger part of their workforces in 1950 than they had done in 1939. For example, women represented 21 per cent of engineering workers in 1950, compared with 34 per cent in 1943 and 10 per cent in 1939. They comprised 12 per cent of the metal manufacturing workforce, compared with 22 per cent in 1943 and 6 per cent in 1939, and they formed 13 per cent of transport workers, compared with 20 per cent and 5 per cent (see Table B.7). Women also held on to their gains in national and local government, where the proportion was 38 per cent in 1948 compared with 46 per cent in 1943 and 17 per cent in 1939. A measure of the permanent expansion of women's employment during and after the war is given by C.E.V. Leser, who wrote that if there had been a return by 1948 to the status quo in 1939, 'the number of insured women would have fallen by more than 400,000. But in fact the number increased by about 350,000.'[5] The overall picture is that whereas women formed 29.5 per cent of the entire occupied population in 1921 and 29.8 per cent in 1931, this had risen to 30.8 per cent by 1951 and stood at 33.5 per cent in 1960. There is, however, nothing to suggest that this post-war expansion departed from the stratified pattern of women's

employment, which, due to the combined efforts of employers seeking cheap labour and trade unionists protecting men's jobs, was barely
disturbed during the war.[6]

The increase in the female participation rate came mainly from the
ranks of older, married women. In 1931, 10 per cent of married women
worked, but 22 per cent did so in 1951. They now represented 43 per
cent of all female employees, the same proportion as in 1943, and by
1958 this had risen to 52 per cent, contrasting dramatically with the
16 per cent of all women employees who were married in 1931. As far
as age was concerned, the pattern of a predominantly young female
workforce was changing. In 1931 41 per cent of women workers were
under 25, whereas in 1951 approximately 34 per cent were in this
age group and 27 per cent were 25-34 in 1931 compared with 21 per
cent in 1951.[7] The age profile of women workers became increasingly
balanced during the war, because of the expansion in the proportion
of older women. Like the change in the marital status of women
workers, this was a permanent legacy of war. (See Tables B.1 to B.4.)

If the experience of mobilising women for war shifted the assumptions and ideologies of policy-makers and employers about women and
work at all, it was in the direction of the idea that women could combine paid and domestic work without damage to industrial productivity
and without undermining the concept that their first responsibility was
to their homes. Part-time and shift arrangements of work, in particular, articulated with the opposing stresses within married women's
lives: the need to earn money to enlarge the family budget and the
need to do the work of caring for the family at home.[8] Its introduction
during the war demonstrates what a good 'deal' it was for industrial
employers, in terms of actual savings on bonuses, insurance, etc., and
of productivity. It could nevertheless be offered as a concession to
women for which, like wartime shopping leave, they should be grate-
ful.[9]

At the same time, part-time and other shift arrangements reinforced
the idea that women were inferior workers, an image whose resilience
we have seen in the way the wartime dilution agreements were operated
to continue the process of sectionalising work by gender rather than to
integrate women's and men's work and pay. Part-time work was offered
to women alone, not to both women and men, reinforcing the stereotyped sexual divisions both of paid work and of family responsibilities.
Women were not 'breadwinners', but were merely supplementing the
family income and they were thus casual workers rather than committed
to work in the way that men were supposed to be. All this was held

to justify the disadvantages women experienced in the workforce: the wage differential between men and women, the concept that training or promoting women was pointless and the idea that any work given to women must necessarily have the attributes ascribed to women themselves. The political defeat within the labour movement of the arguments of trade union leaders in 1945 for equal pay was by no means the whole story of the fate of that development. Though the positions taken on behalf of the AEU and the TUC by Tanner and Woodcock represent an apparent discontinuity with the previous approach of the trade union and labour movement, there were at least three things jeopardising the realisation of the demand for equal pay in practice. These were the unchanging adherence of industrial employers to the principle of the lower wage for women, the weight of prejudice and gender-based thinking within union membership and the limitations of the approach of leading trade union women to attaining parity at work between men and women. They all prejudiced the chances of attaining equal pay through workplace negotiations. This would have been so even if the Labour government of 1945–50 had not refused to give a lead by introducing equal pay in the public services and even if it had not muzzled the demand within the Labour Party and the TUC.

Thus the expansion of employment opportunities during and after the war did not mean that women were offered greater equality at work. In addition there were contradictory pressures on women's responses to these opportunities. During and after the war women were encouraged from some quarters, principally the MOL and some employers, to take the work that was offered, but from other quarters came the message that it was a married women's shame to work and that the right place for her was at home caring for her husband and children.[10] The contradictions were expressed in some of the wartime reports on women's expectations about their post-war roles. Demobilisation started for some women as early as 1943 and was from then onwards a focus of official interest and observation. Both M-O and the Wartime Social Survey collected evidence showing that large groups of women wanted to go on with their wartime jobs and that many other women felt that their decisions were dependent on the conditions of work in the post-war world. But disregarding these views, both bodies stated in their reports that an overwhelming majority of women saw marriage and the family as their post-war destinations. For instance, 25 per cent of women asked by M-O in 1944 said, 'women should be allowed to go on doing men's jobs', and 28 per cent said, 'depends on post-war conditions'. But M-O summed up with the statement:

The most general opinion seems to be that women will want to go back home, or take up the jobs which were usually considered suitable for women before the war, while awaiting marriage.[11]

In the event, the terms on which post-war child care was provided, the arguments in which much of the post-war campaign to increase the birth rate was couched, the ideologies of the 1950s about the psychological damage to children of married women 'leaving' the home to work and the images of domestic femininity stressed in the media under pressure of consumer marketing[12] constituted a barrage of discouragement to working women and reinforced the guilt and anxiety which inadequate provision for domestic work in any case thrust upon those who did undertake paid work.

The post-war pressures do not represent a reversal from the wartime situation, which we have seen was very definitely not one of unmixed encouragement to work, underpinned by the expansion of collective facilities to enable women to do so, for all that this has been part of a (feminist) mythology of the Second World War.[13] Rather they reinforced the lessons of the wartime mobilisation of women for industrial work in the context of limited provision for domestic work. In a 'welfare state', as in a 'warfare state', women who wanted or had to work found that public, collective provision for the work of the home was exceptional. The norm was that they would have to fall back on their own resources and those of their families and friends for help with the domestic work still firmly identified as the private and paramount responsibility of their gender.

It is evident, then, that the expectations that marriage, home and dependency were the appropriate conditions for women not only survived the challenges of war, but were throughout major determinants of policy towards women. The questions which arise from this conclusion, about the long-term implications of the Second World War for women, are thus rather different from those hitherto asked. The supposition that the mobilisation of women provoked the ready provision of universal collective facilities has led to the assumption that they were snatched away at the end of the war and to the search for an ideological 'backlash' and attempt to 'reconstruct' the family. While the idea that women were freed for paid work by the state during the war has been a source of inspiration to the women's movement, the idea that this freedom was lost has been a source of demoralisation because it appears that women 'returned home' without a fight. The evidence of heavy constraints on both collective provisions for domestic work during the war and women's participation in the workforce, resulting from the strength of patriarchal expectations among those with the most power over women's place in social relations, puts the post-war history of women into a different perspective. The question then becomes not one about why women failed to hold on to wartime gains, but one concerning what spaces for future change there were in the actual legacies of the war, such as the partial provision for child care under the 1944 Education Act, the changes in some quarters in retail practice, the increased numbers of women, particularly older married women, in paid work, especially part-time, and the inclusion on the political agenda of equal pay, if as a deferred item. In sum, the issue which needs exploration in the context of the social history of the 1940s and 1950s is what sort of change the redefinition of the double burden during and after the war did produce in women's lives. On the one hand, it may have trapped women more firmly within patriarchal relations at work and at home. On the other hand, it may in the long run have prompted women collectively both to attack inequalities at work and to challenge the sexual division of labour in the home.

Notes

1. E.g. Arthur Marwick, *Britain in the Century of Total War: War, Peace and Social Change 1900-1967* (Macmillan, London, 1968); Gordon Wright, *The Ordeal of Total War, 1939-1945* (Harper Torch Books, New York, 1968).

2. Churchill College Archive, BEVN 2/4, note dictated by the Minister on domestic help, 2 January 1943. See also ibid., note on domestic service, 10 September 1943; PRO Lab 8/860, appointment of Committee on Domestic Service: Standing Advisory Committee on Institutional Domestic Employment, 1943-5.

3. H.C. Dent, *The Education Act, 1944: Provisions, Regulations, Circulars, Later Acts* (University of London, London, 1968), pp. 12-17; Ministry of Health Circular 221/45 and Ministry of Education Circular 75, 'Nursery Provision for Children Under Five', 14 December 1945:

> The Ministers . . . are . . . of the opinion that, under normal peace-time conditions, the right policy to pursue would be positively to discourage mothers of children under two from going out to work; to make provision for children between two and five by way of nursery schools and nursery classes; and to regard day nurseries and daily guardians as supplements to meet the special needs . . . of children whose mothers are constrained by individual circumstances to go out to work or whose home conditions are in themselves unsatisfactory from the health point of view, or whose mothers are incapable for some good reason of undertaking the full care of their children.

4. Political and Economic Planning (PEP), *Planning*, No. 285, July 1948, 'Employment of Women', gives a figure of 44,000 places in 'residential or day

nurseries' in 1948 compared with 59,000 in 1943. See also T. Blackstone (1971), Table 5.9, p. 91: approximately 10% of three- and four-year-olds were accommodated in maintained nursery institutions in 1965, the same as the proportion in 1938.

5. C.E.V. Leser (1952), Tables 3, 4, 5 and p. 335.

6. See Hakim (1978); L. Mackie and P. Patullo, *Women at Work* (Tavistock, London, 1977); S. Walby, 'Gender and Unemployment', (University of Essex Ph.D., 1984).

7. Guy Routh, *Occupation and Pay in Great Britain 1906-60* (Cambridge University Press, Cambridge, 1965), pp. 44-7.

8. See especially PEP, *Planning*, No. 185, July 1948, p. 38: 'Arrangements for part-time work can do much to enable motherhood to be combined with employment without hurt either to the mother or to her children.' See also Social Survey, 'Women and Industry: An Inquiry into the Problem of Recruiting Women to Industry Carried Out for the Ministry of Labour and National Service', by Geoffrey Thomas, 1948, p. 6. He states that in 1947, 30 per cent of women aged 16-60 were in full-time and 9 per cent were in part-time civilian employment.

9. See North Tyneside, CDP, *North Shields: Women's Work*, Final Report, Vol. 5, (Newcastle-upon-Tyne Polytechnic, Newcastle, 1978), p. 39, for quotations from women who saw their employers as generous for making arrangements which enabled them to bear the double burden.

10. For a very thorough discussion see Denise Riley, 'The Free Mothers: Pronatalism and Working Mothers in Industry at the End of the Last War in Britain', *History Workshop*, 11, Spring 1981.

11. M-O, *The Journey Home* (John Murray, London, 1944), p. 64. See also: M-OA, File Report 2059, 'Will the Factory Girls Want to Stay Put or Go Home?', March 1944; Wartime Social Survey, 'Women at Work' (1944), quoted a minimum of 55 per cent and a maximum of 80 per cent of women who wanted to go on working after the war, the majority giving 'economic reasons', and 9 per cent 'may have to'. But the generalised statement of 'Women at Work' (p. iii) was 'If wages are good enough to enable a man to marry and support his wife at what she considers to be a reasonable standard of life . . . she will not, on the average, wish to work.'

12. See Riley (1979); Birmingham Feminist History Group, 'Feminism as Femininity in the 1950s?', *Feminist Review*, III, Autumn 1979; Cynthia L. White, *Women's Magazines 1693-1968* (Michael Joseph, London, 1970), especially Chapter 6.

13. Mitchell (1974); Friedan (1963); Long (1979).

APPENDIX A: EXTENDED EMPLOYMENT OF WOMEN AGREEMENT

Memorandum of Agreement between Engineering and Allied Employers'
National Federation and Amalgamated Engineering Union

*To Provide for the Temporary Relaxation of Existing Customs so as to
Permit, for the Period of the War, the Extended Employment of Women
in the Engineering Industry*

WHEREBY IT IS AGREED that additional women may be drafted into the
Industry for the purpose of manufacturing engineering products, with special
regard for increasing output and to meet war-time emergencies:

1. Women drafted into the Industry under the provisions of this Agreement
   shall be regarded as temporarily employed.
2. An agreed record shall be kept of all changes made under this Agreement.
3. (a) The provisions of this Agreement will not affect the employment of
   women workers engaged on work commonly performed by women in
   the Industry.
   (b) There shall be no objection to the extension of employment of women
   in establishments where women have not hitherto been employed on
   work commonly performed by women in the Industry, subject to the
   general undertaking contained in Clauses 1 and 2.
4. Women workers may be employed on suitable work hitherto performed by
   boys and youths under 21 years of age.
5. In the case of the extension of employment under Clauses 3(b) and 4, the
   National agreed scale of wages of women workers shall apply or the boys'
   and youths' schedule of wages shall be applied, whichever is the greater.
6. Women workers may be employed on work of a suitable character hitherto
   performed by adult male labour, subject to the following conditions:
   (a) Such women workers shall serve a probationary period of eight weeks
   at the women's national schedule of time rate and bonus.
   (b) At the end of the probationary period and for a further period of
   twelve weeks the women workers shall receive an increase as follows:
   (i) The basic rate shall be increased by one-third of the difference between the national women's schedule basic rate and the basic rate of
   the men they replace.
   (ii) The national women's schedule bonus shall be increased in the same
   way by one-third of the difference between that bonus and the
   national bonus appropriate to the men they replace.
   (c) At the end of the 20 weeks and for a further period of twelve weeks the
   women shall be paid:
   (i) A basic rate equal to 75 per cent. of the basic rate of the men replaced.
   (ii) A national bonus equal to 75 per cent. of the national bonus appropriate to the men replaced.
   (d) Thereafter:
   (i) In respect of women who are unable to carry out their work without additional supervision or assistance, the rate and bonus shall be

      negotiable and arranged according to the nature of the work and the ability displayed.

    (ii) Women, however, who are able to carry out the work of the men they replace without additional supervision or assistance shall, at the end of the 32 weeks, receive the basic rate and national bonus appropriate to the men they replace.

  (e) On payment by results the base rate and bonus paid shall be in accordance with Sub-Sections (a) to (d) of this Clause. When the work is carried out without additional supervision or assistance, the male workers' piece work price shall be given. When additional supervision or assistance is provided, the piece prices will be negotiable under the principles of Sub-Section (d)(i).

7. Notwithstanding anything herein provided, women who might enter employment fully qualified to perform without further training and without additional supervision or assistance work heretofore recognised as work done by male labour, shall be paid the rate and national bonus appropriate to the male labour they replace.

8. In the event of a question being raised in relation to the provision of this Agreement it shall be dealt with through the ordinary procedure for avoiding disputes, except that in the event of failure to agree locally the matter shall be dealt with expeditiously by a special central conference held in London.

      Signed on behalf of

          Engineering and Allied Employers' National Federation:

                G.E. BAILEY, *Vice-President*

                ALEXANDER RAMSAY, *Director*

                ALEX. C. LOW, *Secretary*

          Amalgamated Engineering Union:

                JACK TANNER, *President*

                B. GARDNER, *Assistant General Secretary*

22nd May 1940

Source: P. Inman, *Labour in the Munitions Industries* (HMSO, London, 1957), pp. 441–2. (Transcribed *verbatim*.)

APPENDIX B: WOMEN'S EMPLOYMENT STATISTICS

Table B.1   Percentage of Women in Total Occupied Population, 1921–60

Table B.2   Participation Rate of Women in Employment, 1921–51

Table B.3   Women Workers by Marital Status, 1931–51

Table B.4   Women Workers by Age, 1931–51

Table B.5   Pre-war Women Workers by Wartime Occupation, 1943

Table B.6   Women War Workers by Pre-war Occupation, 1943

Table B.7   Percentages of Women in the Insured Workforce in Certain Industries, 1923–50

Table B.8   Proportion of Women in the Different Sections of the Engineering Industry, 1939–45

Table B.9   Average Weekly Earnings of Manual Wage-earners with Women's Earnings as a Percentage of Men's, 1938–45

Table B.1: Percentage of Women in Total Occupied Population, 1921–60

$(\dfrac{\text{women}}{\text{men + women}}$ %)

1921	1931	1943	1951	1960
29.5	29.8	38.8[a]	30.8	33.5

Note: a. In civil employment.
Source: 1921, 1931, 1951, 1960: Guy Routh, *Occupation and Pay* (Cambridge University Press, Cambridge, 1965), Table 20; 1943: Central Statistical Office, *Statistical Digest of the War* (HMSO, London, 1951), Table 9.

Table B.2: Participation Rate of Women in Employment, 1921–51

$(\dfrac{\text{working women}}{\text{all women}}$ in each category, %)

	1921	1931	1945	1951
Single	68.1	71.6	—	73.07
Married	8.7	10.04	—	21.7
Widowed/divorced	25.6	21.2	—	21.06
All females 14–59	33.7	34.2	44.5[a]	34.7

Note: a. In civil employment.
Source: 1921, 1931, 1951: A.H. Halsey, *Trends in British Society Since 1900* (Macmillan, London, 1972), Table 4.7; 1945: Central Statistical Office (1951), Tables 9 and 3.

Table B.3: Women Workers by Marital Status, 1931–51 (%)

	1931	1943	1951
Single	77	49	50
Married	16	43	43
Widowed/divorced	7	7	7
	100	99[a]	100

Note: a. As in original.
Source: 1931: *Census*, 1931, Occupation Tables, Table 1; 1943: Wartime Social Survey, 'Women at Work' (Central Office of Information, 1944), p. 1; 1951: Routh (1965), p. 47.

Table B.4: Women Workers by Age, 1931–51 (%)

	1931	1943	1951
Under 24	41	27	34
25–34	27	31	21
35–44	16	26	21
45–59	16	16	24
	100	100	100

Source: 1931: *Census*, 1931, Occupation Tables, Table 3; 1943: WSS (1944), p. 1; 1951: Routh (1965), Table 22.

Table B.5: Pre-war Women Workers by Wartime Occupation, 1943 (i.e. Where Pre-war Women Workers Went to)

Wartime occupation	Pre-war occupation											
	Prof., admin. Cler. wkrs.	%	Machinists & assembly wkrs.	%	Distrib. wkrs. & waitresses	%	Labourers & domestic servants	%	Miscellaneous	%	Total sample	%
TOTAL	111	100	235	100	171	100	123	100	47	100	687	100
Prof. & admin. workers	8	7	–	–	2	1	–	–			10	2
Cler. workers & draughtswomen	45	40	5	2	17	10	7	6			74	11
Forewomen	11	10	7	3	9	5	3	2			30	4
Inspectors	7	6	23	10	9	5	7	6			46	7
Machine & tool operators	15	13	92	39	58	34	35	28			200	29
Assemblers & repet. workers	6	5	52	22	27	16	22	18			107	16
Labourers & packers	2	1	16	7	26	15	14	11			58	9
Distribution workers	5	4	12	5	2	1	5	4			24	3
Waitresses, barmaids, etc.	2	2	7	3	7	4	14	11			30	4
Transport workers	3	3	5	2	9	5	7	6			24	3
Miscellaneous	7	6	16	7	5	3	9	7	47	100	84	12

Source: Reworked from WSS (1944), Table 14, p. 9.

Table B.6: Women War Workers by Pre-war Occupation, 1943 (i.e. Where Women War Workers Came From)

Wartime occupation

Pre-war occupation	Prof. & admin. wkrs.		Cler. wkrs. & draughts-women		Fore-women		Inspec-tors		Machine & tool operators		Assem-blers & repet. wkrs.		Labourers & packers		Distrib. wkrs.		Waitresses, barmaids, etc.		Trans-port wkrs.		Miscel-laneous		Total	
		%		%		%		%		%		%		%		%		%		%		%		%
Prof., admin. & cler. wkrs.	8	80	45	61	11	37	7	15	15	8	6	6	2	3	5	21	2	7	3	13	7	8	111	16
Machinists & assembly wkrs.	—	—	5	7	7	23	23	50	92	46	52	49	16	28	12	50	7	23	5	21	16	19	235	34
Distrib. wkrs. & waitresses, etc.	2	20	17	23	9	30	9	20	58	29	27	25	26	45	2	8	7	23	9	37	5	6	171	25
Labourers & domestic servants	—	—	7	9	3	10	7	15	35	17	22	20	14	24	5	21	14	47	7	29	9	11	123	18
Miscel-laneous	—	—	—	—	—	—	—	—	—	—	—	—	—	—	—	—	—	—	—	—	47	56	47	7
Total	10	100	74	100	30	100	46	100	200	100	107	100	58	100	24	100	30	100	24	100	84	100	687	100

Note that (a) the women war workers represented here are only those in paid work before the war, (b) the sample is small and the percentages would be misleading if removed from the context of the overall picture and (c) the larger number of categories used for wartime than for pre-war occupation tends to diminish the sample and exaggerate the proportions.
Source: Reworked from WSS (1944), Table 14, p. 9.

Table B.7: Percentages of Women in the Total Insured Workforce in Certain Industries, 1923–50

Industry	1923	1939	1943	1948/50	
Clothing	65	70			70
Textiles	60	60			58
Pottery, earthenware	51	56		56	
Leather	30	38			38
Food, drink and tobacco	40	42			42
Distribution	40	40			48
Miscellaneous manufacturing	31	39			41
Miscellaneous metal industries	30	32	46	34	
Chemicals	25	27	52	31	
Commerce	35	35		38	
National and local government	9	17	46	38	
Engineering	6	10	34		21
Vehicles	9	9	34		14
Metal manufacture	5	6	22		12
Gas, water and electricity	4	5	17		9
Transport	4	5	20		13
Shipbuilding		2	9	3	

Source: Percentages for 1923, 1939 and 1948/50: C.E.V. Leser, 'Men and Women in Industry', *Economic Journal*, 1952, Tables III, IV, V; Percentages for 1943: G.M. Beck, *Survey of British Employment and Unemployment 1927–1945* (Oxford University Institute of Statistics, 1951), Table 41. Both authors used *Ministry of Labour Gazette* as their source. See originals for changes in insurance categories which influence the comparability of these figures.

Table B.8: Proportion of Women Employed in the Different Sections of the Engineering Industry, 1939–45

Industry	Women employed as % total labour force in mid-year						
	1939	1940	1941	1942	1943	1944	1945
Engineering, boiler-making, etc. (incl. marine eng.)	10.5	13.2	21.6	31.9	35.2	34.8	31.2
Marine engineering	2.1	2.5	4.8	9.1	14.7	15.8	12.9
Motor vehicles, cycle and aircraft mfr. and repair	9.5	13.0	23.0	31.9	36.6	36.5	31.8
Construction and repair of railway and other carriages	5.0	5.8	9.7	14.8	16.2	16.3	15.0
Electrical cables, apparatus, etc.	40.6	44.8	50.7	56.1	59.2	61.1	59.9
Scientific instruments, watches, clocks, etc.	37.0	40.6	42.8	46.1	48.4	49.9	50.1

Source: Inman (1957), p. 80.

Table B.9: Average Weekly Earnings of Manual Wage-earners with Women's
Earnings as a Percentage of Men's, 1938–45

Date	Adult men		Adult women		Women/Men %
	s	d	s	d	
October 1938	69	0	32	6	47.10
July 1940	89	0	38	11	43.73
July 1941	99	5	43	11	44.14
January 1942	102	0	47	6	46.57
July 1942	111	5	54	2	48.62
January 1943	113	9	58	6	51.43
July 1943	121	3	62	2	51.27
January 1944	123	8	63	9	51.55
July 1944	124	4	64	3	51.68
January 1945	119	3	63	2	52.97
July 1945	121	4	63	2	52.07

Source: Reworked from H.M.D. Parker, *Manpower* (HMSO, London, 1957),
Table XIV, p. 503. This data is from 'special inquiries made by the Ministry of
Labour and National Service'. The figures represent 'actual earnings in one week
of the months indicated, inclusive of payment of overtime, night-work, etc., and
of amounts earned on piece-work or other methods of payment by results, before
any deductions in respect of income-tax or of the workers' contributions to
statutory insurance schemes'. Not covered: agriculture, coal mining, railway
service, shipping service, dock labour, distribution, catering, entertainment,
commerce, domestic service.

BIBLIOGRAPHY

I Archive Materials

I am giving references in full, both so that other researchers can follow them up easily and to give the general reader an indication of the kinds of sources used.

Public Record Office

Cab 65/20	War Cabinet conclusions, 1941
Cab 67/9	War Cabinet memoranda, 1941
Cab 71/5	Lord President's Committee memoranda, 1941
Cab 78/2	'Manpower', 1941
Lab 8/108	Correspondence concerning the introduction of the 54-hour week and the speeding up of labour releases in the boot and shoe industry, November 1942
Lab 8/378	'Question of Rate of Wages and Recruitment of Women in the Munition Industries and Their Retention in These Industries', March 1941
Lab 8/387	'Special Recruitment for Liverpool Factory of D. Napier and Sons Ltd', February–March 1941
Lab 8/388	'Intensive Recruiting Campaign for the Auxiliary Territorial Service', June 1941
Lab 8/396	'Recruitment for the Women's Auxiliary Services', February 1941
Lab 8/408	'Employment of Women in Aerodrome Construction'
Lab 8/414	'Investigation Carried Out at Casual Wards on 3 and 4 June to Encourage Regular Employment', June 1941
Lab 8/464	'National Joint Council for Building Industry. Wartime Agreement on Employment of Women in Building Industry During Period of the War', 1941–2
Lab 8/470	'Transfer of Women from Retail Distributive Trades', July–August 1941
Lab 8/473	'Employment of Women in the Heavy Steel Trade', 1941–2
Lab 8/479	'Draft Employment of Women (Control of Engagement) Order. Proposals for Restricting Engagement of Women Within Certain Age Groups', 1941–2
Lab 8/492	'Withdrawal of Women from Less Essential Industries under National Service Acts and Registration for Employment Order', correspondence with Board of Trade, April 1942
Lab 8/634	Committee set up to consider the percentage of part-time women to be used in the engineering industry: 'Interim Report', October 1942–January 1943
Lab 8/703	'Development of Part-time and Spare-time Employment and Outwork', general policy, 1942–7
Lab 10/281	'Causes of Industrial Unrest', 3 November 1943
Lab 10/363	DCIC, Scotland, weekly reports to MOLNS Industrial Relations Department, 1942
Lab 10/475	Report of a dispute between the MOS and TGWU over wage rates of skilled women employed at ROF Radway Green, 1944
Lab 26/1	'Welfare Department Publicity', 1940–41

Lab 26/4   'Enquiry into absence from work', reports prepared by the Central
              Statistical Office, 1943–44, August 1945
Lab 26/57   'Provision for the Care of Married Women in Industry; Wartime
              Nurseries', general policy, 1940
Lab 26/58   'Provision for the Care of Children of Married Women in Industry;
              Wartime Nurseries', general policy, 1940–42
Lab 26/59   Deputation of women MPs to discuss the formation of an advisory
              committee for women's employment in wartime
Lab 26/60   'Shop Hours for War Workers', 1940–48
Lab 26/61   'Shopping Difficulties', 1941–43
Lab 26/63   Women's Services (Welfare and Amenities) Committee, 'Recruiting
              of Womanpower'
Lab 26/130   Meetings of the Women's Consultative Committee, 1941
Lab 26/131   'Industrial Efficiency and Absenteeism. Enquiry into Absence from
              Work', 1942–3
Lab 26/132   'Enquiry into Absence from Work'. Papers submitted to the Factory
              and Welfare Advisory Board, March 1945
Lab 26/133   'Provision for the Care of Children of Married Women in Industry;
              Wartime Nurseries', general policy, 1943–4, 1945–9
Lab 26/168   'Provision for the Care of Children of Married Women in Industry',
              wartime nurseries, 1945–9

Mass-Observation Archive, University of Sussex

Wartime Diaries. Especially those of the following women:
    Inspector of Taxes, Purley, Diary No. 5245
    Poultry Farmer's Wife, near Reading, No. 5268
    Ex-shopkeeper's Wife, Burnley, No. 5306
    Civil Servant, Morecambe, No. 5338
    Housewife, Barrow in Furness, No. 5353
    Secretary, Gateshead, No. 5296
    Foreign Correspondent, shipping firm, Glasgow, No. 5390
    Office Worker, London, No. 5443
    Housewife, Bedford, No. 5451

Replies to Directives. These were questions sent monthly to 2,000–3,000 volunteers, to which subjective replies were expected. Those concerned particularly
with women:
    March 1942, 'Wartime Difficulties'
    September 1942, 'Changes in the Position of Women'
    January 1944, 'Married Women and Work Post-war'
    March 1944, 'Shopping in Wartime'
    May 1944, 'Equal Pay'

Topic Collections. These are still being sorted. Up-to-date references for retrieval
are given in parentheses.
Town Box, Coventry, File 3708, 'War Work, Coventry, 1941' (Town and District
    Survey, TC 66/4/C-H)
Box 276. 'Children, Day Nurseries, 1941–2' (TC 19 (Day Nurseries 1941–2))
Topic Collection, 'Industry'
    Box 120, 1941–7
    Box 140, 1941–7
    Box 143, 1938–42
Topic Collection No. 4, 'Shopping' (TC 4)
    Box 3, 'Shops Survey, Ealing, Bolton, Chester, 1942'
    Box 4, 'Shops Survey, 1942'
    Box 5, 'Shopping General, 1939–51' (includes 'Washing Habits, 1939')
Topic Collection, 'Women in Wartime', Boxes 1, 2 and 3 (TC 32)

File Reports. These are numerous and tended to form the basis of M-O publications. Among the most interesting on women workers are:

    290 'Women in Wartime', July–December 1940
    615 'An Appeal to Women', March 1941
    625 'A Note on Womanpower', April 1941
    919 'Female Attitudes to Compulsion', October 1941
    952 'ATS Campaign with Appendix on Munitions Work', November 1941
    1098 'Diary of a Cotton Worker', February 1942
    1151 'The Demand for Day Nurseries', March 1942
    1163 'Women in Industry', March 1942
    1238 'Appeals to Women', May 1942
    1316 'The Women's War', June 1942
    1592 'Women's Opinions', February 1943
    1631 'Absenteeism and Industrial Morale', March 1943
    1970 'Women in Pubs', January 1944
    2059 'Will the Factory Girls Want to Stay Put or Go Home?', March 1944
    2179 'Women and the Vote', November 1944

Modern Records Centre, University of Warwick

MSS 66/1/1/2 Proceedings in local conference between Coventry and District Engineering Employers' Association and Transport and General Workers' Union. 'Interpretation of Relaxation Agreement Relating to the Extended Employment of Women in the Engineering Industry', August 1940
MSS 66/1/1/6 Proceedings in local conference between Coventry and District Engineering Employers' Association and Transport and General Workers' Union, August 1942
MSS 180/MRB/3/2/43 Minute of special meeting of the Regional Board Executive Committee, Birmingham, March 1942

Trades Union Congress: Pamphlets and Leaflets

1940/12 Report of the tenth annual conference of unions catering for women workers, 20 April 1940
1941/6 Report of the eleventh annual conference of unions catering for women workers, 19 April 1941
1942/7 Report of the twelfth annual conference of the unions catering for women workers, 25 April 1942
1943/10 'Part Time Women Workers. The Law Explained'
1943/16 Report of the thirteenth annual conference of unions catering for women workers, 17 April 1943
1944/18 Report of the fourteenth annual conference of unions catering for women workers, 17 and 28 October 1944
1945/11 Report of the fifteenth annual conference of unions catering for women workers, 12 and 13 October 1945

Churchill College Archive, Churchill College, Cambridge: Bevin Papers

Political papers
BEVN 2/2, 2/3, 2/4, 2/5, 2/12
Political correspondence
BEVN 3/1, 3/2, 3/3
General correspondence
BEVN 6/2, 6/5, 6/6

Enfield Rolling Mills Ltd, Brimsdown, Middlesex

Works Council Minute Books, January 1944–June 1945

Interviews with the Author

K.J., Coventry, 30 October 1977
S. MacD., Newcastle, 21 July 1977
Mrs O. and Mrs S., South Shields, 17 November 1977
I.W., Co. Durham, 13 July 1977

II Published Sources

Newspapers and Periodicals

Daily Herald, 1940–45
Engineer, 1940–47
Industrial Welfare and Personnel Management, 1939–42
Lewisham Log: Magazine of the Lewisham Women's Voluntary Services, 1941–45
Ministry of Labour Gazette, 1940–45

Official Publications and Parliamentary Papers

Central Office of Information, Wartime Social Survey.
'An Investigation of the Attitudes of Women, the General Public and ATS Personnel to the Auxiliary Territorial Service' (October 1941)
'Food: An Inquiry into a Typical Day's Meals and Attitudes to Wartime Food in Selected Groups of the English Working Population' (April–July 1942)
'Food. Food Schemes: A Collection of Short Reports on Inquiries Made by the Regional Organisation of the Wartime Social Survey' (May 1942–January 1943)
'Food: An Inquiry into (i) a Day's Meals and (ii) Attitudes to Wartime Food in Selected Groups of British Workers' (June 1943)
Geoffrey Thomas, 'Women at Work: The Attitudes of Working Women Towards Post-war Employment and Some Related Problems. An Inquiry Made for the Office of the Minister of Reconstruction' (June 1944)
'Women's Registration and Call Up' (March–April 1942)
'Workers and the War: A Collection of Short Reports on Inquiries Made by the Regional Organisation of the Wartime Social Survey' (May–October 1942)

Central Office of Information, Social Survey
Geoffrey Thomas, 'Women and Industry: An Inquiry into the Problem of Recruiting Women to Industry Carried Out for the Ministry of Labour and National Service' (1948)

Parliamentary Papers.
Cmd 67, Women's Advisory Committee, 'Report on the Domestic Service Problem' (1919)
Cmd 3508, 'A Study of the Factors Which Have Operated in the Past and Those Which Are Operating Now to Determine the Distribution of Women in Industry (December 1929)
Cmd 5556, 'Twenty-second Annual Abstract of Labour Statistics of the UK for 1922 to 1936'
Cmd 6474, 'Report by a Court of Inquiry Concerning a Dispute at an Engineering Undertaking in Scotland, 1943'
Cmd 6937, Royal Commission on Equal Pay, *Report*, 1946, and *Minutes of Evidence*, 1945–6'
Cmd 7225, Ministry of Labour and National Service, 'Report for the Years 1939–46' (1947)
Cmd 7695, Royal Commission on Population, *Report*, 1949

Select Committee on National Expenditure.
'Twelfth Report, 1939–40, ATS', 21 August 1940
'Seventeenth Report, 1940–41, Labour Problems in Filling Factories', 10 July 1941
'Twenty-first Report, 1940–41, Output of Labour', 6 August 1941
'Seventh Report, 1941–2, Supply of Labour', 26 March 1942
'Ninth Report, 1941–2, Investigation of Two Ordnance Factories', 14 May 1942
'Eleventh Report, 1941–2, Royal Ordnance Factories', 16 July 1942
'Third Report, 1942–3, Health and Welfare of Women in War Factories', 17 December 1942

Census.
Census of England and Wales, 1921, Occupation Tables (London, 1924)
Census of England and Wales, 1931, Occupation Tables (London, 1934)

Books, Articles and Theses

Ahrends, E. 'Women and the Labour Force: The London Metal Industry 1914–38' (Women's Research and Resources Centre, London, 1976)
Allatt, P. 'The Educational Role of the State: Official Policy and Family Ideology in World War II' (unpublished paper, 1978)
Allen, M. and Nicholson, M. *Memoirs of an Uneducated Lady, Lady Allen of Hurtwood* (Thames and Hudson, London, 1975)
Lady Allen of Hurtwood, *New Houses; New Schools: New Citizens* (Nursery School Association of Great Britain, London, 1934)
Amalgamated Engineering Union, *Report of the Proceedings of the 26th National Committee, and 6th Rules Revision Meeting* (July 1945)
—— *Minutes of the First Annual Women's Conference* (1943)
Anthony, S. *Women's Place in Industry and Home* (G. Routledge and Sons, London, 1932)
Beck, G.M. *Survey of British Employment and Unemployment 1927–45* (Oxford University Institute of Statistics, Oxford, 1951)
Birmingham Feminist History Group, 'Feminism as Femininity in the 1950s?', *Feminist Review*, 3, 1979
Blackstone, T. *A Fair Start: The Provision of Pre-School Education* (Allen Lane, London, 1971)
Board of Education *Report of the Consultative Committee on Infant and Nursery Schools* (HMSO, London, 1933)
Bornat, J. 'Home and Work: A New Context for Trade Union History', *Oral History*, V, 2, 1977
Braybon, G. *Women Workers in the First World War: The British Experience* (Croom Helm, London, 1981)
Brittain, V. *Women's Work in Modern England* (Noel Douglas, London, 1928)
Broad, R. and Fleming, S. (eds.) *Nella Last's War: A Mother's Diary 1939–45* (Falling Wall Press, Bristol, 1981)
Bullock, A. *The Life and Times of Ernest Bevin, Vol. II: Minister of Labour 1940–45* (Heinemann, London, 1967)
Bunn, M. 'Mass Observation: A Comment on *People in Production*', *Manchester School of Economic and Social Studies*, XIII, 1944
Burman, S., (ed.) *Fit Work for Women* (Croom Helm, London, 1978)
Burton, E. *Domestic Work: Britain's Largest Industry* (Frederick Muller, London, 1944)
Burton, E. *What of the Women? A Study of Women in Wartime* (Frederick Muller, London, 1941)
Calder, A. 'The Common Wealth Party 1942–5' (unpublished D.Phil. thesis, University of Sussex, 1967)

—— The People's War, Britain 1939-45 (Panther, London, 1971)

Central Statistical Office, Statistical Digest of the War (HMSO, London, 1951)

Churchill, W.S. The Second World War, Vol. III: The Grand Alliance (Cassell, London, 1950)

Cox, M.D. British Women at War (John Murray, London, 1941)

Croucher, R. 'Communist Politics and Shop Stewards in Engineering 1935-46' (unpublished Ph.D. thesis, University of Warwick, 1978)

—— Engineers at War (Merlin Press, London, 1982)

Croucher, R. 'Women and Militancy in the Munitions Industries 1935-45', Society for the Study of Labour History Bulletin, Spring 1979

Darwin, B. War on the Line: The Story of the Southern Railway in Wartime (The Southern Railway Co., London, 1946)

Davies, M. 'Women's Place Is at the Typewriter: The Feminization of the Clerical Labour Force' in Z. Eisenstein (ed.), Capitalist Patriarchy and the Case for Socialist Feminism (Monthly Review Press, New York, 1979)

Davies, R. Women and Work (Arrow, London, 1975)

Delphy, C. 'The Main Enemy: A Materialist Analysis of Women's Oppression', Explorations in Feminism, 3 (WRRC, 1977)

Dent, H.C. The Education Act 1944: Provisions, Regulations, Circulars, Later Acts (University of London, London, 1968)

Department of Employment and Productivity British Labour Statistics: Historical Abstract 1886-1968 (HMSO, London, 1971)

Douie, V. The Lesser Half: A Survey of the Laws, Regulations and Practices Introduced During the Present War Which Embody Discrimination Against Women (Women's Publicity Planning Association, London, 1943)

Douie, V. Daughters of Britain (Women's Service Library, London, 1949)

Dyhouse, C. 'Working-class Mothers and Infant Mortality in England 1895-1914', Journal of Social History, XII, 2, 1978

Ehrenreich, B. and English, D. For Her Own Good: 150 Years of the Experts' Advice to Women (Pluto Press, London, 1979)

Engineering and Allied Shop Stewards National Council and New Propellor Arms and the Men, full conference report, 19 October 1941

Exell, A. 'Morris Motors in the 1940s', History Workshop, 9, 1980

Fabian Society A Letter to a Woman Munition Worker from A. Susan Lawrence, Fabian Letter No. 5 (n.d., 1941?)

Ferguson, N.A. 'Women's Work: Employment Opportunities and Economic Roles 1918-1939', Albion, 1963

Ferguson, S.M. and Fitzgerald, H. Studies in the Social Services (HMSO, London, 1954)

Foley, W. A Child in the Forest (BBC, London, 1974)

Fraser, D. The Evolution of the British Welfare State (Macmillan, London, 1973)

Friedan, B. The Feminine Mystique (Penguin Books, London, 1965)

Frow, E. and R. Engineering Struggles: Episodes in the Story of the Shop Stewards' Movement (Working Class Movement Library, Manchester, 1982)

Gilbert, B.B. British Social Policy, 1914-1939 (Batsford, London, 1970)

Gittins, D. Fair Sex. Family Size and Structure 1900-1939 (Hutchinson, London, 1982)

—— 'Married Life and Birth Control Between the Wars', Oral History, III, 2, 1975

—— 'Women's Work and Family Size Between the Wars', Oral History, V, 2, 1977

Goldsmith, M. Women and the Future (Lindsay Drummond, London, 1946)

—— Women at War (Lindsay Drummond, London, 1943)

Gosden, P.H.J.H. Education in the Second World War: A Study in Policy and Administration (Methuen, London, 1976)

Graves, C. *Women in Green: The Story of the Women's Voluntary Service* (Heinemann, London, 1948)

Gray, J.L and Moshinsky, P. 'Ability and Opportunity in English Education' (1938) in H. Silver (ed.), *Equal Opportunity in Education* (Methuen, London, 1973)

Griffiths, N. *Shops Book, Brighton 1900-1930* (QueenSpark Books, Brighton, 1978)

Hakim, C. 'Sexual Divisions Within the Labour Force: Occupational Segregation', *Department of Employment Gazette*, November 1978

Haldane, C. *Motherhood and Its Enemies* (Doubleday, New York, 1928)

Hall, C. 'Married Women at Home in Birmingham in the 1920s and 1930s', *Oral History*, V, 2, 1977

Hall, E. *Canary Girls and Stock Pots* (WEA, Luton, 1977)

Halsey, A.H. (ed.) *Trends in British Society Since 1900: A Guide to the Changing Social Structure of Britain* (Macmillan, London, 1972)

Hamilton, C. *The Englishwoman* (Longmans Green, London, 1940)

Hamilton, M. *Women at Work: A Brief Introduction to Trade Unionism for Women* (Labour Book Service, London, 1941)

Hammond, R.J. *Food, Vol. I: The Growth of Policy* (HMSO, London, 1951)

Harris, J. *William Beveridge: A Biography* (Oxford University Press, Oxford, 1977)

Haslett, C. *Munitions Girl: A Handbook for the Women of the Industrial Army* (English University Press, 1942)

Hay, I. *The Story of the ROF's 1939-48* (HMSO, London, 1949)

Hinton, J. *The First Shop Stewards' Movement* (Allen and Unwin, London, 1973)

Hodgkinson, G. *Sent to Coventry* (Robert Maxwell, London, 1970)

Holden, B.I.L. *Night Shift* (Bodley Head, London, 1941)

Holtby, W. *Women and a Changing Civilisation* (Lane, London, 1934)

Hooks, J.M., for United States Department of Labor, Women's Bureau *British Policies and Methods of Employing Women in Wartime* (US Government, Washington, 1944)

Ince, Sir G. 'The Mobilisation of Manpower in Great Britain', *Transactions of the Manchester Statistical Society*, 1945

Inman, P. *Labour in the Munitions Industries* (HMSO, London, 1957)

International Labour Office *The War and Women's Employment: The Experience of the UK and the US* (ILO, Montreal, 1946)

Jefferys, J.B. *The Story of the Engineers 1800-1945* (Lawrence and Wishart, London, 1945)

Joseph, S. *If Their Mothers Only Knew: An Unofficial Account of Life in the Women's Land Army* (Faber, London, 1945)

Kalecki, M. 'Sources of Manpower in the British War Sector: The "Real Sources of War Finance" ', *Oxford University Institute of Statistics, Bulletin*, V, 1, January 1943

Klein, V. *Britain's Married Women Workers* (Routledge and Kegan Paul, London, 1965)

Leser, C.E.V. 'Men and Women in Industry', *Economic Journal*, 1952

Lewenhak, S. *Women and Trade Unions: An Outline History of Women in the British Trade Union Movement* (Benn, London, 1977)

Lewis, J. 'In Search of a Real Equality: Women Between the Wars' in F. Glover-smith (ed.), *Class, Culture and Social Change* (Harvester, Brighton, 1980)

—— *The Politics of Motherhood: Child and Maternal Welfare in England 1900-39* (Croom Helm, London, 1980)

Long, P. 'Speaking Out on Age', *Spare Rib*, No. 82, May 1979

Longmate, N. *How We Lived Then: A History of Everyday Life During the Second World War* (Arrow, London, 1973)

Mackie, L. and Patullo, P. *Women at Work* (Tavistock, London, 1977)

Marwick, A. *Britain in the Century of Total War: War, Peace and Social Change, 1900-1967* (Macmillan, London, 1968)

—— *War and Social Change in the Twentieth Century: A Comparative Study of Britain, France, Germany, Russia and the US* (Macmillan, London, 1974)

Mass-Observation *People in Production: An Enquiry into British War Production* (John Murray, London, 1942)

—— *The Journey Home* (John Murray, London, 1944)

—— *War Factory* (Gollancz, London, 1943)

Medical Women's Federation 'The Health of Children in Wartime Day Nurseries', *British Medical Journal*, August 1946

Middleton, L. *Women and the Labour Movement* (Croom Helm, London, 1977)

Milward, A.S. *War, Economy and Society 1939-1945* (Allen Lane, London, 1977)

Ministry of Health *On the State of the Public Health During Six Years of War: Report of the Chief Medical Officer of the MOH, 1939-45* (HMSO, London, 1946)

Ministry of Health *Nursery Provision for Children Under 5*, Circular 221/45, 14 December 1945

Minns, R. *Bombers and Mash: The Domestic Front 1939-1945* (Virago, London, 1979)

Mitchell, B.R. and Deane, P. *Abstract of British Historical Statistics* (Cambridge University Press, Cambridge, 1962)

Mitchell, G. *The Hard War Up: The Autobiography of Hannah Mitchell, Suffragette and Rebel* (Virago, London, 1977)

Mitchell, J. *Psychoanalysis and Feminism* (Allen Lane, London, 1974)

Moss, L. *Live and Learn: A Life and Struggle for Progress* (QueenSpark Books, Brighton, 1979)

Murphy, J.T. *Victory Production! A Personal Account of Seventeen Months Spent as a Worker in an Engineering and an Aircraft Factory: With a Criticism of our Present Methods of Production and a Plan for its Reorganisation* (John Lane, London, 1942)

National Union of Women Teachers *Women Teachers' Demand for Equal Pay*, six pamphlets (1926-1940) held in Fawcett Library

Noakes, D. *The Town Beehive* (QueenSpark Books, Brighton, 1975)

North Tyneside CDP *North Shields: Women's Work*, Final Report, Vol. 5 (Newcastle-upon-Tyne Polytechnic, Newcastle, 1978)

Nursery School Association of Great Britain *The First Stage in Education* (NSAGB, London, 1943)

Parker, H.M.D. *Manpower: A Study of Wartime Policy and Administration* (HSMO, London, 1957)

Paul, A. *Poverty: Hardship But Happiness* (QueenSpark Books, Brighton, 1975)

Pelling, H. *Britain and the Second World War* (Collins, London, 1970)

Phillips, A. and Taylor, B. 'Sex and Skill: Notes Towards a Feminist Economics', *Feminist Review*, 6, 1980

Pierson, R. 'Women's Emancipation and the Recruitment of Women into the Labour Force in World War II [in Canada]' in S.M. Trofimenkoff and A. Prentice (eds.), *The Neglected Majority* (McClelland and Stewart, Toronto, 1977)

Pilgrim Trust *Men Without Work* (Cambridge University Press, Cambridge, 1938)

Political and Economic Planning (PEP) *Planning*, No. 203, 'Nursery Education', March 1943

PEP *Planning*, No. 285, 'Employment of Women', July 1948

Potter, A. 'The Equal Pay Campaign Committee: A Case Study of a Pressure Group', *Political Studies*, V, 1, February 1957

Powell, M. *Below Stairs* (P. Davies, London, 1968)
Priestley, J.B. *Black-out in Gretley: A Story of – and for – Wartime* (Heinemann, London, 1942)
—— *British Women go to War* (Collins, London, n.d., 1944?)
—— *Daylight on Saturday* (Heinemann, London, 1943)
Richards, E.R. 'Women in the British Economy Since about 1700', *History*, 59, 1974
Riley, D. 'War in the Nursery', *Feminist Review*, II, Summer 1979
—— *War in the Nursery, Theories of the Child and Mother* (Virago, London, 1983)
—— 'The Free Mothers: Pronatalism and Working Mothers in Industry at the End of the Last War in Britain', *History Workshop*, 11, Spring 1981
Roberts, E. 'Working-class Women in the North-west', *Oral History*, V, Autumn 1977
—— 'Working Wives and Their Families' in T. Barker and M. Drake (eds.), *Population and Society in Britain 1850-1980* (Batsford, London, 1982)
Routh, G. *Occupation and Pay in Great Britain, 1906-1960* (Cambridge University Press, Cambridge, 1965)
Rupp, L.J. *Mobilising Women for War: German and American Propaganda 1939-45* (Princeton University Press, Princeton, 1978)
Scott, J.W. and Tilly, L.A. 'Women's Work and the Family in Nineteenth Century Europe', *Comparative Studies in Society and History*, 17, 1975
Scott, P. *British Women in War* (Hutchinson, London, 1940)
—— *They Made Invasion Possible* (Hutchinson, London, 1944)
Simon, S.D. 'Married Women in Munition Making', *Industrial Welfare and Personnel Management*, XXII, December 1940
Smith, A.C.H. with Immirzi, E. and Blackwell, T. *Paper Voices: The Popular Press and Social Change 1935-1965* (Chatto and Windus, London, 1975)
Smith, H. 'The Problem of "Equal Pay for Equal Work" in Great Britain During World War II', *Journal of Modern History*, 53, 4 December 1981
Solden, N.C. *Women in British Trade Unions 1874-1976* (Gill and Macmillan, Dublin, 1978)
Spring Rice, M. *Working-Class Wives* (first published Penguin, London, 1939; new edition, Virago, London, 1981)
Strachey, O. 'Married Women and Work', *Contemporary Review*, CXLV, 1934
Summerfield, P. 'Women Workers in the Second World War', *Capital and Class*, I, Spring 1977
—— 'Women, Work and Welfare: a Study of Child Care and Shopping in Britain in the Second World War', *Journal of Social History*, 17, 2, 1983
—— 'Women Workers in the Second World War: A Study of the Interplay in Official Policy Between the Need to Mobilise Women and Conventional Expectations About Their Roles at Work and at Home in the Period 1939-45' (unpublished D.Phil. thesis, University of Sussex, 1982)
Summerskill, E. 'Conscription and Women', *The Fortnightly*, 151, March 1942
Taylor, P. 'Daughters and Mothers – Maids and Mistresses: Domestic Service Between the Wars', in John Clarke, Chas Critcher and Richard Johnson (eds.), *Working Class Culture: Studies in History and Theory* (Hutchinson, London, 1979)
Taylor, S. 'The Effect of Marriage on Job Possibilities for Women and the Ideology of Home: Nottingham 1890-1930', *Oral History*, V, 2, 1977
Thomas, K. *Women in Nazi Germany* (Gollancz, London, 1943)
Titmuss, R.M. *Problems of Social Policy* (HMSO, London, 1950)
Tobias, S. and Anderson, L. *What Really Happened to Rosie the Riveter? Demobilisation and the Female Labor Force 1944-47* (MSS Modular Publications Inc., Module 9, New York, 1973)

Walby, S. 'Gender and Unemployment: Patriarchal and Capitalist Relations in the Restructuring of Gender Relations in Unemployment and Employment' (unpublished Ph.D. thesis, University of Essex, 1984)

—— 'Women's Unemployment, Patriarchy and Capitalism', *Socialist Economic Review*, 1983

White, C.L. *Women's Magazine 1693-1968* (Michael Joseph, London, 1970)

White, D. *D for Doris, V for Victory* (Oakleaf Books, Milton Keynes, 1981)

Williams Ellis, A. *Women in War Factories* (Gollancz, London, 1943)

Williams, G. *Women and Work* (Nicholson and Watson, London, 1945)

Williamson, J.W. *Recollections 1930-1945* (unpublished typescript, 1975)

Wilson, E. *Only Halfway to Paradise: Women in Postwar Britain, 1945-1968* (Tavistock, London, 1980)

Women's Group on Public Welfare *Our Towns: A Close Up* (Oxford University Press, Oxford, 1943)

Wood, E.M. *Mainly for Men* (Gollancz, London, 1943)

Wright, G. *The Ordeal of Total War 1939-1945* (Harper Torch Books, New York, 1968)

INDEX

absenteeism 60, 100, 114, 115,
    124–32, 139, 176
age structure of employed women
    196
    during war 31, 58–60
    pre-war 13–15
    post-war 188
airframe industry 60
Allen, Lady, of Hurtwood 71
Amalgamated Engineering Union 11,
    115, 154, 157–61, 171, 173–5,
    189
Anthony, Sylvia 22, 23
armed forces 30
Assheton 44
Astor, Lady 43

banking 14
Beaverbrook, Lord 33
Bevin, Ernest 34, 35, 36, 44, 185
    and childcare 67, 74, 76, 79, 91,
        93
    and labour 130
    and working hours 137
Board of Education 19, 20, 67
boot and shoe industry 9, 15, 32,
    136–9, 153
box making industry 153
Braybon, Gail 5–6
bread and biscuit industry 9
British Restaurants 100, 101
Brittain, Vera 14, 21–2, 23
building industry 153
Burton, Elaine 46, 58

canteen provision 18–19, 100–3
capitalism 4, 23, 180, 185
chemical industry 9, 29, 151, 153,
    187, 199
Child Care Reserves 74
child care 3, 17, 19–21, 40, 186
    pre-war state provision 1, 19–20,
        42, 67
    residential 82–3
    wartime state provision 67–95
    see also day nurseries,
        childminders
childminders 20–1, 88–95

'Children's Hotels' 82
civil service 12, 14
cleaning 17
clothing industry 30, 32, 33, 153,
    187, 199
commercial services 9, 199
competence 166–7, 176
concentration of industry 32–5
conscription
    female 35–6, 147
    male 31
consumer services 30
Control of Engagement (Directed
    Persons) Order (1943) 142
cooking 3, 17–19
Co-operative Societies 17, 104, 107,
    108, 186
cotton industry 136, 139
Croucher, Richard 134, 157, 159,
    161

Darwin, Bernard 152
day nurseries 19, 93–5, 186
    and childminding 88–93
    demand for 75–9
    hours 81–2, 87
    premises and staffing 70–5
    use made of 79–87
dependence 13, 14
dilution of male labour 3, 60, 74,
    151–80
    effects of 152–3
distribution industry 9, 30, 187, 199
domestic service 8, 10, 48–9, 187
domestic work 16–24
    as private zone 2
    collectivisation of 146
    conflict with war work 38, 40–3,
        45–6
    continuity of pre- and post-war
        attitudes 1, 185, 190
    gender identity 3
    grounds for exemption from war
        work 48–53
    see also childcare, cleaning, cook-
        ing, shopping, washing

earnings see wages

Education Act
(1918) 19–20
(1944) 186, 191
Education (Provision of Meals)
Act (1906) 18
electrical apparatus industry 13, 199
electrical engineering 10–11, 151, 153
electrical industry 9, 29, 199
Elliot, Mrs W. 44
Elliott, Dorothy 44
employment, women's
continuity of pre- and post-war
attitudes 1, 186–7, 190
pre-war 8–12
see also mobilisation
Employment of Women (Control of
Engagement) Order 35–6
Employment of Women, Young Persons
and Children Act (1920) 22
Engineering Employers' Federation 161,
162, 169
engineering industry 9, 29, 151, 153,
154–68, 187, 199
entertainments industry 153
equal pay 1, 154, 159, 180, 189, 191
campaign for 12, 14, 171–3
Royal Commission on 152, 170,
174–8, 180
Essential Work Order 53, 61, 101, 130,
131, 132
evacuation 86
Exell, Arthur 127
exemption from war work 48–53
Extended Employment of Women
agreement 157, 159, 161, 193–4

Factory Act (1937) 22
Factory and Welfare Advisory Board 99
factory stores 110
family allowance 175, 180
family doctor 94–5
food, drink and tobacco industries 9, 30,
153, 187, 199
food rationining 104–8
food, state provision of 18
foundry work 153, 179
Friedan, Betty 1
frustration 42

gas industry 9, 29, 153, 187, 199
Gibson, George 158

Hall, Edith 9
Hancock, Florence 44, 50, 158, 168

Harrod, R.F. 176, 177
Haslett, Caroline 44, 151
health, women's 21–2, 125–6
health visitors 76, 77, 84, 89–90
historical view 185
Holden, Inez 56
home-centred paid work 16
home, definition of 48
Hooks, Janet 33, 152
hosiery-making industry 15, 32, 33,
136, 139, 153
hours of shop opening 103–4
hours of work *see* working hours
Household R category 48, 61, 142
housework *see* domestic work

inessential industries 32, 35, 36, 83, 136
Irish women 58, 59–60
iron and steel industry 153

Jones, Jack 161–2, 166–7

laundry work 10
leather industry 30, 199
leave of absence 113–16, 139–40
legislation 22, 23, 35–6
Leser, C.E.V. 9, 187
Lewenhak, Sheila 11
Limerick, Countess of 44, 49
locomotive construction industry 10
Lord President's Committee 124, 125–6,
129
Loughlin, Anne 174

machine tool industry 58
marine engineering 10, 199
marital status of employed women 196
during war 31, 62
postwar 188
pre-war 13–16
marriage bar 14, 15
Marwick, Arthur 1, 36
Mass-Observation 5, 124
childcare 70, 92–3
demobilisation 189
domestic work 131, 135
factory work 54, 55, 127
husbands' attitudes 41
mobilisation 37
overtime 134
People in Production 55, 93, 128
shopping 101–3, 105, 109
washing 17
women in engineering 156

working hours 129, 136, 146
Maternity and Child Welfare Act 19
Maxse, M. 44
metals industry 9, 13, 29, 60, 151,
    153, 180, 187, 199
    light metals 9–10
Milward, Alan S. 30
Ministry of Food 2, 103, 104
    see also rationing
Ministry of Health 2, 19, 68, 71, 94
Ministry of Labour and National
    Service 2, 3, 60, 123
    and childcare 67–95
    industrial relations 172
    mobilisation of women 29, 33,
        35, 43, 48, 51, 61–2
    Umpire 47
    see also absenteeism, dilution,
        working hours
Ministry of Supply 60, 134, 159
Mitchell, Juliet 1
mobile women workers 42, 45–7
mobilisation of women 2, 3
    compulsion 35–7, 47
    concentration of industry 32–5
    distribution of women 29–31
    perceptions of 53–61
    reactions to 37–43
    volunteers 32
money 135
    see also equal pay, wages
Morrison, Herbert 103
Moynihan House Nursery Leeds 74,
    84
munitions industry 33
    see also engineering
Murphy, J.T. 154

National Service Number 2 Act
    (1941) 35
Nettleford, Miss L.F. 174
non-essential industries 32, 35, 36,
    83, 136
nurseries, day *see* day nurseries
nursery classes 20, 86, 119
nursery schools 19–20, 86, 187
nursing 12

occupational segregation 153
outwork 142, 145

part-time work 115–16, 117, 141–6,
    188
patriarchy 4–5, 23, 41, 170, 175–6,
    180, 191

pay *see* equal pay, wages
People in Production (M-O) 55, 93,
    128
Pilgrim Trust 14, 21
pottery industry 9, 15, 30, 32, 136,
    139, 199
pre-war period 8–24
printing industry 153, 179
'Problem of Absenteeism, The'
    (pamphlet) 129, 130
proportion of women in workforce
    29–30, 151, 196
Puxley, Zöe 68, 81, 82, 87, 89

queueing 111–13

railway work 153, 199
Ramsay, Sir Alexander 159, 174
rationing, food 104–8
redundancy 32–3, 160–1
regional distribution of employed
    women 31
Registered Daily Guardian scheme
    88–9, 92
registration for war work 34–5, 45
registration for food 108
residential childcare 82–3
Restriction of Engagement Order
    (1940) 31–2
retailing 14
    see also shopping
Rice, Margery Spring 14
Riley, Denise 69
Royal Commission on Equal Pay
    152, 170, 174–8
Rupp, Leila 6

Sainsbury, 17
Salvation Army 18
school meals 100–1
scientific apparatus industry 9,
    10–11, 13, 199
Scott, Peggy 86, 151
sectionalisation 11
segregation, occupational 153
Sex Disqualification Removal Act
    (1919) 12
shift work 81, 115–16, 140–1, 188
shipbuilding 10, 29, 52, 60, 153,
    179, 199
shopping 3, 17–19, 186
    conferences on 103
    conflict with war work 99–100
    Co-operative societies 17, 104,
        107, 108, 186

factory stores 110
government policy 100
leagues 116–18
leave of absence for 113–16
ordering schemes 108–9, 110–11
queueing 111–13
rationing 104–8
registration of food 108
Shop Stewards' National Council 153
Shops (Hours of Closing) Act (1982)
    18, 103
single women 13–16, 130, 177
skilled work 156–7
Smieton, Mary 68, 74, 80, 81, 82,
    87, 89
Smith, Fred A. 154
soap making industry 153
social class 55–7
state policy towards women 1–2
strikes 171–2
Summerskill, Edith 43, 44
Sutherland, Mary 44, 51, 92

tailoring 153
Tanner, Jack 174, 175, 189
teaching 14
    elementary school 12
Temple, Ann 36–7
textile industry
    during war 30, 32, 33, 153
    postwar 187, 199
    pre-war 9, 10, 13, 15
Thomas, Katherine 113
Titmuss, Richard 1
toolmaking 180
Trade Union Congress (TUC) 11, 12,
    174–6, 189
    Women's Advisory Committee
        133, 178
    women's conference 82, 92, 105,
        118, 145, 173
trade unions 3–4, 10–11, 22, 33,
    127, 173
Trades Disputes and Trade Union Act
    (1927) 12
training, job 168–9
Transport and General Workers
    Union 11, 153, 161–3, 171
transport industry 9, 29, 153, 187
Tribe, F.N. 44, 45
turnover of women workers 132, 139

unemployment 32
    benefit 15

unskilled work 162–6
    see also skilled work

Vaughan, Janet 174
vehicle industry 9, 29, 153, 187, 199
voluntarism 36–7
volunteer housewives 89, 91–2

wages 22, 135, 169–70, 172
    see also equal pay
Wakefield, Charles Cheers 14
war work
    conflict with domestic work 38,
        40–3, 45–6
    exemption from 48–53
    part-time 141–6
    perceptions of 53–61
    see also mobilisation, working
        hours
War Work Weeks 37–40, 53–4
Ward, Irene 43–4
Wark, Lord 172
Wartime Social Survey (WSS) 5, 37,
    49, 53, 57, 99, 101, 105, 145,
    189
washing 16–17
water industry 9, 29, 187, 199
welding 168
white-collar jobs 11–12, 30
White, Doris 141, 156, 158
Woman Power Committee 43, 44, 60
Women's Advisory Committee (TUC)
    133, 178
Women's Cosultative Committee
    44–53, 143
Women's Employment Federation 32
Women's Health Enquiry Committee
    17
women's movement 190
Women's Voluntary Service 117
Woolworth, F.W. 17
work *see* employment, mobilisation,
    war work
working hours 53, 80
    and absenteeism 124–32
    and satisfaction 129
    and sickness 125–6
    extension of 132–3, 136, 139
    part-time 115–16, 117, 141–6
    regulations 132
    shifts 81, 115–16, 140–1
Working Women's Organisations
    Standing Joint Committee 22,
        91–2